ALSO BY ROY BLOUNT JR.

Roy Blount's Book of Southern Humor
Camels Are Easy, Comedy's Hard
First Hubby
About Three Bricks Shy . . . and the Load Filled Up
Now, Where Were We?
Not Exactly What I Had in Mind
Webster's Ark and Soup Songs
It Grows on You
What Men Don't Tell Women
One Fell Soup
Crackers
About Three Bricks Shy of a Load

Be Sweet

Be Sweet

A Conditional Love Story

Roy Blount Jr.

Alfred A. Knopf / New York / 1998

Grateful acknowledgment is made to the following for permission to reprint
previously published material:

Warren Bankston: Excerpt from "When You Give It All" by Warren Bankston
(originally published in *PROLOG*, National Football League annual for 1978).
Reprinted by permission of Warren Bankston.

Harper's Magazine: William F. Buckley Jr., excerpt from interview with Lewis
Lapham, copyright © by *Harper's Magazine*. All rights reserved. Reprinted by
special permission of *Harper's Magazine*.

Harvard University Press: Excerpt from poem number 1741 from *The Poems of
Emily Dickinson,* edited by Thomas H. Johnson (Cambridge, Mass.: The Belknap
Press of Harvard University Press), copyright © 1951, 1955, 1979, 1983 by the
President and Fellows of Harvard College. Reprinted by permission of the
publishers and the Trustees of Amherst College.

Hal Leonard Corporation: Excerpts from "Wild Thing," words and music by
Chip Taylor, copyright © 1965 (Renewed 1993) by EMI Blackwood Music Inc. All
rights reserved. International copyright secured. Reprinted by permission of Hal
Leonard Corporation.

The Plain Dealer: Excerpts from article on males named "junior" by Dr. Murline
Gatewood, copyright © 1978. Reprinted by permission of The Plain Dealer,
Cleveland, Ohio.

PolyGram International Publishing, Inc.: Excerpt from "Her First Mistake" by
Lyle Lovett, copyright © 1996 by PolyGram International Publishing, Inc., and
Lylesongs. All rights reserved. Reprinted by permission of PolyGram
International Publishing, Inc.

Russell & Volkening, Inc.: Eudora Welty interview in *The Paris Review* by
George Plimpton (*The Paris Review,* Spring 1995, number 134), copyright ©
1995 by *The Paris Review*. Reprinted by permission of Russell & Volkening, Inc.,
as agents for the author.

The Washington Post: Excerpt from May 18, 1997, letter ("Ombudsman"
column, *The Washington Post,* byline Geneva Overholser). Copyright © 1997 by
The Washington Post. Reprinted by permission of The Washington Post.

Library of Congress Cataloging-in-Publication Data
Blount, Roy.
Be sweet : a conditional love story / Roy Blount Jr.
p.   cm.
ISBN 0-679-40054-0
1. Blount, Roy—Homes and haunts—Southern States—Humor.
2. Humorists, American—20th century—Biography—Humor.
3. Blount, Roy—Childhood and youth—Humor.   4. Southern States—Humor.
I. Title.
PS3552.L687Z465   1998
818'.5409—dc21
[B]   97-49352   CIP

Manufactured in the United States of America
First Edition

For my sister

Humorists recoil with horror from analysis. Humor is fastidi-
ous, will not be touched. And since this curious art has an
absolutely impenetrable defense—a prickly wall of gags
mounted by desperate men—it is usually best just to leave it
alone. —WILFRID SHEED

"I didn't mean—"

"That's just what I complain of! You should have meant!
What do you suppose is the use of a child without any meaning?
Even a joke should have some meaning—and a child's more
important than a joke, I hope. You couldn't deny that, even if
you tried with both hands."

"I don't deny things with my hands," Alice objected.

"Nobody said you did," said the Red Queen. "I said you
couldn't if you tried."

—LEWIS CARROLL, *THROUGH THE LOOKING-GLASS*

The most merciful thing in the world . . . is the inability of the
human mind to correlate all its contents. —H. P. LOVECRAFT

Contents

1 / Orientation   *3*

2 / Memories Are Made of This   *22*

3 / Who Dat Say Who Dat When I Say Who Dat?   *24*

4 / Language! Language!   *36*

5 / And Now, This   *39*

6 / You Had to Be There   *44*

7 / A Day in the Life   *48*

8 / Got to Get a Handle on It First   *61*

9 / The Primal Scene   *71*

10 / Funny Peculiar, Funny Ha-Ha   *75*

11 / Attitude   *83*

12 / The Bottom, Ontogenetically   *91*

13 / Going Down   *97*

14 / An End of Something: I Am Born   *102*

15 / Back, Back, Back to Where We Once Belonged   *110*

16 / A Date with Destiny   *121*

17 / The Next Morning   *130*

18 / Sauce for the Genders   *137*

19 / Juniors   *146*

20 / Ball   *182*

21 / The Story So Far   *198*

22 / Reverse English   *208*

23 / A Road Not Taken   *220*

24 / I Go Home Again   *229*

25 / The Family Curse   *236*

26 / When I Was Happy, I Thought   *250*

27 / I'm Not Here Right Now   *261*

28 / Sweet Bye and Bye   *265*

29 / Upleaf   *272*

30 / What the Author Has to Tell Us   *282*

     Acknowledgments   *289*

Be Sweet

CHAPTER 1 / **Orientation**

. . . essays, poems, interviews and such from . . . William F. Buckley Jr., John Updike, Pauline Kael, Charles Bukowski, Fred Chappell, Bill McKibben, Louis D. Rubin Jr., William Steig and the inevitable Roy Blount Jr. —*WASHINGTON POST,* MAY 5, 1992

I was supposed to be an angel. From a distance, onstage, I would no doubt have resembled one, in the costume my mother had made for me—halo, wings, the works—but I wasn't onstage. I was sitting in my dimly lit basement-floor third-grade classroom, which was where I had insisted my parents drop me off. That was where, as I understood it, we children were to gather before the Christmas pageant.

"Are you sure, Bucky?" my mother had asked me when we got to the classroom and no one else was there. They called me Bucky Bug, for a now long-forgotten cartoon character who had big dark eyes. Which makes me sound more adorable than, frankly, I look in old snapshots. If you ask me, I look evasive. But determined.

There was no one in any of the classrooms. I assured my parents that I knew what I was doing, told them to go on upstairs to the auditorium.

Half an hour later, I was still the only one in the room. Faintly, from up above, I could hear sacred music. But I held my ground.

So this is nice, you're shaping the richly recollected raw material of your childhood into a narrative. You're telling a story.

Could you not make it sound so cozy? *Storytelling, closure* and *unconditional love*—those are the three universal needs of today. People calling themselves professional storytellers wear storytelling *costumes* at storytelling festivals. When I was a child, one definition of "telling a story" was lying. And stories ran free as foxes and snakes. Today people go on and on fondly about storytelling as if that is *the* word for what words are meant to do.

A story is like a sandwich—you know what it is, you can get a grip on it, but it can still be full of Velveeta. The *truth* is something that makes us wonder, "What . . . in the world . . . is *that*?"

I've been as guilty as anybody. I tell stories—and mine, for reasons that we may or may not get to the bottom of, are generally humorous. Which means I have left things out. But now I am fifty-five: roughly the age when humorists stop being funny. It could happen any minute, maybe in the middle of a sentence. So this time I'm putting everything in.

My grandson Jesse Roy Dellea was eighteen months old when he told his first story. I was looking after him one day in his house in North Carolina while his parents were at work. He didn't know me very well yet, since I live in New York. He was fiddling unsteadily with a folding glass screen in front of the fireplace. "That thing might hurt you, Jesse," I said. I went to close it flat—and his finger got pinched. He looked at me astounded, as though I came from some bizarre tribe of people who felt it necessary to *prove* to children that something could hurt. I felt terrible and hugged him and apologized with as whole a heart as mine probably ever seems to be. Accustomed as he was to something more tongue-in-cheek from me, he was startled back into trust. Right there was when we bonded. When his mother—my daughter, Ennis—came home he held up his finger, showed her the little blood blister and told her, "Papa, boo-boo."

So far, just an anecdote. After he and Ennis dropped me off at the airport the next day, he made it a story. Held up his finger and said, "Papa, boo-boo, bye-bye."

Your basic three-part story structure. Papa boo-boo bye-bye.

Jehovah's dictate: Papa. The eating of the apple: boo-boo. Expulsion from the Garden: bye-bye.

King Lear, the Papa, makes a boo-boo and the rest is one long agonizing bye-bye.

Hamlet's late Papa (Big Hamlet) shows up to say bye-bye and then it's one boo-boo after another.

Oedipus kills a man. Thinks it's just a bye-bye. But it also gets him into deep boo-boo. Which at length begins to dawn on him: that was *Papa* . . . ?

In *Casablanca*, Rick is the Papa. The double boo-boo is Rick's losing

Ilsa and France's loss of itself to the Nazis. The bye-bye at the airport is a resolution of sorts.

But no one would suggest that in any of these cases, the story as such is the whole or even the main thing. There's atmosphere, feeling, mystery, Mama. Could be bitter, sweet or bittersweet, depending on the tone, the subtext, the characterizations involved. "I love to tell the story, 'twill be my theme in glory . . . ," my mother used to go around the house singing. But often when we asked her about something, she would say, "There's no telling. There's just no telling."

I want to get into the no-telling part. If it makes a story, fine, but who knows what it *might* make. A friend of mine was visiting her mother in a nursing home. Many of the other residents had Alzheimer's, but the mother's mind was unclouded. Except by remembrance, and envy. "They've forgotten their stories!" she said of the others. "They can say anything!"

Okay, no story, so: insights. What you're saying is that all your life you have been sitting in that dimly lit basement classroom, but now, at last—

Insights! You mean diagnosis. *How I Figured Out What My Problem Is—No, Was!—and You Can Too.* If there is anything I learned from my mother, it is that there is more to life than that. After my younger sister, Susan, and I grew up, we hinted around to Mother that she might like to talk to a psychotherapist. She gave that notion about as much consideration as Rasputin might have, or Jeremiah. When she was in the hospital for the last time, two chipper young hospice women came by and tried to engage her in the sort of conversation they thought she needed. "They wanted to talk to me about dying!" she said. "Imagine!"

"I think of Mother as someone sitting on a volcano of emotion," Susan says, "that she constantly was working to keep the lid on. Every once in a while she would say, 'I could just scream,' and scream. She did this once in England." (Susan was married then to my friend Gerald Duff, who was teaching English there for a year. She and I are both single now, and have been, for years.) "We were driving in a Volkswagen bus to London with a few students along. Their eyes bugged out."

So evidently not everyone's mother screamed. When we were children, who knew? We thought the volcano was our fault. We still feel the heat. And who can we complain to? "Don't you talk back to me," Mother would say.

And now . . . I ask that you give me a little slack here. In consideration of my late parents' memory. And my children's future. And my grand-children's. (I have two grandchildren. The second, Noah, born in 1996, will likely not remember the twentieth century.) You needn't feel any responsibility for the imminent loosening of my grip on humor—which, oh, I guess I could do without it, don't worry about me, we're just talk-ing about my livelihood, my redeeming social value, my access to sanity, that's all. I ask only that you give a moment's thought to this: I tried to go blind.

You're kidding.

No. My mother— Well, first, one quick story. A friend of mine had an uncle Edward who prided himself on keeping up with every branch of the family. There was no forebear so distant nor cousin so removed that Edward could not come up with exactly how he or she was related to everybody else and where he or she lived and whom he or she had married. Usually it is a woman relative who keeps up with that sort of thing, but in this family it was Edward. Edward was a walking family Bible. Then one day his brother Charles went to bed and wouldn't get up. Doctors were summoned. Edward showed up and said, "What's wrong with Charles?"

His sister Anna Laura looked at him as if he were an idiot.

"Edward," she said, "as much as you know about this family, I'd think you'd know what's wrong with Charles. Like nearly every other male member of this family, Charles is a bad alcoholic."

Tears came to Edward's eyes.

"Well, don't take on so, Edward," Anna Laura said. "You don't drink."

"It's not that," Edward said. "It's . . ." And he began to weep outright. "Mama was dead six days," he said between sobs, "before I knew she had a glass eye."

Nobody in my family could have said that. My mother lost an eye to cancer right after Susan was born. . . .

One of the three or four conversations I can remember with my father was after the cancer was diagnosed. I was seven. "We're going to have to be especially sweet to your mother now," he said, in an oblique, constricted voice. And my blood ran cold.

"Now, you be sweet," she would tell me when I was little. And from her, nothing ever seemed just a figure of speech. When I would try to argue with her in adolescence, she would go in a flash from fierce to pitiful and whimper, "Be sweet to me, Bucky." After I went away to college, I started, never finished, finally threw away, a poem called "Sweetboy."

> *I am a sweet*
> *Little jolly old elf.*
> *I'm so sweet*
> *I can taste myself.*

I can't be sweet on command! I can't be sweet on purpose, even. I can be polite, I can be sympathetic. But being sweet, like being funny, is a freedom-of-choice issue to me.

My father had one man-to-man with me about my love life. I was home from college. He took me to lunch. I was seeing a classmate, Ellen, steadily. Gradually it dawned on me that this relationship was the reason for our get-together. And that my mother wanted him to talk me out of it. I had brought this remarkable young Waxahachie, Texas, native home to meet the folks, and we had all watched *The Grapes of Wrath* on TV together, and none of us could think of the name of this particular character actor in it. My parents went to bed. Ellen and I stayed in the TV room and commenced to make out, Lord, Lord. It may be that generations after mine will never know the deep purple musk-turgid vastnesses of prolonged demi-virginal pre-Aquarian making out.

"Hans Conried!" came my mother's voice, in its sweet, sharing, utterly-out-of-it mode. And then her sharp intake of breath.

"Mom!" I said.

What did she think we were doing in there?

"No," I added shakily, the actor's name having come to me—mysteries of the mind—in the interval. And then firmly, with disdain, I informed her: "It was John Carradine!"

She vanished in a huff. A sulphurous huff.

And now, at lunch, my father—who conversed readily, equably, unassumingly yet authoritatively with decent folks of all walks of life, but who would rather have chewed off his arm than get down to cases with me on any delicate or indelicate matter, which was fine with me, at the time—was saying . . .

I wonder how my life would have developed if he'd said, "Son, we *like* Ellen. And you know I love your mama. But I wish I'd gotten to know a little more about myself and . . . women, before I got married."

If he had ventured just a bit into the no-telling area. A *confidence* would have meant something to me. But we didn't confide in each other. What he said was, "You're not serious about this girl, are you?"

"No," I lied quickly, and that was that. A year or so later we were married; she is the mother of my children. One of the things that attracted me to her, I realize in retrospect, was her incapacity for demonstrative motherliness. She sang a funny song about it at our daughter, Ennis's, wedding, many years after our divorce: "You know I'll miss you, / Even though I never kiss you," something like that. In the context of our not only extended but improvisational, multihelical, and some may say gerrymandered family, it was appropriate, it went over well. Hey, functional families are all alike.

We were crazy to marry each other or, so young, anybody else, but we have had a congenial ex-marriage. That's what a humorist *would* have, a congenial ex-marriage, you may say, and you may be right. But . . . we can say this: our children aren't anywhere near as crazy as we were.

The only conversation with my father that I remember distinctly and with pleasure was when I was, I don't know, eight? We were driving in the family car past a construction site and he asked me if I could figure out why there were strips of tape on the windowpanes of the house that was going up there.

"So they'll know there's glass there and won't break it," I said, after a moment.

He gave me a nod that I treasure still.

I could *think*. But how can anybody just up and *be sweet*?

I *know* it was hard on my mother to have a glass eye.

And then she got glaucoma in the other eye. She said the doctor told her not to read much, so she wouldn't strain that eye. She loved to read. She said he also told her, for the same reason, not to cry much. And she loved to—well, at any rate, she had so many things to cry about.

When my sister Susan asked the same doctor about my mother's glaucoma after her death, however, he said, "What glaucoma?"

Then, a couple of years ago, I was diagnosed with glaucoma. In the same eye as my mother's glass one. (There's the seed of a sentimental ballad: " 'Twas the same eye, as Mother's glass one,/That you winked at me in such a roguish way./And that's how it came to pass one/Evening, that you stole my heart away.") And I thought to myself, All right! At last, some gravitas! But the doctor told me just to use these drops regularly and it should be all right.

And I did and it was. But while I was thrashing around trying to write this book, I stopped using them. If I went blind, it would be an excuse not to write this book. If I went blind in one eye, it would put me under the same handicap—okay, okay, under one of the same handicaps—as my mother.

A mother who was this unhappy: not only wouldn't she let her loved ones have the satisfaction of persuading her that they loved her, she left her children with matricidal guilt.

Uh . . . this dimly lit classroom. Where was it, exactly?

Decatur, Georgia. Ponce de Leon grammar school. It's not there anymore, the town fathers (before my father became one) tore it down because it was so close to a black neighborhood that they would have had a hard time justifying the continued exclusion of black children. The federal government built a post office there, and staffed it with black men.

I never went to school with a black person until I went north to graduate school.

Does your mind always jump around like this?

Yes. Like dreams, ballplayers nowadays and the Internet. I contradict myself, I contain multitudes, give me a break. I'm fifty-five years old! I live alone! I work, at home, alone. I get up in the morning and start writing and it's two-thirty in the afternoon before I realize I'm sitting here naked, unshowered, unshaven, I've knocked half a cup of strong coffee over on my father's Packard Motor Car Company psychological profile, the wizardry of Windows 95 (may it burn in hell) has seen fit to go *WOOOOP* and take the last few hundred words I've written and string them out over sixty-some-odd pages, like this,

o

n

e

c
h
a
r
a
c
t
e
r

p
e
r

l
i
n
e
,

and I haven't had any lunch. You say my mind jumps around? My mind could give a shit. Let's work with that, is what I'm saying.

The dimly lit classroom . . .

You might think someone would have come looking for me, but there was no shortage of angels, and certainly no one regretted the absence of my singing voice. Many years later, having become a humorist, I would speak out about the plight of the singing-impaired, but at the time it would not have occurred to me to suspect that I had been purposely told to report to the wrong place. In fact, I had a kind of reverse persecution complex—I suspected that I was being shielded from something dark, something hinted at but never acknowledged. I was looking for clues, meanwhile trying to fit nominally into third-grade society. People looked at me oddly sometimes. Once, in my presence, my mother asked Wesley Freese, of all people, if I was "one of the, you know, regular fellows." He gulped, and said I was. As a result of that question, though, he may be somewhere today still worrying whether *he* is. My mother called everything into question. How in the world she can have thought she was rearing a regular fellow, I can't imagine. She was rearing a writer.

After the pageant, my teacher, Mrs. Martin, and my parents came to get me. Mrs. Martin was a wrenlike, frizzy-headed woman who devoted a good deal of classroom time to reaming us out for talking too much during lunch. I of course preferred those teachers who seemed to find me appealing in an off-beat way, but the readily offended ones, like Mrs. Martin, who thought I was a smart aleck—

In Georgia?

Yes. We had smart alecks in Georgia. I say Georgia and people assume I rode a mule to school and we all sat around in overalls with one strap broken. In fact, I went to good suburban public schools all the way to college, thank you, and we had smart alecks, yes. By today's standards, to be sure, we appeared to be highly corrigible. For the most part our teachers believed in keeping a lid on our self-esteem, and some of them were crazier than we were.

For instance, Miss Shirley, in eighth grade, was a large, confused but obdurate, percolating but never quite fully brewed woman who blew things out of proportion. One day she couldn't make it to school, and her hastily summoned substitute arrived a little late, to find a festive class. One of us happened to be looping the window-shade cord around another one's neck. Loosely. Not in earnest. The next day Miss Shirley was back, raging up and down the aisles between our desks like Lear on the heath.

"I can't be out for a single day without you-all trying to murder each other!" she cried. "How do you think Forrest's mother felt when he came home with his eyes bulging out?" Then, to make sure we were all listening to what she was about to say next, she swung around too quickly there in the aisle, and got wedged in between two desks.

You could have heard a bug crawl, except that all the bugs were listening. Everyone looked straight ahead, especially the two students sitting on either side of Miss Shirley. She was breathing heavily. A substitute teacher was one thing, but we didn't want our regular teacher to lose control. What would we do? We were unlike children of the Baby Boom in that we had sense enough to know we did not want mere anarchy to be loosed upon the world.

"Turn to page eighty-four," Miss Shirley said.

As we pulled our texts from under our desks and rustled to the specified page, Miss Shirley shifted herself, bit by bit, back and forth, rocking, like a driver working his stuck car out of the mud, until she was free.

She strode to the front of the class. "You'll learn!" she said. "You'll find out!"

The fearsome teachers like Mrs. Martin and Miss Shirley squared with what my mother had led me to expect. My mother's teachers, by her account, had been unrelievedly withering. When mine weren't, I suspected there was a catch.

I was a good conventional speller, but sometimes I slipped up and spelled words by instinct. For instance, *what* with the *h* first. When Mrs. Martin marked this wrong I conceded her point—*w* first was officially correct, and I would not get far in the world if I persisted in giving precedence to the *h*. But I wanted her to see my point. I explained that I had spelled the word the way it was pronounced. Mrs. Martin said that was crazy.

Crazy? Before I was school age my mother had taught me to read by sounding out the words.

I went to the classroom dictionary and looked *what* up. I was confirmed. Preferred pronunciation, *hwot* or *hwut*. Mrs. Martin never forgave me.

She also disapproved of the slouchy way I sat at my desk. "You are too lazy to get comfortable," she told me.

I believe I have always had a high discomfort threshold. I assume that other people have more right to complain of suffering than I do. (Though when they say what is *making* them suffer, I often think, *That's all?*) For me, in my work, discomfort is raw material. I don't take it kindly when other people assure me that it's grist for my mill—but it's true that a humorist, though he can never expect sympathy, does have the recourse of moping (*vigorously*) until he can transmute his affliction into humor. The moping doesn't appear on the page (except in this book), but in life it takes up a good deal of the day, and it is hard, I have found, for a woman to live with.

In the third grade, I didn't have all that worked out yet. I expected no sympathy from Mrs. Martin, but I did from my parents still, and although they were a bit ruffled after craning their necks looking for me throughout the angel portions of the pageant, they were comforting. My father, not explicitly. He had made a deal with my mother that he would make the living if she would raise the children.

My father gave me slack, which I appreciated, but I don't think he knew what to make of me. It seems to me possible that he had expressed concern to my mother about my regularity, thereby prompting her question to Wesley Freese. My father would sometimes bring me wonderful presents from his business trips—a ball autographed by the 1950 Yankees, for instance, which I still have. (Everyone has faded except DiMaggio.) But sometimes he would bring me a white short-sleeved shirt suitable for Sunday school or something else really lame, and I would pout, and he would look hurt and my mother would tax me with making my father feel bad. Mother once told Susan that she bought, and packed into his suitcase before he left, the presents Daddy brought home. "Why did she create the myth," Susan wonders, "if she was going to destroy it?"

Most of my painful childhood memories are of being made aware that I had hurt my parents' feelings. I don't recall there being any question of their hurting mine. I missed my mother enormously on the very rare occasions when she went somewhere without me for a few days, probably to nurse a sick relative or maybe once or twice on a business trip with my father. Mostly I was in her bosom. We played canasta, a card game. Then I did something bad, I don't remember what (how bad could it have been?), and to punish me, that was the end of our canasta. She was tough.

She read to me—the Mother West Wind stories, all the Winnie the Pooh books (though I found the wispy verses of *Now We Are Six* rhythmically nice but too sticky—so that when, in high school, I started reading urbane humorists, I was not too jolted to find Dorothy Parker, as Constant Reader, remarking of that Milne book, "Tonstant Weader fwowed up"), and particularly the Uncle Remus stories. The most formative literary experience of my life was getting a phonetic grip on the printed word as my mother read to me Joel Chandler Harris's versions of those old African-American animal tales. You needed to know the dictionary spellings of words, but if you were trying to capture spoken language on the page, you could spell by dead reckoning. "To be sure" as "tooby sho," "by and by" as "bimeby." I don't think I could have done anything bad enough for her to cut off the reading.

Early on, though, I began to read to myself. I no longer needed my mother for what was then, and still is now, the most intimate pleasure I know. Reading was our bond, but as soon as I was doing it myself, and doing it up a storm, we began to grow apart. That was okay. But I felt unfaithful when I showed her something funny I had read and she didn't get it.

That's all there is to the angel episode?

On the way home in the family car I began to cry. My mother got me ready for bed and held me on her lap for a long time, rocking me and singing, "Too-ra-loo-ra-loo-ral, That's an Irish lullaby"—which I now realize she must have picked up from *Going My Way*, which won the Best Picture Oscar in 1944. A warm-hearted young priest played by Bing Crosby sings a cranky old priest played by Barry Fitzgerald to sleep with that song. Knowing, as we do now, that in real life Bing was a cold-hearted parent enables me to watch this scene with some detachment. Bing is mellow, sure, but there's a bad streak there, you can see it in his condescending smile as the old man slips into dreamland.

The subsequent reunion of the old priest with his Irish mother, on the other hand, is so raw I can hardly stand it. The old lady is played by Fitzgerald's real-life mother. You don't know whether you're watching a movie or what. She enters, tottering, with "Too-ra-loo-ra . . ." in the background. He hasn't seen her in forty-five years. The Bing character has raised money to bring her from the old country as a surprise. The old man's face just barely changes expression when he recognizes her, and yet he's beaming. She takes his head in her hands and kisses him. As unsteady as she is on her feet, he buries his head in her shoulder, and she whispers something to him as if comforting a child. He gives her a grin and shakes his head bashfully. When he was making that movie Fitzgerald was fifty-five, the age I am now.

You want to be sung to sleep, then?

No, I have a ways to go before second childhood. I am, however, fifty-five. Can you imagine?

Yes.

· · ·

That *I'm* fifty-five, you can imagine. But that *you're* fifty-five? Even if you are? *Especially* if you are. One bitter night last winter at the bottom of the steps to my subway stop (I live in New York City, mostly, now), I saw a thin, whacked-out woman wearing nothing but a dress, hugging herself and shaking so hard that I thought she was going to tear herself apart. As accustomed as I am to bypassing misery in the Manhattan streets, I couldn't stand to see that, and I was only fifty yards from where I live, so I took off the ratty down jacket I was wearing and gave it to her. A gnarled, gimpy old man walked by and said, "Thass right. Get to be our age, you wanna do something good for a change." I knocked him down and took his coat.

How hard did you take not being an angel?

It was a loss, because my mother had instilled in me a taste for dramatic performance. She had me reciting "The Night Before Christmas" and a comic number entitled "Life Gets Teejus, Don't It?" to her Sunday school class by the time I was five.

But it was sweet, my face wet against her blouse as she crooned. I could have gone on all night. Although there was no such thing then as rock and roll, we were rocking.

There was a catch to it. Even then, I think, I had a sense that there was a catch to it. But it was, as they say, empowering.

Forty-six years later, on September 1, 1995, I was inducted into the Rock and Roll Hall of Fame.

Wait a minute . . .

Okay, that's stretching it. I was *admitted*, on that day, into the Rock and Roll Hall of Fame, along with a few, well, thousand other people. The first day it was open. In fact I would have been given a special tour through the Rock and Roll Hall of Fame the day before it opened to the public, if my trip to Cleveland had not been delayed by the hellbent rocker's life that I feel obliged to uphold as a beacon to future, or more precisely present, generations. That is, I had to drive my children somewhere. My children, and also my elder grandson. (He is very small. Mick has one too.)

I did help *found* the Rock and Roll Hall of Fame, on September 1,

1995, by blowing away a million-dollar benefit crowd with my solo on one of the five hundred songs that most shaped rock and roll.

Well, that's stretching it. I'm not so sure myself that "Wild Thing," originally by the Troggs—it is not for me to say that I have made it, or part of it, my own—was all that influential a song in rock and roll history, although it was selected as such by a board of experts in connection with the opening of the Rock and Roll Hall of Fame.

Which I perhaps didn't help found, exactly; *found* may be too strong a word. But my band and I (I am in a band) were the sole entertainment at a banquet, in a "Gala Pavilion Tent" erected outside the Rock and Roll Hall of Fame, which raised a million dollars (a thousand people at $1,000 a pop) to help fund the Rock and Roll Hall of Fame. The banquet crowd included Elton John. I didn't actually see him, but he was said to be there. If so, Elton John paid $1,000 (well, maybe he didn't have to pay—I didn't) to hear me sing:

"I luhv you."

Right exactly bang on when I was supposed to, pretty much. For the first time. The audience, perhaps sensing that history had been made, went wild.

Also on September 1, 1995, I became quite possibly the first person ever to steal something from the Rock and Roll Hall of Fame, as we shall see.

I have always had in mind being in a hall of fame someday. When I was a lad I assumed that it would be the baseball one, but that did not come to pass, though I lettered in high school. My friend Ruff Fant is in the Bird Dog Hall of Fame, in Grand Junction, Tennessee, but only because he happened to be standing near an all-time great dog when the latter's picture was being taken. Once I was mistaken for a Hall of Famer. I called up Billy Martin to interview him, for *Sports Illustrated*, and when he heard my voice he said, "Mick? Mick? Is this the old Mick?" When I said I wasn't Mickey Mantle but just me, Martin and I were both let down.

My chances of being enshrined in the Rock and Roll Hall of Fame have never been strong, because I got into rock-and-roll performance, as such, too late. I got into it in 1991, as an original member of the Rock Bottom Remainders, an author's band that has now sort of semi-disbanded, but that's what bands do, so let's just say that it also includes Stephen King,

Dave Barry, Amy Tan, Ridley Pearson, Mitch Albom and—our founder—author escort Kathi Kamen Goldmark. (It used to include Barbara Kingsolver, but she "got a life.") I am the emcee, and also part of the Critics' Chorus, in which I am joined by Dave Marsh, Matt Groening, Griel Marcus and Joel Selvin. We in the chorus sing titles, mostly. For instance on "Gloria" we sing "GLO-RI-A!" Some of us also sing "G-L-O-R-I-A," but I have never quite gotten the rhythm of that right, so I hang back and wait for "GLO-RI-A!" Also, I marry Amy on "Chapel of Love" and try to light her cigarette when she is wearing black leather and carrying a whip on "These Boots Are Made for Walking."

But "Wild Thing" is my big vocal number. The rest of the band goes:

> *Wild Thing, I think I love you.*
> *But I want to kno-ow for sure.*
> *So come on and . . . hold me tight . . .*

Then there is a pause.

No sound at all.

Just everyone waiting.

You may think it is easy, hanging back coolly as every rhythmically prescribed split second of this pause ticks away, ba-dum, ba-dum . . . , and then, and only then, coming in with:

   "I luhv you."

But it isn't. Easy. Because it isn't rock and roll if it isn't natural, and by nature I am reflective. While I am noiselessly muttering "ba-dum, ba-dum . . ." to myself (and one problem I have is that I have never been quite sure how many "ba-dums"), I get to reflecting noiselessly back over the years.

I reflect back, as tension mounts, on my career as national chairman of the League of the Singing-Impaired, an organization whose ranks are as enormous as they are unofficial. I have tried not to put too much emphasis on the singing-impaired (also known as the hard-of-singing) as victims. I have stressed the importance of research into what on earth causes people not to be singing-impaired. For instance, I read somewhere that Enrico Caruso could hold an entire egg in his mouth without anybody else knowing it was in there. He could be standing around at a party, just rocking back on his heels and keeping his own counsel, and until he opened his mouth and either an egg or an aria came out, no one would be the wiser. Try holding a whole egg in your mouth sometime without attracting odd stares, and see if you don't begin to wonder whether it is perhaps those who can sing well who constitute a freakish minority.

On the radio, on "A Prairie Home Companion," I have sung songs of my own composition. For instance, "A Cat's Song," to the only tune I can play on any instrument, "My Dog Has Fleas":

I don't like dogs.
Dogs don't like me.
I wish dogs would
Go climb a tree.

If I were big
And dogs were small
There wouldn't be
No dogs at all.

I'd eat them like
I ate the par-
Akeet that used
To perch up there.

But since dogs have
An edge on size,
I concentrate
On looking wise.

The time will come
When cats take charge
And there'll be no
Point being large.

That's all I have
To say for now
Except for purr,
Pfft and meow.

(The "I" of the song, of course, is a cat. I myself do like dogs, and it's mutual except when I'm singing.)

Here's something I have learned, in singing with live musical accompaniment: that it is harder than most people realize, not only to hit the right notes, but also to jump in at the right time. You assume you can jump in at the right time because you are used to singing along with records. You hear the recording artists jumping in and you think you would've known to jump in yourself, without them. When you're up there doing a solo, however, you find that the musicians will play along to the point when you're supposed to jump in, and then you don't. Did your father ever teach you to water-ski? He'd try to pull you up, and when you didn't make it he'd have to tow the rope wayyyyyyy back around to where you could grab the handle again. And then maybe you wouldn't quite grab it. So he'd have to tow it alllllll the way back around again. That's the way it is sometimes, when a singing-impaired person is performing with musicians.

When I'm doing "Wild Thing" with the Remainders, I'll be reflecting back over all the times I haven't jumped in on time—and suddenly I realize that I've lost track of my ba-dums. So I jump in.

And until September 1, 1995, I had never jumped in at quite the right moment with my solo:

"I luhv you."

But that night, for the first time, I jumped in, for all intents and purposes, on the nose. As I say, the audience ate it up. My bandmates eyed me with, if not new respect, at least a different sort of consternation. And as what I had done sank in, it struck me that what I ought to do, next, right there on stage, was die.

It would have been my closest brush with immortality. The Rock and Roll Hall of Fame is chockablock with unforgettable memorabilia—for instance, Keith Moon's high school report card and a piece of the wreckage of Otis Redding's plane, both of which give off an air of tragedy. (I have no fault to find with the Rock and Roll Hall of Fame except that the alphabetically arranged shrine of the inducted greats, upstairs, is kind of dinky, and unless they've fixed it since I saw it, Doc Pomus is not in the P's with Wilson Pickett but in the D's with Fats Domino.) But surely somewhere in that great elysium of vibes there is room for a niche where a small plaque might be placed in commemoration of a man who, though musically he qualified for handicapped parking, yet managed to give his all for rock and roll in one shining moment, in the Gala Pavilion Tent, and then his heart burst and, having found the beat at last, beat no more.

As it happened, I didn't die. Before I could finish considering it, the second verse came around, and I jumped in a little too soon with my second solo:

"You moove me."

So it's a good thing, for my place in history, that I had the foresight, that afternoon, to steal a T-shirt from the Rock and Roll Hall of Fame gift shop. My bandmates didn't seem to approve, but my thinking was, Hey, rock and roll is transgressive. If some other claimant should come forward, as having stolen something from the Rock and Roll Hall of Fame gift shop before 4:38 on the afternoon of September 1, 1995—let's see some proof. I have witnesses.

The next night, at the Rock and Roll Hall of Fame inaugural concert of a lifetime in Cleveland's Memorial Stadium, featuring Chuck Berry, Bruce Springsteen, Jerry Lee Lewis, the Kinks, Bob Dylan, Ray Charles, James Brown and just about everyone else who, like me, isn't dead yet, I of course jammed and hobnobbed backstage with the best of them. Okay, that's stretching it. I watched Aretha eat. As we on the inside have long known, she can evermore put it away.

That is how I make a living, doing things like that and writing about them. My father was a great home builder.

So that little boy who didn't get to be an angel—

That boy went on to a life of farcical efforts to get away from his mother's undying, unreciprocable love. Let's say, for the sake of argument.

"I just want to raise up you children," she would say, "and then I want to die." While we were trying to think what to say to that, she would add: "and you'll grow up and forget about me."

"No we won't, Mom."

"Yes you will, too." Jolly her out of it, right? You didn't know my mother. She'd get that deep, wise, nobody-knows-me look in her eyes: no, no, the pain is too deep, who could stand to remember me? If you argued with her, she'd just get angry, and if you gritted your teeth and insisted you damn well would (only you couldn't say damn) remember her, she would draw further back up into herself in a way that permeated the house with her, and if that made you splutter and tear your hair she'd say, "Don't fuss at me, Bucky."

Don't be croool. To a heart that's true.

That time she rocked me may have been the last time I cried to her. I remember running outside at about that same age, tripping, falling on my face. My first reaction is to jump up and run inside for sympathy, but then . . . no, I don't need that, there's a catch to it.

I jump up happy, running. See, that's what I like, that jump.

I'm eight. When my mother was that age her father died, leaving her with no parent but a stepmother who, as my mother would recall suddenly at unsettling moments, "would beat me till the blood ran."

If I'm eight, it's 1949, and my mother has already lost her eye, to the melanoma that resurfaced and killed her in 1981. She died without the consolation that I would be joining her in heaven. What was I going to do, lie? To my mother?

How much longer can I keep on jumping?

The time has come for me to lift the family curse.

CHAPTER 2 / Memories Are Made of This

Why not say what happened?   —ROBERT LOWELL (JR.), ON WRITING

What happened?   —ROBERT LOWELL (JR.), MANY MORNING-AFTERS

Any memoir leaves much to be said about memory. In my earliest memories, though they are far fresher than my recollection of where I put that pad on which I wrote down whatever it was that I remembered last night, there is an element of speculation. But if you can't stand behind your earliest memories, what can you stand behind?

Which reminds me of driving past a barbershop with a sign outside that said, "We Stand Behind Your Haircut," and my mother saying, "Honestly! I wouldn't want anybody standing behind my haircut."

"I believe that's the joke, Mom."

"Well, I know, but . . ." She went so far as to look over her shoulder and shudder. I also remember Steve Garvey, the baseball player, telling me that he wanted to live his life as if a twelve-year-old boy were always standing behind him. Later, he, Garvey, not the twelve-year-old boy, fathered children by two different women he wasn't married to.

Nobody's perfect. We memoirists do the best we can, by trial and error—science—and in the hope of grace. Unearned endowment. The difference between science and art.

Which is not to pooh-pooh science. Before realizing, in the tenth grade, that my destiny was to be a humorist, I gave some thought to becoming a biologist, and I still would love to make a contribution in that field. Not long ago, at a party given by my bandmate Amy Tan, I presented my hair theory of human evolution to the eminent evolution expert Stephen Jay Gould.

Briefly: that human beings are the only animals whose head hair grows so extraordinarily long that at some point our ancestors had to stand upright, develop front paws capable of brushing their hair back, and

22

grow a brain large enough to interpret the environment visually rather than—since they were too far off the ground to sniff it—olfactorily. For the full theory see my book *It Grows on You*.

Gould allowed, sociably, that my theory made "as much sense as any other." We humorists know that brush-off. In the course of the same conversation, Gould maintained that, because he had been allowed to keep to himself and pursue ideas, he had had a perfectly happy childhood. "Even his parents say that's not so," said his wife.

"Yes," Gould said, "each person has his own version. And mine is right."

Maybe Gould would have taken my hair theory of evolution more seriously if I hadn't, improvisationally, hazarded the ill-considered speculation that if all tiny dogs, such as Amy's, were fitted with silk bat wings, as Amy's had been for the evening, eventually they might evolve real wings because . . . Well, I got carried away there, I realize.

What do scientists want from me? Methodology? Research? Maybe I should have come to the party disguised as a disturbed street person, ranting and raving—like the disheveled woman my son Kirven sat across from in a library once. She muttered and pulled at her hair and then turned to the man who was with her and said, indignantly, "Why do you bring me to places like this?" If I had managed to pass myself off as such a person as that, then a scientist might pick up on my insight, because then he could compliment himself on selecting something genuine out of chaos. Whereas nobody wants to be caught taking a humorist straight.

Hey, humor is trial and error too. Keep on churning till the butter comes. But let's get one thing straight: nothing anybody says about his or her childhood is science.

Not that I'm making this up. If I were, it would have to make more sense. I am just being honest. As a Faulkner character in a fever of recollection puts it so well in *Absalom, Absalom!*: "There is no such thing as memory: the brain recalls just what the muscles grope for: no more, no less: and its resultant sum is usually incorrect and false and worthy only of the name of dream."

CHAPTER 3 / Who Dat Say Who Dat
When I Say Who Dat?

For a year, I felt real terrible. But after a while, I kind of just let
it leave my mind. I know what kind of person I am.
—BRIEN TAYLOR, WHO HAD A GREAT FUTURE AS A BASEBALL PITCHER
UNTIL HE INTERVENED IN A FIGHT BETWEEN HIS BROTHER AND
ANOTHER MAN AND HURT HIS SHOULDER, SHATTERING,
AS SPORTSWRITERS SAY, HIS DREAMS

You know when you're in a one-person rest room or stall and someone
outside, a stranger, tries the door? And tries it again, gives it a rattle,
not sure it's locked?

You hate to say, "I'm in here."

That is saying both too much and not enough. It raises issues of identity and intimacy that neither of you wants raised. The person who is trying the door thinks:

I? I who? As if I wanted to know! Anyway, I am I, and I am not some
kind of . . . toilet intruder!

And what if the door rattler responds, "Who is I?"

"Buster Melrose," say, the answer is. What then if the rattler, unim-
pressed, resumed rattling?

Maybe "Do that one more time and you're a dead man" would be effec-
tive, but who wants violence at such a time, when a moment of peace is
what is desired? To say not a word but to make a terrific voiding sound is
not always possible.

"Could I please have some privacy" sounds effete.

I have been the one who tries the door. Once, when I was in Iceland
covering the Boris Spassky–Bobby Fischer chess match for *Sports Illustrated*, I went into the men's room (*Snyrting*) in Reykjavik's Loftlieder
Hotel, checked both stalls vigorously, because you never know how these

24

things are set up in a foreign country, and both were locked but silent. I went back to stand against the wall and wait my turn.

There was a young Englishman there already, who said, "Both of them quite full, has been my conclusion."

One of them, it eventuated, contained Arthur Koestler.

Another time, many years later, do you know who was inside? Daryl Hannah.

I was interviewing her for *Harper's Bazaar*. Short piece, quick job, in and out, nice enough dollar, publicity for her forthcoming TV movie (*Attack of the Fifty-Foot Woman*). That's how a free-range writer makes a living, in between bouts of One's Own Work, but I can't do it unless it has a certain personal spice. I have had an affinity for the celluloid Daryl Hannah (and that little tan-all-over French girl, Valerie Quennessen, whatever happened to her?) since the sweet-young-threesome-on-a-Greek-isle scene in *Summer Lovers*, which I didn't mention to her. I've never mentioned it to anyone until now. As I told you, I'm telling everything.

She suggested we meet at the carousel in Central Park. We walked to a little café there in the park and had a beer. She was very nice, in a sylphlike kind of way. "A combination of carnality and moonglow," Pauline Kael called her in *Roxanne*, and even in person she seemed a little ethereal—but not, you know, trying to be. Tall, willowy, intelligent, no makeup, unstudied outfit, no airs. She reminded me of someone I was once actually happy with for several years.

She got up to visit the rest room, and after a minute or so I realized I had to go too. I found two closed doors, undifferentiated as to gender.

What could I do but try one of them? I didn't want to be lurking there when she got out. Furthermore, I didn't want to think of myself as a person who, you know, had some kind of issue that would prevent him from straightforwardly trying a rest-room door. . . . A friend of mine told me that he was so shy about bathrooms as an adolescent that when he had to resort to one at a party at someone's house, he knelt down when he peed so he wouldn't make a splashing noise that might be heard, and one time the lock on the door wasn't working and someone opened—look, I am not self-conscious about natural functions, generally, but every now and then you feel like you're back in high school, you know what I mean?

I tried one of the doors—wouldn't you know, the wrong one. From somewhere on the other side of it, a sylphlike voice said, "Excuse me."

No no no, excuse *me*. But I didn't say anything. Maybe she wouldn't know it was me. I went into the other room. Back at the table, neither of us mentioned it.

Filming *Splash*, she said, she would be thirty feet underwater for eight hours straight. Everyone else had on scuba gear, but she wore nothing but her mermaid tail. As she waited out the long delays between takes she would take hits off an air hose. And she's nearsighted, so she could hardly see. For a scene in which she was supposed to be fleeing a pursuer, the director, Ron Howard, indicated with hand gestures how she was to swim full speed past the camera, and the crewperson (mermaid wrangler?) who held the air hose would be waiting just beyond. But she misinterpreted the direction and missed the air man—who couldn't catch her, because the mermaid tail gave her such a powerful kick. She kept kicking, looking, lost, needing air, heading out to sea. She could have drowned. But Ron Howard got an angle on her, managed to intercept her just as her lungs were bursting, and they buddy-breathed off his mouthpiece.

Opie and the mermaid. That's nice, isn't it? Nice, it's a series! But it isn't life.

There was so little space allotted to the piece I wrote that I didn't have room for the diving story. The magazine mainly wanted to know what was up with her and John Kennedy Jr. (She wasn't sure.) We met a second time, went to a film festival on Long Island. I slipped her into the place without the paparazzi noticing, and she gave me a little cool-move gesture. That makes a fellow feel good, a little cool-move gesture from a sylph.

But no woman you're actually involved with—I'm not saying this is news to anyone, I'm just saying—is simply a sylph.

Filming *At Play in the Fields of the Lord*, Daryl said, she slept out in the jungle for months. At one point she confided to Kathy Bates, her costar and the only other woman around, that she was embarrassed doing a nude scene and Kathy Bates said, "Why do you think you're here?"

Every woman I've told that to has identified with Kathy Bates. A woman may dress and eat as though she aspires to be a sylph, but inside she is Kathy Bates—unslender, hungry, needy, aggrieved: the self.

The characters Kathy Bates plays (especially in *Misery*—she who so cherishes a man, a writer, that she breaks his legs to keep him captive) give men the shudders, but women love those characters. A man's got to do what a man's got to do, and one thing he's got to do is embrace a woman's Kathy Bates. And nature has given him no aptitude for it.

Later JFK Jr. called me to write something for his political magazine, *George*. "I know you wrote a story about my old girlfriend," he said.

That took me aback. I mean, I didn't need for him to say, "I have long admired your political insights," but . . . You have a sense of yourself as the sum of your experience, but every time you cross paths with someone else you realize you are just a little blip on his or her experience. When I meet people and they say in recognition, "Oh, yes" (not that they always do), I don't know what they are recognizing.

It's like—you know when you put on a T-shirt in the morning and don't think about what it says? And later you go outside and a complete stranger catches your eye and asks you, "Was it colder than you expected?"

And you stare at him wild-eyed and think to yourself, "What in the name of—"

And you see him looking at your chest and you look down and realize you're wearing the T-shirt that says, "I Swam the Nile with the Buffalo Gals," a T-shirt you've always liked because you never understood what it meant and you can't even remember who gave it to you?

Public recognition is like that. (Private too, sometimes, alas.) At least in my case. Because for a while in my checkered career I was a Southern newspaper columnist going back and forth between making fun of the forces of hate and dabbling in limericks inspired by the names of towns in Georgia:

> *There was a young lady of Climax*
> *Who cried out, "Why are you so shy, Max?*
> *Why why why why why*
> *Why why why why why*
> *Why why why why why why why* why *Max?*

And:

> *In the house of the Lord down in Glory,*
> *They tell the old, old story*
> *Of original sin:*
> *That judgments of men*
> *Are finally made* a priori.

Then for a while I was a *Sports Illustrated* writer covering college football games and doing profiles of Vida Blue and so on, and then I was freelancing long Gonzo-journalism magazine pieces about getting really drunk and staying up late with musicians or Billy Carter or somebody, with one hand, and obliquely humorous "casuals" for *The New Yorker* with the other.

I grew up dreaming of becoming a *New Yorker* writer, and that magazine took several pieces of mine, including a poem, and encouraged me to do more. At one point Mr. William Shawn, the legendary editor, referred to me as "our Mr. Blount." But Mr. Shawn also rejected a piece I wrote, in which a woman got superglued to a dry-cleaning apparatus, because he worried about how she would go to the bathroom. I'd be told that something I'd submitted was awfully funny but just not quite right for *The New Yorker*. A humor piece that was almost right for *The New Yorker* was probably not at all right for anybody else, which meant that I'd wasted two weeks of twisting my tongue exiguously around in my cheek and would have to run off and get drunk with somebody famous and write it up pell-mell so the children could have shoes. Finally, when William Whitworth left *The New Yorker* to edit *The Atlantic* and asked me to write for him, I decided, Fuck what was right for *The New Yorker*.

For several years I made up a cryptic crossword puzzle accompanied by Reagan-and-Bush-baiting commentary for the largely baffled readers of *Spy* magazine, then I settled pretty much into being a sporadic bordering-on-grizzled humorist in such a variety of magazines that no one, including me, could be expected to keep up with what I was doing. (Altogether I have written for 117 different publications, had regular columns in 11.) And then I wrote a moving picture—which (not "moving picture" but "wrote a moving picture") is a contradiction in terms, compounded in this case by the fact that it starred my friend Bill Murray, who prefers not to be too familiar with the script, and an elephant, who never gave the script a look.

Then too I reviewed country music regularly for a while, and I wrote a book about the Pittsburgh Steelers and another one more or less about the Carter administration and another one about hair and another one of verse about food and animals. I've been on "A Prairie Home Companion" a number of times over the years, badly singing songs I wrote or portraying Orpheus or Millard Fillmore or the Prodigal Son or a foolish virgin in sketches by my friend Garrison Keillor or playing the dozens with Paula

Poundstone, and for a few years there I was fairly often on *The Tonight Show* trading quips with Johnny or Jay. Then I wrote in *Spy* magazine that sitting there between Johnny and Tennille or somebody and Ed was "like being on Mount Rushmore, only we are all capable of some movement," and I was never asked to be on the show again.

I did a one-man show off-Broadway, talking for an hour and a half (my friend Calvin Trillin, who did a similar show, gave me credit for inventing the dramatic genre of "a middle-aged guy talking in a sportcoat"). I was on the lecture circuit for a while, and it was lucrative enough that I had in mind printing up a card that said "WAXING, ALL KINDS: FLOORS, LEGS AND ELOQUENT"; but I got to where every time I swung into a tried-and-true anecdote a voice in my head would expostulate, "Oh God! You're not going to tell the piranha story again!"

There was a period there where I specialized in personal-adventure stories, rafting the Amazon and riding camels in Kenya and scuba diving with sharks. William Hazlitt in "On Personal Identity" says we all wish at some time or another that we were someone else, but we don't want to stop being ourselves into the bargain, because then we couldn't enjoy being the other person. I did things other people do, things I wouldn't do, and wrote about them. But I had a bad experience in a huge tank of water at the Redstone Arsenal—let's just say I washed out of the space program.

At one point I was just on the verge of getting famous, because I was doing a weekly five-minute off-the-cuff essay on the CBS *This Morning* show, but then I delivered a dissenting view on condoms and honored the TV newswriters strike although I didn't have to and met an English foreign correspondent named Christabel and started making frequent trips to London, and for one or all of those reasons I got canceled. I passed up a couple of chances to make guest appearances in sitcoms—the truth is, I didn't want to be a TV guy. I have had bit parts in three movies, and Andie MacDowell sang one of my songs, about pie, in *Michael*, but no one would know that except that I tell everyone I meet. For three years or so I wrote a right lively column, if I do say so, in *Men's Journal*, and then one day they called up and said they had a new woman publisher and they were going in a new direction. (I like to think the publisher, whoever she is, was offended by my writing, in response to a statement in the *New York Times* that women were making men go see *The First Wives Club*, that I would never have thought of making any women go see *Deep Throat*.) As the Parthenon proves, columns come and columns go.

Every time I get a niche, I get an itch. Because I am terrified of getting trapped in a nurturing (by the environment's standards) environment. If I'd become firmly established at *The New Yorker*, I'd either have been dumped, like some of my friends there, or I'd have quit, like most of the rest of my friends there, and Tina Brown would have called up and made me feel guilty. I'm not tough enough for that. I don't ever want to feel as rotten again as my mother and my wives (in very different ways—the consistent thread, no doubt, was my fault line) made me feel.

The upshot is that I never know what hat, if any, I may be wearing in a given person's eyes. It gets even more confusing when a Kentucky newspaper describes me as "a Randy Newman lookalike whose father wrote for *Sports Illustrated* for years" (ah, the confusions of being a junior).

A few years ago, the New York Public Library named me a literary lion, which meant that generous supporters of the library paid in the low four figures apiece to dine formally with a number of distinguished authors, including (how can I put this modestly enough, but not so modestly as to suggest that there must have been some mistake?) me. I behaved with as much distinction as was possible, I believe, considering that it was my credo in those days to drink enough free cocktails, champagne and wine as to leave no doubt in my mind that I had amortized, at least, the tux rental. I noticed that most people in New York who could afford to dine with me on such an occasion had to look at my name tag before asking me what I was working on, and I wrote a little essay about the experience for, oddly enough, *Vogue*, and reprinted it in a book of mine under the title "We Feed, We Lions," an allusion to a Philip Levine poem that I doubt anyone caught.

Then the tenth anniversary literary lion gala came around. Ten batches of lions, some two hundred in all, assembled at the library. We had cocktails with the patrons, then we were led to a hallway outside the glittering dining hall. Meryl Streep said a profound thing once to the graduating class of Vassar: "You're leaving college now, and going out into real life. And you have to realize that real life is not like college. Real life is like high school." Sometimes, in fact, it is like grammar school. For in that hallway a harried man with a clipboard lined us up alphabetically.

There we stood, waiting to make our individual entrances. I now know where I stand in the contemporary pantheon: between Harold Bloom and Judy Blume. I got along fine with Judy, but Harold and I didn't really hit it off. I thought I would break the ice by mentioning *The Book of J*, a new translation of an ancient scroll alleged to be the kernel from which not only the Old Testament but also the Koran and the Torah eventually derived. Bloom had contributed an introduction, in which he contended that it was in this prototype sacred work that the original Jahweh character was created, and that the author of the work must have been a woman.

So I say to Harold, lightly, "That must be a good way to meet women, to be able to say, 'Hello. I'm the man who says that a woman made up God.' "

"No!" he replied, I had it all wrong. Feminists didn't even like his theory, he said, and he went on to decry the decline of the Western sense of humor, meanwhile looking around for someone more congenial to hob-nob with.

That sort of thing was happening all up and down the line, apparently, because L's were drifting over to chat with A's, N's with S's and so on. To the consternation of the man with the clipboard.

"People!" he cried. "I can't do this if you won't stay in order! And please, shhhhhhh!"

Well, when you're a literary lion you hate to be shushed, somehow, but it was all in a good cause, so we muttered and got back in line and behaved.

As the man with the clipboard peered through a crack in the door to the glittering dining hall, he would grab the first lion in line, wait for just the right moment, and then thrust him or her into the great room.

Being a B, I was among the first to be seized and injected. I stepped into the great, gala space there and heard a highly amplified familiar voice. I looked to the podium and saw that my introducer was, by gosh, Barbara Walters. Cool. Feeling, I must admit, heightened, I strode—no, let's choose exactly the right word: I proceeded, as literarily as possible, toward the table to which I was pointed.

"AND NOW," I heard Ms. Walters saying, "A HUMORIST . . ."

As I proceeded past a woman in what appeared to be a gown of sewn-together black pearls, I believe I actually winked.

". . . A NOVELIST . . ."

Very nice. Barbara Walters was aware that I had written a novel.

". . . AND, INCIDENTALLY, A VERY GOOD COOK . . ."

That threw me. I have done a number of things over the years, at night, that I couldn't remember the next day. One morning I awoke in my New Orleans hotel room, hauled myself unsteadily to the bathroom and looked into the mirror.

There, in the middle of my forehead, was a big, thick gout of dried blood.

Well, I thought to myself, I am going to have to change my way of living. I thought back over the preceding evening. For the life of me, I couldn't remember having been shot.

Then I switched on the light and looked more closely, and saw that it wasn't blood. I had just slept on my complimentary mint.

I do have a dim recollection of helping my late friend Pete Axthelm talk a stripper named Misty into lending him her pistol one night in Augusta, Georgia, so that he could take it outside and fire it into the air* as part of our coverage of the Masters golf tournament. And I believe I did help Larry L. King and Marshall Frady talk an editor out of shooting his aged and suffering border collie one night at about 4:00 a.m. in his New York apartment (back when that sort of thing was part and parcel of the writing life), but the editor maintains that part of my argument was a recitation of "Old Shep," and I can't even remember ever knowing "Old Shep" by heart.

At any rate, I couldn't imagine, as I approached my table in that gala library hall, that I could possibly have cooked dinner for Barbara Walters and forgotten it. For one thing, I was pretty sure I had never met Barbara

---

*Not a good idea. Bullets come down. When Axthelm died in 1991 of liver failure—he'd been told twice to quit drinking or die, and he'd quit twice and started again—it was the end of an era. In high school and college I was a teetotalling straight arrow, and then I was a graduate student drudge, and then I was a regular if apparently uninspired family man, so it wasn't until I got divorced that I realized I had a talent for carousing in the line of duty—the duty being to find out what rowdy people were really like and somehow remembering, later, what they had said and done. My health held out (partly, no doubt, because I got started late) long enough for me to slow down. Ax, three years younger than me, died. A couple of years ago there was a TV movie about Earl "Goat" Manigault, an immortal of Harlem playground basketball who was too cool for organized ball. He's in prison, at low ebb, and a guard asks him if he knows that he figures big in a book. He's surprised. The guard gives him a copy of *The City Game*, Axthelm's sports-classic reportage about the courts where the Helicopter was dominant. Manigault, transfixed, struggles to read his own legend. Ax's actual physical book—you can see the title and everything—has a big emotional scene in a *movie*, in *jail*, and Ax isn't alive to see it. It made you hope there is a heaven and good-humored alcoholic degenerate gamblers get to go there and it has cable.

Walters. For another thing, I can whip up a pretty interesting soup or spaghetti sauce, but a great cook? No.

". . . NORA EPHRON!" concluded Walters.

Somehow, for all the careful planning that must have gone into this very impressive occasion, the list of lions had gotten jumbled. Barbara Walters went through the first half of the alphabet, and then Tony Randall took over and did the second half, and every name was wrong. At one point Randall said, ". . . GEORGE PLIMPTON!" and a diminutive Indian woman (the very engaging and accomplished novelist Bharati Mukherjee) walked out.

Often, I have found when I rattle the door, a voice inside says this:

"There's someone in here."

Someone. It's self-objectifying. You're putting yourself in the other person's perspective. And at the same time, it's too poignant. Writing about yourself, you come down somewhere between someone and I.

Several years ago I was walking down Broadway when I noticed a man coming toward me and sort of . . . recognizing me out of the corner of his eye. You don't want to smile and make direct eye contact in that situation for several reasons, but he kept cutting his eyes toward me, so I was about to give him a slight, gracious nod when I realized that he looked familiar, and then I realized that he was the (now late) actor Raul Julia, and he was thinking that I was recognizing him.

I will say this for myself. Many a person might have lost all focus, from being perceived so diffusely. The only thing that has kept me keeping on is that I don't blame myself for the amorphousness of my place in the culture, I blame the culture. I have always been writing and talking about the same thing. Probing for the same frisson. Just nobody has noticed.

Even when I was writing full-time for *Sports Illustrated*, which was interesting work but not exactly the kind of expression that was the need of my soul, I was getting at certain things. Down in Mansfield, Louisiana, I interviewed Vida Blue's high school football coach:

"I remember when we played Booker T. Washington in Shreveport. They were always our chief obstacle. We were ahead 13–0 at the half and it started raining cats and dogs. So Vida ran it the whole second half— every play we had the ball except when we punted, he ran. He wouldn't throw it or hand it off. He could take a beating. They'd get up saying, 'We know we killed Blue,' but he'd get right back up and run again. We won 13–0."

And then Vida Blue's mother:

"That game was the night Mr. Blue passed. He'd had a heart attack and been sick about six months. Junior didn't want to go to the game, he said he'd stay with me. But I told him, 'You can't hurt your father if you go and you can't help him if you stay, so you go on and play ball.' "

Not long after that night, Vida signed a big-league baseball contract. His owner, an unabashed jerk named Charles O. Finley, asked him to change his name, for reasons of promotability, to True Blue. He refused, and after that Finley seemed to make a point of underpaying him and breaking his spirit. "Finley took the little boy out of Vida," his teammate Reggie Jackson told me (he also said he liked to hit on days when Vida pitched because big crowds came out to see Vida and that made the air in the stadium warmer, which meant Reggie's home runs would travel farther), "and you can't play this game without some little boy in you." Blue was the best player in baseball when he was twenty-one, but after that he struggled, got into drugs, eventually served a prison term. Maybe he had his Great Moment too soon, that night against Booker T. Washington.

A media notion is the Defining Moment of a presidency. The time the rabbit attacked Jimmy Carter, that sort of thing. But I think it more likely that a person's destiny derives from a Great Moment, good or bad, which may come early in life, leaving the person frustrated by anticlimax in his or her prime.

Imagine that your family is the Blues, and you're black, and your first name is Vida, which means life, and you're Vida Blue Jr., and on a dark and stormy night, in your adolescence, Vida Sr. passes away while you are not only refusing to pass but also rising up again and again as people do their best to kill you.

On another *Sports Illustrated* story I was out in Cortland, Ohio, talking to the Job family. "The Impatience of Mrs. Job" was the headline on the eventual story. The Job children all developed into champion swimmers, because their mother drove them to it. Brian Job went so far as to become a world-class breaststroker. He told me:

"There's always a fear. You know you're not going to die, but you know that if you swim a fast time it will hurt so much, and you're afraid of that. But I . . . always hated to have somebody right next to me, keeping right up with me, and I used to work to where I could stay way out in front of everybody. But there would always be somebody else keeping up. So I would progress in stages.

"My breaststroke today is exactly the same stroke my mom taught me back in the lake. . . . No coach has ever touched my stroke.

"I hated my mom. I can remember lying on my bed and wondering how God could be so mean as to give me a mom like her. All the other kids had nice moms, I thought, why should I have her?

"I hated swimming. I mean, I know I don't hate my mom. . . ."

You can't hate your mom. That would be your whole character right there, you sorry son of a bitch. When you're the person inside the rest room and someone is trying the door, your first instinct would always be to cry out, *"I'm in here leave me alone I don't hate my mom!"*

CHAPTER 4 / Language! Language!

Dancing fleas, for example, are actually just scurrying around trying to get out from under their tiny flea formal wear.

—*SKY,* THE DELTA IN-FLIGHT MAGAZINE

GET YOUR FILTHY NASTY DIRTY HAND OFF MY NICE STOMACH!" I shouted one day to my sister Susan—just kidding, we were actually playing nicely, pretending to be siblings picking on each other. We never felt free to go at each other in earnest because it bothered my mother so. We had better love each other, she would say, because we were going to need each other when she was gone. Anyway, I was seven years older, so Susan was too little and cute to hit.

I always thought the seven-year gap was a measure of my mother's reluctance to risk childbirth again, but Susan informs me that "Mother had fertility problems, tipped uterus, and had to have all sorts of treatments, including her tubes blown open."

We were never in the same school at the same time, which seems kind of a shame. The only downright mean things I can remember doing to Susan were grabbing her physically and dragging her away from my friends and me once when we didn't want a little girl around, and yelling furiously at her when I was thirteen and she was six and she had spoiled, by way of playing what she innocently thought would be a funny trick, a potential hole in one at the miniature golf course by blocking the chute that the ball rolled down, toward the hole, if you hit it just right. I felt recurrent sharp pangs of fierce guilt over those moments—she was a sweet little girl, who looked up to me—until I told Susan so, just a couple of years ago, and she said neither incident had bothered her much. I was almost disappointed.

Anyway my pretend yelling had been so loud that my mother exclaimed, "Good gracious alive, Bucky! The neighbors will hear you!" She was always concerned that we give every impression of being just as reputable as, in fact, we were—but she was smiling. Then she saw what our black-and-white mixed terrier, Chipper, was doing. "And Chipper's just sitting there, chewing on the chair leg!" she said. Chipper looked up and gave us a smile that was sort of ingratiating, but not exactly. Some people have mean dogs, some people have pretty dogs, we had funny dogs.

Our dogs were greatly indulged, but they also put up with a lot, emotionally. They often walked around looking as if they were talking to themselves, probably because we talked to, and for, them too much.

"This is the craziest family!" my mother cried, happily. Things were out of her hands, and yet things were all right.

I thought of that moment years later, the year before she died, when I was tentatively trying to talk some things through with her and she asked me, "Don't you remember *anything* good?"

She took me by surprise. I hadn't been *complaining*.

I resented being put on the defensive. I couldn't think of anything to say. If I had offered her that little craziest-family vignette. . . . I think she had in mind something more like the last scene in *I Remember Mama*. Irene Dunne plays the unselfishly supportive mother of an aspiring writer (Barbara Bel Geddes). "Write about Papa," Mama says when the daughter is urged by an editor to write what she knows. The movie ends with daughter reading aloud to the family what she has written—fondly, publishably, to Mama's astonishment—about Mama. Unsought gratitude is sweet. That movie came out in 1948, the year cancer took my mother's right eye.

My mother needed me to warm her heart, that year before she died. But I wasn't in a heartwarming frame of mind. Something funny would have been good, but . . . here's a terrible thing: my mother and I didn't have very compatible senses of humor.

> *There once was a lady, Louise,*
> *Whom no one could ever quite please—*

There are no last three lines to that limerick that my mother would have enjoyed.

Life isn't comic, you know. I know, you know, say no more—just so we're straight on that.

For the life of me I couldn't come up with a sweet reminiscence for my mother, that time in the last year of her life, and the conversation drifted off painfully, and not long afterward, the cancer resurfaced. In the space of six months she appeared to age twenty years, wasted away to nothing and died.

I didn't save her. She would have saved me.

We never talked things through, either. I did tell her, on her deathbed, that I loved her.

"Do you, son?" she said.

She also said, "I hope so, because I sure love you," but what I can't get out of my mind—it pisses me off, it leaves me out over an abyss—is, "Do you, son?"

And, you know, here's the thing: we *were* crazy.

Well, functional families are all alike.

Once, after I made a speech in Dallas, a man came up to me and said, "Your father could make a roomful of men laugh longer without ever using bad language than any man I ever knew." Daddy was dead by then. I was astonished.

I don't mean I was astonished that he was dead, although I was, and still am. He died in 1974, twenty-three years ago, at sixty. My mother went sixteen years ago at sixty-six. Before I could get to know them.

I mean I was astonished that my father had such a humorous reputation. I heard him tell two jokes my whole life. "I knew a man who ate so much okra he couldn't keep his socks up." And "You think I'm stoopid—my father used to walk like this," and he'd take a few steps all humped over. He was good.

At my first wedding rehearsal dinner he got up and told a long joke, pretty funny as I recall, and mildly spicy, but I don't remember a word of it. Because it doesn't fit my sense of him.

God damn it.

I'm not astonished about his not using bad language. We didn't swear in our house. My mother thought the F word was *fib*. I thought she was going to die of indignation when my daughter Ennis, at age four, dropped her ice cream and said, "Damn!"

"Where did that child learn gutter language?" my mother wanted to know.

Of course when Susan and I were kids, my mother would sometimes get so frustrated with being a housewife that she would yell at us, "You put me through pluperfect hell!" Or, "double-jointed hell!"

But that was because she *believed* in Hell. The place.

CHAPTER 5 / **And Now, This**

"How'd you get to be a pickpocket?"
"How'd I get to be a pickpocket! How'd you get to be what
you are? Things happen, that's all!"

—JEAN PETERS AND RICHARD WIDMARK,
RESPECTIVELY, IN *PICKUP ON SOUTH STREET*

So many things that you'd think would go without saying, don't. I have
learned that the hard way, over the years. So here's what a woman
would say to me, probably:

"Why don't you start saying those things, then?"

For one thing, I never seem to know which things, until too late. You
don't want to go around saying every obvious thing you can think of every
minute of the day.

For another thing, so many things that are said don't go over.

I remember one evening in Atlanta nearly thirty years ago, when
Ellen, my first wife, asked me what I thought love was, and I said: "Mutuality." (A word I had seen in an ad in *The New Yorker* for a new edition of
Webster's unabridged.) And she looked at me as if I had confessed that
what I really wanted out of life was sex with dead people.

I may be exaggerating. I may be too sensitive to a woman's looks. I
have come to believe that those men whom women call sensitive, in a
good sense, are in fact men who are insensitive enough to take the hit of a
woman's look and then unflinchingly behave in a way that women regard,
approvingly, as sensitive. These men get a sense of what women want
them to sense, and then they pretend to sense it.

At any rate, Ellen looked at me as though I'd put into words the abyss
that yawned between us. Which I guess was true. But I thought I was, you
know, relationshipping. And jeez, we were married and had a baby. We had
another baby after that.

39

And I still think the notion of mutuality is romantic. Romantic as in impractical, I guess.

I was a fifties person. I thought this was what people did: you met someone in college and married her so you wouldn't burn (my mother often quoted the apostle Paul), and then you hunkered down and tried to be, if not sweet, at least nice. Now, *now,* I see that to be a severely limited expectation, but tell me this: where could I have been expected to come by a less limited one? As far as I could tell from the culture, Lucy and Ricky were as good as it got. What I didn't know was that people got married and then broke up. Ever since that first divorce I've been improvising.

I was in love with a beautiful actress. We were talking about our relationship and she said, "I just believe in following the script."

I said, "There's a script?"

The look on her face then!

Maybe there is a script, and everybody but me got a copy. When I was seventeen I embarrassed myself by letting it slip, in conversation with a girl who was cute and two years younger than me, that I didn't know what a church key was. She looked at me in disbelief. "You're so smart," she said (I made good grades), "and you don't know anything."

I have made it my business since to know about church keys. As in beercanopener. Not as in a key to a literal church. Your mother ever call you an infidel? Mine called me one. An infidel. Not kidding, at *all.*

That's the kind of unexpected word, a literary word, that will hit a son in just such a way that it really registers.

I have myself always had a tendency, according to women, to be too literal.

> To too sharply focused Pierre,
> A lady protested, "I swear.
> Don't be so literal.
> When I speak of clitoral
> I mean all around down in there."

But how do you ever find anything out any other way? Still, I am driven by the desire to get things, in the hip-to sense. Primarily, to get what women have in mind when they say, "You just don't get it."

An expression which I don't find helpful. Did Gandhi say to the British empire, "You just don't get it"? Maybe he did. But I'm not the British empire! I'm a human being!

"I just don't argue with women," a friend of mine told me not long ago (his second marriage is pleasant to be around—but then, so was his first), and there, it hit me, is wisdom.

I have several provocative insights about relationships, myself. But paramount among them is that you can't base a relationship on provocative insights about relationships. A relationship is based on the man throwing up his hands. Sweetly. Anyway, nicely.

But I can't help it! I have a deep-seated need to thrash things out with women. To get down to brass tacks. And they look at me as though I am leaning too hard on tender buttons. I guess because, willy-nilly, I am thinking, to a considerable extent, with my you-know.

Five years ago some of my friends threw me a fiftieth-birthday party enlivened by a sketch in which the ladies among the company portrayed, one by one, the exotic cavalcade of women I had broken up with in my forties—serial fizzled relationships. On that occasion I made two resolutions.

One: to do as many as possible of the few things I had never done so far (drive a race car, scuba dive, go to China, paddle way back up into a swamp, write a movie that would actually get made). I have done those things, and more—have had two grandchildren, have mocked an incumbent president of the United States live on national TV while he made an acceptance speech on the same screen, have run for president (vicariously, with my friend Lamar Alexander), have sung "Gloria" on stage with Bruce Springsteen (he stepped in with us Rock Bottom Remainders). . . .

Two: to figure out why I couldn't seem to get what a woman might call "a life." Five checkered years later . . .

> *A take-it-slow lady named Sybil'd*
> *Rather be nuzzled and nibbled:*
>   *"Why is it when I'm*
>   *Approaching sublime,*
> *You're coming down off of ribald?"*

> *Jeanne, when plied with a gem*
> *And a magnum of Chateau d'Yquem,*
>   *Said, "I haven't used a-*

Ny soap since last Tuesday.
Guess you go for my eau de moi-meme."

. . . have I made any progress? As a great philosopher once said, "I'm trying to think!"

Does everybody else have a copy of the script? Or does nobody, really, and as they say in moviemaking, "That's a writer's problem"?

Will I ever get to the bottom of those questions?

Will I ever get to the bottom of that question?

You might say that humor is bouncing up as if there were a bottom.

Is there a bottom?

Is there a source?

A few years back, yet again out trying to ensure that a book of mine would reach and touch as many souls as feasible (given the fact that my thinking is evidently more unusual than it seems to me), I met a woman. But briefly. She was coming off a radio talk show in Atlanta as I was coming on.

She was the hooker who had recently blown the whistle on Jimmy Swaggart, the TV preacher. No, that's not right: a brother in Christ had blown the initial whistle. But having been brought to the realization of who her client had been, this fallen woman had been willing to cast—not in malice, but in the interests of full disclosure—what must have struck Reverend Swaggart as follow-up stones.

Let us say, without dwelling on the details, that she made no bones about the fact that Swaggart (fateful name!) had on more than one occasion paid her to provide him with active, illicit, visual stimulation.

I don't remember her name, I'm embarrassed to say, and I don't think I ever got exactly what it was that she was promoting. Just virtue, maybe. But I'll never forget what she said to me.

She said, "When I was coming on, you know who was coming off? Jimmy Carter." He had given her, she was pleased to report, a gracious hello, one guest to another.

"Little did I know," she said, "when I was showing my you-know to Jimmy Swaggart, that it would lead to meeting the president of the United States."

Former president, to be more precise, and I can't deny that it put me off just a little bit that she was not gracious enough to add, "and you too of course"—but the question is, what was the purpose behind that sequence of convergences? Jimmy Swaggart wasn't *idly* seeking a you-know to look at. He wasn't *casually* out scouting around for somebody who would show him hers. He *needed* to see a you-know, right then. God made him need to see one. Maybe God was tired of being preached at in that particular kick-ass TV tone. Maybe God wanted to tempt, in a roundabout way, Jimmy Carter one more time. Maybe God wanted to give me an anecdote with which to nudge along this book.

Little do I know.

CHAPTER 6 / **You Had to Be There**

No, not at all. If it was a mistake, I wouldn't have written it.
—NEW YORK JET WIDE RECEIVER KEYSHAWN JOHNSON, WHEN ASKED
WHETHER HE CONSIDERED HIS BOOK *JUST GIVE ME THE DAMN BALL,*
IN WHICH HE INSULTED SEVERAL TEAMMATES, TO BE A MISTAKE

You know the feeling, "There's something I'm supposed to do today—what is it?"? I've had that all my life.

At the same time I've had the feeling that I'd better not do it, whatever it is.

One day my mother was at the front door paying the bread man, and she looked down at the loaf of bread he had delivered (this was back when such things were done), and my sister Susan, who was two or three at the time, was sitting on it.

"Why on earth," my mother asked her, *"would you want to sit on a loaf of bread?"*

I wasn't there. But I can see it from both points of view. A loaf of bread—the mooshy white kind in a wrapper, probably Merita brand where we lived, back then—would be inviting to sit on if you're low to the ground and it's right there. Yet you'd have a hard time explaining why you did it, once the strangeness of it was brought to your attention. Aren't so many things we do in life like that?

From the parent's standpoint, there is something weird about a child who sits on bread. Especially if it's your child. You wonder, does this derive—surely not—from some buried proclivity of mine? If not, then where from? Is the child testing me in some way, out to get me, to show me up?

And my mother went through the Depression: you don't sit on food!

Now. On the other hand. I can remember times when I expressed perfectly understandable dismay about something weird Susan was doing, and my mother would say, in a certain humorous tone, "She's not hurting anything. If it pleases her to put syrup on her peas [or whatever], let her do it."

I attended Sunday school regularly at a formative age, so to this day when I don't know what to do about something, I think of what Jesus would do—or rather what he would want me to do, since he'd be busy—and I think, I'm not about to do *that*. But I feel bad about not doing it, and the upshot is that it's never quite clear *what* I did, unless a woman tells me, and then it often doesn't sound to me like what I did, and I can't help arguing about it. This is hard on a relationship.

And another thing: one Sunday morning while we were singing "Red and yellow, black and white, they are precious in his sight, Jesus loved the little children of the world," it occurred to me that all of us were white. I didn't make a stink about it. Jesus would have, but I was only nine, and I doubt there were any red or yellow children in Decatur at the time, and the black ones were in a separate world back then, and since I didn't fit into that class very well as it was, who needed complications? I just wondered, Why did they teach us that song if they didn't mean it? As I mentioned before, one of my problems is, I take things literally. And then I realize that I shouldn't, not so literally, but then how do you know *how* literally?

Later, in my teens, I was going to invite some African Methodist Episcopalians to visit our Methodist Youth Fellowship, but our pastor got wind of it and told me not to. So, I didn't. One way of being literal, without having to do anything, is to write.

But what?

Whatever lifts the family curse. I have begun to feel that I may be able to do that—now, just as I'm reaching the stage in life when every couple of weeks somebody I know who's about my age dies. You don't get a foot in the door till you've got one in the grave.

That's the kind of thing my mother would have written, if she had been the writer.

She should have been. But she never told me, even, the story of her life, except for horrifying snippets.

And yet it falls to me . . .

I'm going to level with you now. I did some research for this book, and found something out. It's quite possible that nobody even told *her* the truth about a key part of her life story.

If I found out about it, she could have. Or she could have told what she *thought* was the story. She had the requisite alcoholic father and sainted mother. She even had a wicked stepmother. That story tells itself, bing bing, Oprah would have eaten it up.

As opposed to my story, the story of a boy who nearly kills his mother at birth. Show me the precedent. Show me the fairy tale, show me the Greek tragedy, about a boy who nearly kills his mother.

Instead of laying that story on me, she should have been the writer.

Then, okay, I would be someone to whom people say, "Your mother is *Louise Floyd* Blount? *The* Louise Floyd Blount? Author of *My Life: A Living Hell*, not to mention *Every Little Breeze Seems to Whisper 'Louise, There Is a Reason You Were Singled Out for Unparalleled Misery'*?"

As it is, I am a humorist. At dinner last night, a humorist friend of mine was dolefully recounting, at some length and to his own considerable morose satisfaction, a deeply dissatisfying experience he had had, when a woman in the company exclaimed, "But I read what you wrote about that! And it sounded like so much fun!"

"Yes. But now," he intoned, "I'm among friends."

Other people's life stories are so clear-cut. Abused by superior court justice father, abandoned by bareback-rider mother, true parents discovered living in an alcove behind the furnace all these years. These are life stories you can run with.

Most of the things I have done of general interest, I have recounted—having done it in the first place in order to have something to recount—soon afterward, for a living.

Meanwhile, lurking beneath everything I do is this curse that I just *inherited*.

I daresay it's what made me funny. I don't care. I want to lift it.

First I've got to reconstruct how it has affected me, which won't be easy because, except for certain personal and embarrassing moments that fall into the category of I Don't Believe I'd've Told That, I don't remember much unless I was taking notes at the time.

And I believe it is wrong to take notes at moments in one's actual personal life—toilet training, say, or marriages. That would be a form of betrayal. I remember once, long after I had given up going to church, when my sweet second-wife-to-be, now ex-wife, Joan and I took my mother to Christmas Eve services in the New England village where Joan and I and my children were living happily (I thought) in sin, and during the doxology I couldn't help myself, I had such a rush of bizarre Methodist-Oedipal recollection that I started scribbling on the program, and afterward my mother asked me, "What were you writing, son?" and Joan said, "He was taking notes." I threw those away. It was the only honorable thing.

Over the years I did record, in notebooks, bits of my mother's voice. For instance:

"Why, land, that man was all over the stage. He's just as funny as he can be; right caustic with it at times, but—"

Why did I write that down? Because it was so nice to see my mother so delighted, but also, I'll bet, because whomever she was talking about was somebody I had a different perspective on. I have sat here for an hour now, trying to think who it might have been. She liked Dick Van Dyke, who started in Atlanta mugging and lip-synching to records on a local TV show, *Merry Mutes*. Together we enjoyed the old Sid Caesar show, and Martin and Lewis, and George Gobel, Red Skelton, Jack Benny.

Whomever she was talking about, he can't have been any too caustic. My mother lived to see two of my books. Neither of them was as lurid as what she laid on me, but both of them disturbed her.

And yet why have I pursued humor to such an absurd extent—to the point of vocation—if not because I grew up desperately wishing I could do something to keep my mother from being so sad and angry?

Here's something else that I recorded, something my mother wrote me while I was in college and Susan was in high school: "Susan is struggling with *For Whom the Bell Tolls*. She doesn't like it much. I think Mrs. Russell could suggest something that would mean a lot more to a fifteen-year-old girl."

That I'm sure I set down as an example of my mother's parochialism. My mother who asked me once what Hemingway's first name was.

We now know, though, that my mother was right about *For Whom the Bell Tolls*. One of the key female characters is as rough as a man, and the other is palpable and mute as a globed fruit.

We now know, furthermore, that it was a pretty raw deal to be a fifties mom.

But I've gotten to the point where I'm loath to let a woman cook a meal for me, lest I incur an onus that I'll never hear the end of.

Oh cursed spite, that ever I was born to set it right.

CHAPTER 7

A Day in the Life

Believe it or not, children like the Family Circus. And children don't mind stale jokes, because they haven't heard them before. Many stale jokes have become stale because they're funny enough to be repeated many times. If you no longer print stale jokes, how will the culture of jokes be passed on to the next generation?

—FROM A LETTER TO THE OMBUDSMAN
COLUMN OF THE *WASHINGTON POST*

I awoke this morning to a rewinding noise.
     And the smell of my own underarm. Know it anywhere. Prefer some-one else's. Someone else's something else. But what if she were accusing me—with reason—of not expressing my feelings and of not validating hers? And what if I were resisting—manfully—the feeling that she woke up in a mood to make me feel like everything I say makes her feel worse?

I knew who I was (you are who you are when you first wake up), but where?

Oh. Home. Insofar as I have one. And the rewinding noise would be my answering machine.

A severe, perhaps Swiss-accented woman's voice that grows righteously angrier and angrier:

"Well, what's your name? You don't say your name! How can you expect that anyone will leave a message if you don't say your name? Well. This is . . . Why should I tell you who I am? I am calling for Danielle, but, huh, I am not going to leave a message, *pffff,* if you don't say your name!"

Click. My outgoing message is not so outgoing as to say who I am, since I assume, vainly, that anybody who is calling me knows. I don't know anyone named Danielle.

The phone rang. A woman at the *Harvard Health Letter*, whatever that is. "Are you Ray Blount [to rhyme with count]?" Close enough. "Well, we have someone quoting you on oysters, and I can't find where you wrote this, so I wonder if you could tell me if you're quoted correctly. Here is the quote: 'Never eat anything that swallows faster than you do.' "

To myself, I wondered what that meant exactly. Goes down faster than you can swallow it? Is likely to reach out and swallow something hazardous from the atmosphere before you can close your mouth on it good? Did I ever write such a thing, and even if I didn't, should I go ahead and take credit for it on the off chance that it might get me into *Bartlett's*? Should I try to think of something that I have, in fact, written about oysters? Should I say something, now, offhand, about oysters? Well, I try to be scrupulous about attribution.

"To the best of my knowledge," I said, "I didn't ever say anything remotely like that at all."

"Oh," she said. "We'll take it out, then." I'll never get into *Bartlett's*. My friend Garrison Keillor is in *Bartlett's*, the son of a bitch. I tried not to swallow hard as the *Harvard Health Letter* said good-bye.

Then I got up and started trying to put my life, or anyway, my apartment, in order. Within moments, I was brought up short. On my writing desk is a sort of vase, made of a slashed and fluted Fanta can, where I keep ballpoint pens that may not be quite dead yet. When I dumped the pens out to decide which ones I could in good conscience dispose of, along with them came three short, thick, hollow-nose bullets, marked ".38 Auto."

My daughter, Ennis, bought the vase for me from a man on the street, several years ago, before she started working with assaultive teens and hapless mothers in North Carolina and got married and gave me grandchildren.

But how did bullets come to be in it? I don't remember. Who knows what else I have forgotten?

Do I forget some details on purpose for the sake of humor? How lame is that! The other day a man told me about a time when he was standing in the back of his pickup sawing off a limb, and for some reason his wife started up the pickup and drove off. He did a complete somersault in the air with a live chainsaw. "I'm laughing now," he said, "but it wasn't funny then."

I hear that. But bullets? I wouldn't use bullets on anybody, even myself. I lack the killer instinct. My mother took sleeping pills once, but she threw them up.

They say you can unrepress your memory by having yourself hypnotized. But I don't know. I had polyps removed from my sinuses a while back in what the surgeon told me was "a twilight state." Whatever I was injected with left me conscious enough to talk to the doctor, but oblivious afterward. I don't want the details of *that* to come back. A man reaching way up inside my head, snipping things. It was spooky enough during his diagnosis, when he stuck up my nose a probe that was a television camera, and on the screen I watched all these jellyfish-like blisters appear as the probe went around corners.

Apparently I got these polyps from sitting next to a woodstove for hours every day writing, in the country, during the oil crisis. I thought I was outslicking the Organization of Petroleum Exporting Countries, but what I was doing was parching my mucus membranes, and these polyps were rising up in protest.

I had never been televised internally before. I'd gone *on* television many times, perhaps too many. You have to watch that being on television. It is liable to turn you into a personality. While back home some little gal is singing:

> *Being on television adds ten pounds,*
> *A chicken only weighs about two.*
> *So why not get off television*
> *And let me cook a chicken for you?*

I wish. Or do I? My mother could evermore fry good chicken, but that chicken was *fraught*. I feel less pressure being on TV than eating home-cooked chicken.

Over the years, I have been hosted, or guest-hosted, by Johnny Carson, David Letterman, Jay Leno, Garry Shandling, Dick Cavett, Larry King, Charlie Rose, Tom Snyder, Bob Costas, Conan O'Brien, Bill Maher, Dr. Sonya Friedman, Forrest Sawyer, Al Franken, Pat Sajak, Richard Belzer, Jon Stewart, Robin Leach (on the food channel, not *Lifestyles of the Rich and Famous*), Tom Brokaw, David Hartman, Charley Gibson and Joan Lunden, Bryant Gumbel, Katie Couric, Studs Terkel and Calvin Trillin (a short-lived "Studs and Bud" cable show), David Susskind and Helen Gurley Brown. (I was supposed to jet to the Coast to "bounce off Shelley Winters" on *Merv Griffin* once, but weather stranded me in New York. I was scheduled to do *Chevy Chase* but his show was canceled.)

What were they really like? you're wondering. I don't know. Some were terrible company, but I'm not going to say which ones because they might not invite me back. And now I'm worried about the order I've listed them in. I mean no disrespect to the ones toward the end. But, hey, how close to the top of the show have I generally appeared? On the nighttime shows, I am almost always dead last, in the author's slot, though once on *The Tonight Show* I was next to last. I forgot to move over when the time came and Linda Hopkins, the singer, who followed me, very nearly sat in my lap.

I can remember when normal people could be expected to appear buttoned-up and awkward on TV. Even newscasters didn't seem to feel at home, exactly. (Dan Rather still doesn't, of course.) Nowadays no one would be surprised to turn on a daytime talk show and find six or eight salt-of-the-earth types sitting around together quite comfortably showing each other and the world their chigger bites and patches of athlete's foot, scratching themselves and each other and saying to the host, "I'm glad you asked me that, Jenny. This inflamed place over here on the back of my leg, I've had that for, oh, gee, I'd say . . ."

But for a *thinking* person, it's not always as easy as it looks. The first thing you have to deal with is whether to tell friends that you're going to be on. If you don't, they'll hear about it afterward and look at you as if you must perceive your relationship with them as awfully superficial. "Seems like you would have told us, so we could watch and not hear about it secondhand. So what did you say?"

"Oh, I don't know," you say. There is nothing less entertaining than trying to tell people what you said on television. They look at you like, "They let you go on television to say that?"

But if you notify them ahead of time, they say, "Well, uh, that's kind of late for us to stay up, with the kids to get off to school and all, but if you really want us to watch . . ."

And if you do give them notice, chances are you'll rub your cheek on the air and smear your makeup dramatically ("You have very nice skin, let's just cover up a couple of little red spots," the makeup artist will have told you, before covering your entire nose—and believe me, you do need makeup, or you'll look like the only dead person on the show) and that's the only part they'll remember. Or else you'll get rescheduled or bumped, and people will be calling to say, "What happened? We stayed up till two in the morning, and Toni Tennille went on and on and we kept waiting for you, and . . ."

One of the differences between being a guest on someone's talk show and a guest in someone's home is that in the latter case you are not likely to get bumped. Or pressed to embarrass yourself. Some years ago I was sitting between Lash Larue, the old cowboy-movie star, and Larry "Bud" Melman in the *Letterman* green room. "I want to read my poetry," Lash was saying, "but they want me"—he gave his trademark bullwhip a morose twitch—"to do a whip act." Larry "Bud" wasn't saying anything at all. ("The worst green room I was ever in," Art Buchwald told me once. "There was a chimpanzee in there with me, and a woman was changing its diaper.")

"Just remember," a *Tonight Show* booker, Bob Dolce, told me once, "this is a performance, not a visit." A late-night host may feel like a boredom-dreading, atrocity-fearing head of household trying to be witty himself while keeping deranged or soporific relatives confabulating cheerfully around the Thanksgiving dinner table, but to the guest, the host is one facet of a multiplex audience that also includes the other guests, the band and the crew, the live studio gallery semi-visible through the lights and the prospective home viewers who will begin to receive the show across the country—westerly from time zone to time zone—within the next couple of hours.

And my first inclination, when the host asks what I'm up to lately, is to blurt out the truth: "Well, right now I'm sitting here on national television and omigod I can see myself on the monitor and omigod my hair is sticking up in some kind of bizarre way and now omigod I'm frantically smoothing it down and it won't stay, and meanwhile you may be interested to know that on one track of my mind I'm saying to myself, Drop this line of talk right this minute and start saying 'As you know, my latest book is entitled *This Should Appeal to Everyone from Nine to Ninety* . . . ,' and on yet another track I'm telling myself, Oh, no, no, no, don't tell me you're going to tell that mouse-in-your-hat story again. . . ."

It's a mistake to see yourself on the monitor. Especially when you're live on CNN. What you see on a CNN monitor, because of the way the signal is bounced off a satellite, is yourself an instant ago. It's bad enough to see yourself as the world is seeing you now. To see yourself as the world saw you in the immediate past is to see yourself tantalizingly just beyond any hope of redemption. Once I saw a guy reporting live from the field on CNN and you could see the monitor behind him, showing him as he was in the previous moment. Presumably within the image on that monitor was another monitor, and within the image on that monitor . . . If I'd had a big enough screen and a strong enough telescope, I guess I could have looked all the way back to an afternoon in 1927 or so when Philo T. Farnsworth of Beaver, Utah, got his "dissector tube" or "orthicon"—the first working model of what we now know as television—up and running.

On the screen, talk-show hosts seem eminently comfortable. Seeming that way is their job. At close range a host's eyes are crying out to the fates, "Please, please let this guy hit something resembling or halfway setting up a punch line within the next couple of split seconds, please." At the chuckle, the feed, the reaction, the setting of tempo, Carson was a less ebullient Magic Johnson. He was there to keep you rolling, and he seemed genuinely glad when you scored. Yet I often had the feeling that he was sharing with me his deep-seated awareness that we could both die right here at any moment, doing this.

Once I groused about being on an author tour with sinus trouble. I said I was afraid I might get hooked on nose spray. A writer ought to be addicted to something more glamorous, like opium, I said. The word *opium* was bleeped, and it was a long time before I was on with Johnny again.

Once I was hustling toward the wings, trying to look like a person who in a matter of seconds was to be brought out onto the set of *The Tonight Show* for, like, the fifteenth time, when a security guard stopped me and asked me what I was doing backstage.

"I'm a, you know, guest," I said.

"Yeah, whose?"

"Johnny's," I said.

"What do you mean, 'Johnny's'?"

"On the . . . show." Only when the guard saw that I had makeup on the backs of my hands (I tend to wave my hands around in the vicinity of my face, so they have to be color coordinated) did he let me proceed.

Once I followed Carl Reiner, who had presented Johnny with a loud tie, and Johnny had donned it, loosely, right there on camera, and it had been good, friendly television, and as I was about to walk on someone whispered a suggestion: "Trade ties with Johnny."

I didn't do it. Quips, hey, my privilege. But ties? I kick myself now, because someday when my grandchildren are rummaging through my antique neckwear, I will be able to say, "That one? With the, um, yes, the naked—that's from the seventies. You've heard about the Summer of Love?" But I won't be able to say, "And that one. . . . Oh, Johnny Carson gave me that one off his own neck."

I doubted I had the interpersonality skills. Johnny had probably traded ties with Cary Grant, Morgan Fairchild, Fernando Lamas, perhaps all in the same night. My tie was one with boll weevils on it, which my sister had bought me in Memphis.

The first show I was on, years ago, was Dick Cavett's. At the end, when the cameras pulled back, and I could almost feel the credits rolling over us, and we leaned closer for a private chat, I said, "I always wondered what the guest and host, at this point, when you can't hear them anymore—what they're talking about."

"Frequently," said Cavett, "this."

But. Yes. Sometimes, during the breaks, Johnny actually seemed to want to talk. At one of our first breaks together, he told me, "So many funny writers aren't funny talkers. S. J. Perelman."

I was struck dumb. Perelman is one of my literary heroes. And I had seen him on television, and, to be sure, his discourse had not fit the medium. Johnny didn't seem to have anything else to say on the subject, and now the break was over and we were back in the presence (or near future) of that manifold crowd, which would not be interested in this topic. And in closing, we guests were telling where we would be appearing soon (the others, the Sands or somewhere, I, back at my writing desk), and that was that.

At another break, after the supposedly live house had scarcely responded, Johnny observed, "There should be a chill factor for comedy." At first I thought he was criticizing my intensity (he hadn't laughed much either—the show's various layers of audience tend to synergize, or not), but on reflection I decided it had to do with maintaining your feel for risibility in the presence of blank faces, and I found it comforting. By that time I was out in the parking lot.

Then one evening as I began to expand on having written something about the thirty-nine things that make a woman sexy, we ran out of time. Johnny wrapped up by saying, "Come back and we'll pick this up again."

Just politeness, I figured. Four or five months later when I was back on the show, and had gone over with Bob Dolce what I had written most recently and was assuming that, as usual, the questions would come from that, Johnny opened our segment by saying, "The last time you were on, you were telling us the thirty-nine things that make a woman sexy."

I just barely managed to remember a couple. (Fortunately, or not, I was sitting in a chair still warm from Joan Collins.)

So Johnny was thinking, did remember. There is, maybe, a God.

Another show, when I had been taking off on various semi-personal woes, Johnny murmured, just to me, during the break, "So often, comedy is rooted in sadness."

I was astounded. I couldn't think of anything to murmur back. We had only a few seconds. I didn't think I ought to start telling him about my mother.

I dreamed once that I was on the show with Johnny, and the break came, and he looked over at me, and said, "We will never see each other again. You may ask me one question."

And I blurted out—

"Johnny! Quick! My father never gave me any pointers. Tell me what to say to a woman when she asks me how something felt!"

And Johnny looked at me, sadly, and said, not with that Nebraska-droll on-screen expression of his but with the rooted-in-sadness-during-the-break expression: "Just say, 'You can imagine.' "

But can I imagine where I got those bullets? No.

When I was a boy I loved bullets, but ever since the army I don't. You'd think I'd remember having these in my apartment; in fact, I almost think I do, but I don't. The last time I remember dealing with bullets was several years ago when a woman interviewed me in a Southern city.

She attracted me intensely and I got the feeling, vice versa. She took me to a gun shop that had a firing range in the back, where she and I fired Uzis. *Brrrrrp. Brrrrrp.* Great-looking woman with burning eyes, but then someone told me, "You know she is *extremely* religious." Which may, in part, be why I was so attracted to her, and is certainly why, when she wrote me that she was coming to New York, I didn't answer.

Surely I didn't bring bullets home with me by plane. Maybe someone else left them in my apartment. I don't live here, or anywhere else, full-time, and various people including me have stayed in my apartment. Once Bette Davis was on my answering machine, returning the call of a friend of mine who wanted to interview her (she didn't let him), and another time it was Sam the Sham (of Sam the Sham and the Pharoahs, who sang "Wooly Bully"), different friend, same reason. I have interesting friends.

I used to see a pretty woman in Paducah, Kentucky, who carried a pistol, but not when she was with me because it made me nervous. She was a pistol, herself. Dottie Barkley, the late vice-president Albin Barkley's granddaughter. Thirty-one cats, she had, one of them named Royboy, for me. One time, she took me to a funeral home in Paducah. "I want you to see Speedy," she said.

When we entered the home, there was no one around.

"Oh, well," I said, "we'll come back later. These folks are probably—"

"Anybody home?" Dottie called out. "We want to see Speedy!"

An accommodating man came up from the back.

"Yeah, uh-huh," he said. "Speedy right here in the closet."

Speedy was upright, leaning against some furniture, next to a folded-up easel. The man brought him out and brushed some dust off his head.

"Yeah, Speedy a hundred and twelve years old. He died back in 1928 and he was about fifty then, uh-huh. He was drinking and walked right out into the river an drowned. He didn't have any family, so Mr. Hamock used his embalming fluids on him that he had developed, uh-huh, and kept him around. Back in the sixties the river rose so high till it came in here and floated Speedy right out the window. He was floating along having a terrible time. People thought he was a log. Yeah, uh-huh, Speedy been in the water twice.

"Been wearing this tuxedo since he was on *That's Incredible*."

Dottie's mother was a Ziegfeld Follies girl and her father belonged to Mensa.

All the women I have known—which is by no means to lump them together—have been that interesting. In fact, that's something a male friend of mine said once, after meeting a new girlfriend of mine: "Another *interesting* woman." Well, they're supposed to be interesting. One or two of them have been sweet. Well, they've all been sweet in one way or another, but at least one of them was sweet-natured. It drove me crazy. I kept wanting to wave my hand up and down in front of her eyes.

Enough. There is no way a man can come off savory—there is no way a man can come off as anything other than a dog—talking about all the women he has known. So. They have all been that interesting.

I have been *married* to women from Waxahachie, Texas, and Cambridge, Massachusetts. I have been in love with a woman who, at moments when you or I might say "Lordy, Lordy" or "Oyoyoyoy," would intone,

"Meher Baba, Meher Baba," and with another who would say, "Now I've fucked the dog."

Enough. I remember something cautionary that Geraldo Rivera said. Gerald is a sort of angel of the lurid.

"Hark!" Geraldo angel sings,
"Glory be! Such awful things!"

Once when I was in Elaine's, a New York restaurant where famous people go, Geraldo walked by and somebody at our table who knew him said hello and we all got to talking about the trials of O. J. Simpson—trials to which Geraldo had devoted years of nightly shows—and Geraldo said, "My fantasy is one night I'm in here and he comes in, and we go at it one-on-one."

And there was more than a hint, in his stance, of: physically if necessary. Maybe not with knives, but, hey, let's get it on.

But the cautionary thing I have in mind I heard him say on TV, on his talk show. His guest was Lawrence Schiller, who had earlier helped Simpson write his protestation-of-innocence book and now had written another book on his own, which revealed all sorts of embarrassing secrets—for instance, that Simpson had badly failed a lie-detector test. And the question sort of hanging in the air was whether Schiller had sold a wife killer down the river, so to speak. Collaborated and told. Suddenly, recalling an autobiographical work of his own, Geraldo said this:

"When I wrote about my loves, it shamed me, and that will live with me till I die."

In that moment, you could hear memoirists in progress all over the world saying: "WHOA. If *Geraldo* feels that way . . ."

At any rate, the upshot is that I live alone. I am a single grandfather. That doesn't seem *right*, does it?

I didn't want to put the bullets down the garbage chute in my building, because what if the compactor caused them to fire? Could happen, seems like. I didn't want to put them out on the street because they might get back into circulation. I went to lunch.

Huevos foo yung at this Cuban-Chinese place I've been going to for twenty-five years, off and on. Chinese who had restaurants in Cuba and left when Castro took over; there are lots of Cuban-Chinese places on the west side of Manhattan. No look of recognition has ever passed between me and the waiters in there, whom I've watched get older.

Then I walked through Riverside Park to the Hudson, leaned against the fence and tossed the bullets into the water one by one, trying to hit a straw hat floating about fifteen yards off shore. As each of them sailed through the air, I made the kind of whistling-trajectory noise I would make as a boy.

This one is for rue.

Tiuuuuuuuu . . . sploop.

This one for remembrance.

Tiuuuuuuuu . . . sploop.

And this for the little girl who lives in the lane.

Tiuuuuuuuu . . . sploop.

Just missing the hat each time. And the big question boiled up in me again:

Why can't I be like other men? Why can't I go on ahead and grow up and singlemindedly pursue career and hearth-health forthrightly? Or, else, go on ahead and shoot somebody?

After it boiled back down, I went and sat on a bench. A man came up and began talking animatedly to a Hispanic-looking couple on the bench just uptown from me:

"Young kid . . . arm stiff out like this . . . just up the walk . . . it's a mess . . . just found him."

"*Ayaye,*" said the woman of the couple.

"Drugs. It must be the drugs," said the man of the couple.

The man with the news came on toward me and I said, "What was that?"

He didn't look eager to tell me because I don't sound like I'm from the city.

"Cops found a kid dead," he said. "Been shot."

"Just now?"

"They just found him," he said. "He was done overnight."

Done overnight. Killers could advertise: "Doing Done Overnight." That doesn't sound clipped enough, however—the present participle, "doing." Open-ended. Once I made a speech in Wyoming, which sounds like a present participle itself. The infinitive would be "to wyome." What you been doing? Just wyomin' around.

If only the lifting of the family curse could be done overnight! Why does it fall to me to lift it? Did I bring it down upon myself? No. I guess I know who did bring it down, but what can her motive have been? She just figured, if she was going to be a stepmother, she might as well be a wicked one? She just got off on beating somebody else's little girl?

It's a long story and I don't know how to start.

Just jump in. In Wyoming, a Friend of the Library acquainted me with a new concept: webeing.

"The men around here love to hunt; they'll go off a couple of weeks at a time. The wives start to feeling like huntin' widows, so they go out webein': 'We be gettin' dressed, we be goin' out, we be gettin' drunk and we be gettin' laid.' "

Be with me now, Wyomin' wimmen! I need all the muses I can get!

Maybe that's why I live alone.

Are those women's husbands actually hunting? I talked to a man named Robert in Washington, D.C., who said he had a cat that stayed home only at night, was out hunting all day. Then one day Robert was canvassing in the neighborhood, rang a doorbell, a man opened the door, and there next to the man stood Robert's cat, who saw Robert and ran.

"That cat!" said Robert.

"Yeah," said the neighbor, "he's a big old tabby, isn't he? He just stays home in the daytime. He's out hunting all night."

There's a story, you may say. But to the cat, perhaps not. Certainly the cat would not be quick to feel that an explanation was in order.

Nor have I been quick to feel that way, when people asked me, "Why are you funny?" I have always brushed that question off, because I was afraid a door would open and I would see myself standing there. And the game would be up.

But then I decided to do some research. I knocked on the door, so to speak, of the grandfather I never knew, and there was the family curse.

It's going to take me a while to take you with me to that point, though. I've got to get us there in such a way as to *lift* the curse. The road will not be straight.

Yesterday as I was walking up Broadway, a young woman was coming toward me bouncily carrying a little boy. As they passed me they caught each other's eye and smiled so engagingly—chummily, congenially as well as bondedly—that I smiled, myself, in what I felt to be a corresponding sort of way. They didn't notice me, but my eyes met those of another woman coming behind them, who saw me smiling and could also tell what I was smiling at, and she and I in passing exchanged a smile—two people who will never know each other from Adam's house cat, as my mother used to say, sharing a fleeting intimation that life can be sweet. Behind that woman, then, came another one, who may not have taken in the whole series of reactions but had apparently been able to catch enough of an inkling of its amicability that she, too, exchanged smiles with me, smiles more tentative than the ones before, but nice. Then came another woman who gave me a quick, stony glance—for all she knew I was grinning at every woman who came along—and the chain was broken. And I felt bad.

Maybe by that point my smile was beginning to look forced. It could be that all my ups and downs can be traced back to one thing, my comic flaw: I can't smile convincingly on purpose.

But no, there's something more.

Once I asked a man in Mississippi if he would mind telling me his age. "I'm seventy-two years old," he said, *"already."* I'm fifty-five now, and no telling how old I might turn any minute.

> *Before this getting older gets any worse,*
> *Before I start needing a registered nurse,*
> *Before they come to get me in a Cadillac hearse,*
> *I be lifting the family curse.*

CHAPTER 8 / Got to Get a Handle on It First

> Children cannot be surprised by the extraordinary who have not
> been made aware of what is ordinary. A generation knowing top
> hats only as props for conjurers does not think it so remarkable
> when rabbits emerge from them.
>
> —IONA AND PETER OPIE, *THE OXFORD BOOK OF CHILDREN'S VERSE*

I remember discovering my feet.

"Awww, look at his little feet," I had heard huge, looming presences say, one HLP to another, as if my feet were present but I wasn't. Remember how it felt to be little, with no way to speak out besides bawling or smiling, and all around you flourished a conspiracy of presumptively superior beings who talked knowingly among themselves, right in front of you, about how precious and impossible you were? *And they didn't sound all that well-informed!* But you had to reject that notion—if they weren't well-informed, who was?

Sometimes you'd be dozing off and you'd hear a chorus of overbearing oohs and awws and an enormous voice would say, "Aren't they sweet?" (*They?* I'm *"they"* to *them*?)

And another such voice: "In their sleep."

Chuckles, and then they would slip away, quietly, so as not to disturb me.

The other day I saw a mother leading a tiny boy in a hooded sweat suit into a seafood store. The proprietor, an older man—well, he was probably my age said, "Can I see how it feels to pick up a little boy like this?"

The mother nodded proprietarially.

"Isn't he solid?" the mother asked.

"Why yes," said the seafood man, hefting him.

"He's just a *chunk*," she said.

The man looked like he had about exhausted his curiosity with regard to the boy, but when the mother said "chunk" he hefted him again, and said, "Mm."

"He's just as chunky as he can be," the mother went on. "All my children are solid like that. He's as solid as a little rock."

"Why yes," said the man, setting him back down. And dusting his hands, an odd gesture.

"Of course he's spoiled rotten," said the mother.

On the boy's face there was no expression. He didn't look all that solid to me, nor that rotten. *Stolid*, yes—on the outside. On the inside, who knew?

I believe we remember things from birth, but we don't realize what we're remembering because we had no way of knowing what was going on at the time—just that it was so outlandish, the most outrageous thing until, presumably, death. We remember *flashes* from birth, and everything else we remember collects around those flashes.

But a foot is fairly solid.

"That's your foot," adults said, or "See your foot? That's Little Roy's foot." What? I would feel them touching me, pointedly, somewhere.

I could tell the difference between contact with a person, no matter how insensitive, and contact with the side of a crib, say. But it wasn't at all clear to me that the difference was of quite the *requisite quality*. It wasn't clear to me that this touch was taking me adequately into account. I cried a lot. It made my mother anxious.

I was too critical. The boy who cries "Bull!" It's a bad strategy. Because what comes back is, "You're so critical!" or even, tragically, "I don't please you!" and now I've got to apologize, the issue is me, my complaint is lost. I pretty much don't complain anymore. I live alone.

But I hadn't worked all that out yet, then.

"Noey has officially begun crawling," Ennis E-mailed me the other day. Noey is what we call my second grandchild, Noah. "He waited until the day after he discovered his penis—which took up most of his spare time." When I was an infant, adults did not encourage that sort of thing.

And I guess there wouldn't have been much point in their telling me, "There's your nose," because I couldn't have seen what was indicated—no there there. But a foot: voilà.

My attitude, however, was: You just keep me fed and refrain from crushing me until I figure things out, and then I'll decide what is or isn't my "foot."

Then one day—after a lot of random scanning, back and forth, and putting things together bit by bit, same way I figure things out today, when and if I do—I got a grip on it: the thing, and the concept. Foot.

I liked it. The word *foot* connected admirably with the thing itself. I have never been such a chauvinist, so to speak, as to assume that Anglo-Saxons were the only people capable of coming up with the right words for things (I'm Norman-Celtic genetically, and lococulturally Celtico-African), but there's something gratifyingly solid about *foot*. *Le pied* is too . . . prancy; *der Fuss* puts on heavy airs.* Whereas getting the word *foot* is like receiving a nice easy pitch in a well-broken-in catcher's mitt. Foot.

I could feel it. And I could feel it feeling me. Mutual contact. Of a sort that did have a certain clarity. The toucher, the word, the touchee: a complete loop. Feel foot, foot feels back, ergo: my foot. But wait. I felt a qualm. It was empirically mine, this foot, but was it not also said to be the foot of someone else? Of someone else who was a smaller version of some *third* party? Contact should lead somewhere. This time—*because of* the qualm—it led to this: my foot is Little Roy's foot.

Then I must be Little Roy! I was seventeen.

No, I'm kidding, I was just an infant.

Then these, I thought to myself, would be my fingers . . . hand . . . arm . . .

And what is this other thing that looks just like my foot? Oh, duh. Other foot.

I lay there, turning these things over in my mind. I didn't think of it as my mind then—I still don't with any clarity. Expecting anybody to know how his or her own mind works is like asking a dollar to make change. I could turn things over in it, though:

I have body parts. Ergo, I have a body. This is my body, which I have, and also am: where would I be without it?

Wait. Somewhere along in there I started making this up.

"Write it as fiction," my fellow rock musician Stephen King once advised me. "Then the other people who were there at the time can't tell

---

*All three, of course, come from the same Indo-European root, *ped-*. I won't go into deep background here except to mention that *foot* is connected to *sin* through the Latin verb *peccare*, meaning "to stumble," and connected also to *pajamas*, by way of Middle Persian. I don't scorn French or German by any means: *amour* is fine, and there's nothing quite like *das Ding an sich*. You'd think, though, that the French would have come up with something less cumbersome for *footnote* than *note en bas de la page*.

you it's wrong." But I have some kind of block against that. When my fellow sportswriter Dan Jenkins was a kid, he and his friends made up fake names for themselves, in case they ever got in trouble with the law. His fake name was Bob Roberts. Then one time he did get picked up for some sort of mischief, and the cop asked him his name and he said, in a small, muffled voice, "Bob Roberts."

"What?" snapped the cop.

"DAN JENKINS," he blurted out.

But a memoirist needs details. So, finally, I did consult a hypnotist.

"You want the implants?" he said.

"Certainly not. All I want is a little hypno-suggestive help in getting past whatever blocks have kept me from retrieving the richness of my past as it actually was, the texture of it, the way a single broken live-oak leaf slanted down . . . made its lop-winged way . . . along a something ray of crisp September sunlight and, whatever, you know—as I took my first faltering steps toward school that fateful day in the second grade when—"

"Were you paying attention to this leaf and this ray at the time?" asked the hypnotist.

"No, I had things on my mind," I said.

"I can get you the implants."

"How can you possibly implant the stuff of my own unique history?"

"I know a guy," he said.

I do remember certain moments, over and over. Once I heard Merle Travis remark, on a recording, to a banjo player who was working out real strong: "They say if you pick it, it won't get well." But I can't help it, I keep going back, worrying at these memorable moments, wondering, Did that really happen that way and that's why I am this way, or do I just think it happened that way because I am this way?

And I don't even remember what I was like at these moments. People say, "If only I knew then what I know now." But in that case, you wouldn't have learned anything since. What I'd like to know now is what I knew then. I'm at least as insubstantial in my recollection, myself, as everything else is. I don't think I have ever been any more solid, inside, than, say, soup.

I remember wetting my pants, dramatically, in the second grade. Okay?

During reading period. There I was, in a circle of chairs with all the other fast readers at the front of the room, in plain sight of the slower readers as well, and suddenly . . . Little kids wore short pants in those days, and I was splattering the floor. I'd like to say that I saved the situation with a quip, but I didn't. I assumed the closest thing to a fetal position you can assume while trying not to attract attention. Mrs. Lindsay was a kind teacher. She told the class, "Roy is sick," and let me go home. I remember wondering in the darkness that night, How will I be able to go back? But I did. Hunkered down, got back on the horse, buried myself in my work. Life went on.

So that won't serve as my defining incident. Generally you can find in the childhood of a significant humorist some event so absurdly traumatic that there's no way to make straightforward sense of it. Mark Twain looked through a keyhole and saw his father being autopsied—his organs being lifted out and held to the light. Richard Pryor looked through a keyhole and saw his mother turning a trick. Robert Benchley, when his brother died, overheard his distraught mother crying, "Why couldn't it have been Robert?" How can I be a significant humorist if I can't lay claim to any such moment?

You could make a case for the time when I was, I don't know, five?, and my mother walked into the bathroom as I sat in the tub innocently swushing soapy water around my nether area in a pleasurable way, and she said, "No, we don't do that."

The qualm kicked in. (*Qualm*. A word of unknown derivation.) It seemed a shame, but I respected her judgment. She wouldn't say anything to hurt me, would she?

Then, since I had brought the matter up, she took the occasion to tell me this:

"When you were born the doctor cut a little too much off your, you-know. I don't know why in the world he wasn't paying better attention!" She sounded vexed. On top of all the other difficulties of my birth, she had had that to worry about. She bustled on off with an armload of laundry.

I sat there and thought to myself, Well, gee.

That's all I remember.

There ought to be more to this scene. Boy's mother tells him something's wrong with his you-know, and leaves him sitting there in his bathwater. The moment must have made an impression on me, since I still remember it after fifty years. For one thing, it was the first time I'd heard anything about anything being cut off of anybody's you-know. It was also the last time, until I was in college and read in a magazine that people were beginning to argue that there was really no very clear medical reason for circumcision. And it wasn't a Methodist thing.

But you know, I think I just sort of took it, gradually, bit by bit, on board.

I told a woman I was going out with about that moment once and she said—this is what she would always say, as in a catechism:

"How did that make you feel?"

I don't know. I was five. I don't even know what it made me think, other than, Well, gee. In retrospect I am inclined to believe that my mother was not what you might call a phallophile. But would I have wanted her to be one? No.

You can't expect a woman to empathize in that area. Once when a friend of mine's daughter was a tot, she walked in on her father when he was taking, as we guys would say, a leak.

"Well, that's a silly way!" she said.

Hey, okay. That's natural.

I *was* a little put off recently to read this by Rebecca Pepper Sinkler, in a review of a book by Carolyn G. Heilbrun: "Ms. Heilbrun, like many of us, is quite fond of the particular men who share her life, but mistrusts the genotype."

But, hey. Okay. Sexist, surely, but quite possibly wise. My first wife hated the idea of mutuality as a basis for marriage. But maybe mutual mistrust would work. Someone once said to me, with regard to two unsavory people we knew, "They hold each other in mutual contempt. Which speaks well of both of them." Mutual mistrust is something that two people just might be able to depend on. Would they ever get naked, though?

At any rate it wasn't a man who beat my mother. Her daddy was sweet, she said, the few times she mentioned him to me. He gave her a quarter that she kept all her life.

Certainly I don't judge my mother by contemporary parenting standards, at least as represented by Nancy Friday, author of *Women on Top*: "I'm always saying, raise your little girl to masturbate—it's the best sex education, and it's the safest education she can get in her life." (When girls do it, is it called jilling off?) Personally I think masturbation should be left to the individual. It seems to me nothing would put more of a crimp in it than a parent calling upstairs, "Have you masturbated yet, dear? No television for you, young lady, till you've at least made an *effort*. . . ."

We don't do that. A classic parental expression. I admit, I've said it myself. When, for instance, one of my children would lie right down in the middle of the dirty grocery-store aisle, wallowing around on the floor so that people were steering their carts around the child in question. That's something I don't think I ever felt entitled to do as a child, but there must be something distinctly gratifying about it, if only because it galls parents so distinctly. The other day in the hardware store there was a man trying to pay for some spackle and his little girl was lying flat out on the floor pulling on his ankle.

"We don't do that," he said to her. Well no, *we* don't, but *she* did.

"You don't love me!" the little girl shouted.

I would never have dared shout that to one of my parents. They were always saying that to me.

I must say, however, that it does seem to me that any parent, male or female, even in Georgia back in, like, 1946 or whenever this was, however much she may have been offended by the sensual swushing, might have thought to herself, Well, I don't want to make a big deal of this, don't want to dwell on it with him, but I do want to take the time to make it clear—I won't even have to go into the whole thing of how he will be calling upon it down the road—that there's nothing wrong with his you-know, it's just a little more skint back than other people's.

That's pretty much what I worked out on my own. But only over a period of some years, during which I could have been learning to play the guitar.

Oh, I probably didn't handle the thing—the situation—right. That old male thing of keeping things inside, not being willing to talk things through. How would a girl—well, let's say, how would an articulate child have reacted, after his mother dropped her bombshell and bustled out the door? "Mom . . ."

I wasn't calling her Mom at that point. I didn't start calling her Mom until after I grew up and her first grandchild, Ennis, had started calling her Mumu, which is how we all began to refer to her in the third person and still refer to her now that she's gone. (She had asked to be called Grandma, but that's what Ennis decided to call her other grandmother— my mother never got what she wanted.)

"Sugar . . ."

No, I can't feature that. Maybe that was the moment I stopped calling her Sugar, in fact, when she told me my you-know was in some way trun-cated and then bustled on out the bathroom door. I know, she had an arm-load of laundry, parents always do, genuinely do, have an armload of something.

After I quit calling her Sugar, I called her Mother. Sounds formal, but that's what I called her. Then I think when my sister Susan came along she started calling her Momma and so did I and eventually I shortened that to Mom. But this was back before Susan was born, I was still an only child—who sometimes felt like an only human being. I remember the first time I encountered the word *solipsism*. Aha! I thought to myself. Why didn't *I* think of that?

"Mother. . . . Please come back in here, because what you have told me makes me feel bad." That's what a child of today would say, I guess. You know what my mother would have said to that? "Oh, don't be such a swoose."

That was a word she used: *swoose*. Sometimes in a snippet of song: "Or would you rather be a swoose?" After childhood I happened upon *Going My Way* on television and heard Bing Crosby's mellow-priest char-acter (catch *him* molesting an altar boy) sing "Swinging on a Star." Its tune is the same as my mother's snippet (to the extent that anybody in our family could carry a tune), and in its lyrics swinging on a star symbolizes spiritual aspiration, the alternative to which is stubborn heathenism: "Or would you rather be a mule?" (That song won an Oscar. When I was a child, theism was as firmly entrenched in the popular culture as perfect breasts and pecs are today.)

I believe that when my mother said, "Don't be a swoose," she meant don't get bogged down on a mundane, fleshly level. I don't think she ever saw any reason for me to feel bad, emotionally. It would have been a reflec-tion on her.

Unless, of course, I felt bad for a reason she could identify with and not feel responsible for, like being left out of the Christmas pageant, cute little angel down there all alone, *toora-loora-looral*. That's the way I have been with women, I realize now: I sympathize with their feelings when those feelings are feelings I have had myself and don't feel accountable for. Sym-pathizing with myself, in other words. The fallacy of the golden rule. What people *want* is for you to do unto them as they think they would do if they were you.

The essential joke of all jokes is what the old boy said when asked if he believed in infant baptism—"Believe in it? Hell, I've seen it done." That's about as objective as anybody gets, which is why nobody ever quite loves anybody the way the beloved wants to be loved—the way the beloved sub-jectively assumes should be the perfectly obvious way. But you do have to get that objective in order to love anybody. My mother was *sometimes* that objective, as when she exclaimed, "This is the craziest family!" And it was sweet. I am trying to be that objective about her. Maybe if I can man-age to be detached about my own you-know. . . .

Evidently the doctor didn't cut anything functional. No one has ever accused it of looking a little overtrimmed, even. It has been a pretty good old you-know for me over the years, taken all in all. (To treat myself on my fifty-sixth birthday I may well go to Honduras and get one of those neoprene-and-chamois spring-loaded jobs implanted in my hip, but only as a backup or lagniappe.) In its way it has been more reliable, and I hate to say this, than my mother. Or than several other women I could name. But undoubtedly I have asked more of women than I have of my you-know. And I didn't make enough of an effort to be sweet to them. That's the thing about your you-know, you don't have to be sweet to it. It's a guy; you do things with it.

I've been able to think with it. Not clearly.

I think I shrugged the foreskin thing off, pretty much. I grew up shrugging things off, pretty much. It's a secondary, if not primary, male characteristic. Without it we'd go crazy. Because let's face it, it's not only males who don't want to know how they're feeling. Females don't want to know how males are feeling either. And yet complain because we're not emotional enough!

Men are sensitive! Bill Clinton, for instance, feels people's pain. And yet what has been the most distinguishing mark of his presidency? The first president whose . . . You know.

Sir Laurence Olivier is on tour reading the sonnets of Shakespeare. The house is hushed. He begins: "Let me not to the marriage of true minds admit impediments—"

A guy stands up in the back row of the last balcony and hollers, "HEY, LARRY OLIVER! SING 'MALAGUENA'!"

Unaccustomed as he is to being heckled, let alone heckled nonsensi-cally, Sir Laurence stops. Waits a moment. Begins again:

"Let me not to the marriage of true minds—"

"HEY! LARRY OLIVER!" cries the guy in the back. It is clear he is drunk. "SING 'MALAGUENA'!"

It's not as though Olivier has any need, generally, to have a squelch prepared. Rather than dignify this guy with a response, he pauses again, pointedly, and then, again, begins:

"Let me not to the marriage—"

"HEY!" the guy screams, "LARRY OLIVER! SING 'MALAGUENA'!"

Olivier can no longer rise above this. "Sir," he says, and the richness of his voice is to the coarseness of the heckler's as Armagnac is to Mountain Dew, "in the first place, my name . . ." He hates to have to say this. ". . . is not 'Oliver,' it is Olivier. In the second place, and more important, I am not here to sing, I am here to read certain sonnets by William Shakespeare.

"And in the third place . . ." Somehow he can't forbear to make this point as well. ". . . 'Malaguena' is an instrumental. I couldn't sing it if I wanted to. So, if you don't mind, 'Let me not—' "

And the guy stands up and hollers, "WELL, SHOW US YOUR DICK THEN!"

CHAPTER 9 / **The Primal Scene**

I'm selling my pork chops, but I'm giving my gravy away.

—MEMPHIS MINNIE

Jacksonville, Florida, 1935. Jeanette MacDonald, looking a bit like Bette Midler—prettier, but a lot less fun—is a French princess dead set on chucking royalty for backwoods love. Nelson Eddy, looking a bit like Howdy Doody's Buffalo Bob, but less animated, is a "frontier scout" who is evidently just the man to enjoy a committed relationship with an ex-princess—a relationship based entirely on singing—without in any way forsaking the life of a frontier scout. Looking as deep as may be into each other's eyes, this golden couple bursts like two great canaries into

Ah, sweet mystery of life at last I've found thee,

just as Roy Blount reaches his arm, for the first time, around Louise Floyd.

Louise is a twenty-one-year-old shop girl, Roy a twenty-two-year-old clerk. She is a petite five four and a half, has deep dark eyes, looks a bit like Vivien Leigh. Eventually he will resemble Spencer Tracy, only more stately, but at this point—deep in the Depression—he is bone skinny: six foot two, one hundred thirty pounds. They're both rigorous Southern Methodists. This is their first date.

And, at last, I know the secret of it all—
All the longing, seeking, striving, waiting, yearning. . . .

Roy's hand touches Louise's sleeve. A sleazy-crinkly, crispy-silky texture: crepe de chine. Softer to the hand than crepe paper or the hard-finished black crepe cloth that people wear for mourning; but not as soft as you might expect. Its character results, according to *The Columbia*

Encyclopedia, "from the peculiar arrangement of the weft, which is formed of yarn from two different bobbins twisted together in opposite directions or uses alternately a right-twisted and a left-twisted thread." He has never felt anything like that before and is overwhelmed; his arm retracts.

He doesn't know *what* he had ahold of. Indeed he doesn't, and neither does she.

At this point there is ample literary precedent (Saul Bellow, Delmore Schwartz) for me to expostulate:

"Leave it at that, folks! Find other partners! Have some other child!"

But that would be silly. Had those particular bobbins not twisted together, there would have been no such expostulator.

The only other thing I know about their courtship, except that they acted in plays put on by young people of the church (what I wouldn't give to see a video of Louise and Roy in one of those plays in particular, entitled *What Every Woman Knows*) is that the morning after that first date, the morning after *Naughty Marietta* ("It's an atrocity, of course, . . . and yet it has . . . a mad sort of appeal"—Pauline Kael), Louise's mean aunt Pearl lit into her because of what had happened on the porch as she and Roy lingered over good night. Louise had picked all the leaves off a perfectly healthy fern.

My sister Susan is a product manager for a big Houston computer firm (since I am Southern, you probably assumed my sister to be an overwrought chicken-parts processor named Urethra or Gabardine, but no). She tells me that Louise would refer to sex, in mother-daughter talks, as "the magic and the mystery," but all I ever heard from her was, "You're playing with dynamite."

Well, I take that back. Susan and I took turns sleeping with her when Roy was on the road, and one evening Louise gave me a little book to read, a pamphlet prepared under Methodist auspices, a pamphlet which didn't clear up any of the questions raised by conversations among my peers (What was a morphodite? Did Red Koreans really drape POW's balls over one brick and then drop—*ooo*—another brick on top? Have you ever been using the pencil sharpener and gotten a hard-on in front of the entire class?) but which nonetheless shocked me to the core (your own parents, two people who could not even legally use the same public rest room . . .); and that night in bed she said, "If there's anything else you want to know about . . . sex, ask me." Oh, right, Mom. I never slept with her again. I never heard the first peep about the facts of life from Roy, thank God.

She was afraid of everything, and yet—or therefore—she was liable at any moment to come out with something that would curl your hair. ("She used to say things to me that she wouldn't have said to the dog. Of course that expression is different in our family because the dogs had such elevated status. She had so much anger directed at me but she was at peace with Chipper.") He, Roy, wasn't afraid of anything but her. Well, of her and of discussing intimate issues.

In 1938 they were married. It must have been my fault.

I don't mean to suggest that they, you know, had to—I wasn't born until 1941. The reason Louise didn't get to have a real wedding, had to slip away for a quick civil ceremony (her wedding dress lies, still unfinished, in Susan's attic) was because her uncle Archie, the mild-mannered husband of her mean aunt Pearl, with whom she lived for most of her girlhood, died of a heart attack (while tending a railroad bridge) shortly before their wedding date. Aunt Pearl announced her intention to take Louise back to Mississippi where she came from, so my parents got married quickly to liberate Louise. Pearl got sick. She was living with us when I was born. I don't really remember her, but I'm told that I would stand for hours next to the bed to which she was confined as she told me stories. I don't remember any of them. But maybe those stories planted a literary seed (Aunt Pearl had been a columnist for a railroad house journal), and maybe also they instilled a meanness; I don't know.

Nor do I mean to suggest that my parents didn't wholeheartedly want to get married. There was chemistry. "It was right embarrassing, to see how much Roy was in love with that girl," my aunt Neetie in Tallahassee told me after they died. Children get a jaundiced view of their parents' marriage, from not having been around it until after it is corrupted by children. But I can't imagine they were bound to spend the rest of their lives together (all of his, most of hers) for their sakes. I remember him trying to kiss her and her saying, "Oh, go away."

Susan, however, says, "Mother used to put her head in Daddy's lap and he would scratch her head while they watched TV. I caught her sitting in his lap one time when they were in their late fifties. After Daddy died and I would visit Mother, she wanted me to sleep with her. Then she would talk and talk and talk and tell me all kinds of things. I was so grateful for the dark so she couldn't see my face. It was in one of these sessions that she asked me what lesbians do. I'd be switched if I was going to tell her. I figured if she couldn't even bring herself to tell me what heterosexuals did, I wasn't going to tell her what homosexuals do. But she said one night that she and Daddy had decided that it was a good thing she had trouble getting pregnant because otherwise they would have had a whole bunch of children."

I can't believe I'm doing this. Dragging my parents out of a sound sleep, blinking in their pajamas, to hold them up before strangers! Would they have done that to me?

Okay, they would have, but only to show people how cute I was. They loved me. They sacrificed for me. And this is how I repay them? "We don't talk about family things to people outside," my mother would say. Why not? What was wrong with us?

Roy was a natural-born leader of solid, community-minded folks. Certainly those folks would have included Louise among their number, but she needed attention he was unsuited to give. "Nothing I do works out right. I think I must be a freak of nature," she told us kids and no doubt him.

What can have been the logic of such a union? Given my inevitability, it had to be me. Susan too, but I'm seven years older, I'm primarily responsible—and Louise told me she risked her life to give birth again so I wouldn't have to be an only child.

"You know, I nearly died having you, son."

Thanks, Mom.

Do you know what Roy told me at a terrible juncture in my life, when I had finally gotten up the nerve to tell my parents I was getting divorced from the mother of my children because she couldn't stand me anymore?

"Be a good man."

Thanks, Dad.

The idle hopes, the joy and burning tears that fall . . .

I'm not responsible for Jeanette and Nelson, though. That was Louis B. Mayer or somebody.

CHAPTER 10

Funny Peculiar, Funny Ha-Ha

Beatrice: But I beseech your grace, pardon me. I was born to speak all mirth and no matter.

Don Pedro: Your silence most offends me, and to be merry best becomes you; for out o' question, you were born in a merry hour.

Beatrice: No, sure, my lord, my mother cried.

—*MUCH ADO ABOUT NOTHING*

When I am hustling across America trying to advance one small piece of literature, my latest book, interviewers often ask me:

"Do you feel you have to be funny all the time? When people meet you, do you feel pressure to come up with something funny?"

Here is my standard answer:

"No."

After an awkward pause, interviewers press the issue. They ask what *made* me funny.

Do they have any idea what they're asking? I'd have to write a book.

"Self-loathing" is of course the easy answer, but people want more—they know that if self-loathing alone were enough, everyone employed by a corporation would be funny. And people don't respond well to the notion that you can use your self-loathing as a resource. "Oh. I see. Project it onto others, I suppose. Onto me, for instance. So that means I have to deal with my self-loathing and yours too. Well, let me tell you something, mister . . ." There's not much constructive you can do with self-loathing other than make humor. I have toyed with the idea of working up a whole series of motivational speeches and how-to books based on harnessing the power of self-loathing—*How to Go Fuck Yourself for Fun and Profit*. But there you are—I've just been toying with it.

Got to have that self-lo working. That's what we call it in the humorist trade: sefflo is how it has come to be pronounced. The others won't admit it, in fact, they'll probably shun me now for breaking ranks, letting you behind the scenes of the secret life of humorists. . . .

Last Sunday, on Broadway, I came up behind a fiftyish father and a nineish daughter as he was grinning at her and saying, "That's a good one, Emma," and old Emma was looking quietly, legitimately pleased with whatever line she had gotten off (I believed right away that it *was* a good one; the father was one of those semi-burly casually intellectual some-what-bushy-haired probably Jewish New York guys that I always think are cool), and I actually got misty-eyed, thinking, Old Emma won't *have* to be a humorist.

Old Emma won't have to be the bumbling, conflicted little fuckup for whom nothing goes right. Whose job is to put his or her face right down into the sefflo and project it as sweet. "Think of what you hate the most about yourself and hate them for it," Bill Murray cracked the other night when we were talking about how to address an audience. He was being tongue-in-cheek of course, but.

Can't be just *flat* self-loathing. Got to be fluid, and with a sense of self. The flo and the sef, those are good things, you don't want them to become servants of the sefflo. That's when humorists get bitter and hard, stop being funny.

The ordinary person doesn't need the sefflo so much, the ordinary person . . .

Listen to me! It's so easy to lose your bearings. Nobody *needs* the sefflo. We go to humor to get away from it. But if you go to humor enough, you got to refresh the sefflo, maybe. Got to keep on having something to go to humor from. Humor ought not to be an end in itself, but when it's a vocation and a living and a job, hey, sometimes you got to prime the pump.

Is that why I keep fucking up and breaking up? If so, I'm sorry, all you unlumpable-together-except-in-this-context women I have been in love with, I am truly. (Truly! Is ever there another word that rings less true? I hear my mother saying mockingly, "I'm s'ry," mocking my childish apology—as if I could possibly come up with an apology that would ease all her pain. Or, let's be fair: as if I meant my apology at all. I probably didn't mean it, shithead child that I was.)

But I don't think I'm perverse enough to keep my life sad so I can be funny—I don't. I think I keep breaking up to keep ahold of the sef and the flo.

However that may be, loathing yourself is like anything else, you've got to do it with feeling, or no point in doing it at all. And you've got to master certain key humorous techniques:

1. Irony. You know. We may define this as "how detached you are from your mother." An aspect of this is the Dead Pan, the Straight Face.

2. The Straight Face, or Dead Pan. Humorists have fine laughs—not broad, not gleeful, but high quality. Did you ever see a picture, however, of Mark Twain or James Thurber or E. B. White or S. J. Perelman or Garrison Keillor or Calvin Trillin or Fran Lebowitz all lit up by a smile? Or Charlie Chaplin or Buster Keaton or Bill Murray or Woody Allen? No. I suspect there is something about a funny person's mouth.

Supposedly it takes more muscles to frown than to smile, but in that case why do most people in repose or walking down the street look dour? Especially humorists. Humorists are notorious for looking gloomy.

Partly because they *are* gloomy, but also I suspect there is a physio-logical factor. The boxer George Foreman once said that before he got religion himself, "I always thought preachers was low-lifes, weak people. It always looked like some kind of weirdo deal to me. Even their mouths looked funny to me."

Preachers' mouths look funny—as in funny peculiar—because, well, as the old Georgia politician Marvin Griffin once said about Jimmy Carter, "He's like a man wearing a serge suit, and he's peed in it. He's got a warm feeling, but nobody else knows what's going on." One reason humorists are funny is that they are congenitally deadpan.

According to a story in the *New York Times* there is a syndrome called the Moebius Syndrome, which afflicts about a thousand Americans who are born without a facial nerve that transmits commands to muscles that control smiling, frowning and pouting. People think they are aloof or bored. Their parents, in particular, are frustrated. According to this story in the *Times*, a seven-year-old girl in Ohio somewhere was going to have an experimental operation in which a muscle and nerve would be removed from her leg and transplanted to one side of her face. If it worked, they were going to do it on the other side. I don't know whether it worked.

Humorists are not that severely impaired, but William F. Buckley Jr. once recalled that when he was running for mayor of New York (Buckley is not a humorist, but he can be funny, especially when running for office, and his son, Christopher, is a humorist), "I was in a televised debate with Abe Beame and John Lindsay. Somebody pointed out that when the announcer said, 'We will now have a debate between John Lindsay and Abe Beame and William Buckley,' Lindsay smiled and Beame smiled and Buckley didn't smile. Somebody said, 'For heaven's sake, Bill, smile!' So I tried and—I couldn't do it. No matter what I did, I couldn't smile on command. It was awfully depressing. A couple of years ago I was terribly relieved when some brain specialist told me that the static smile is controlled by a different hemisphere of the brain than the extemporaneous smile. So to create a synthetic smile you are asking certain muscles to work for you. And they didn't work for me. I smile a lot, but not synthetically."

My mother's smile was . . . oh, me. I don't think I can go into that right now. My father's was genial, but it was always the smile of a man who's in charge.

The Blount upper lip, which I inherited, is sort of dead. Thin, straight. My father's mother looked a lot like a Gilbert Stuart painting of George Washington.

Dr. Johnson on Jonathan Swift: "He had a countenance sour and severe, which he seldom softened by any appearances of gaiety. He stubbornly resisted any tendency to laughter." Ever see a picture of Mark Twain pre-mustache? Check it out. Dead upper lip.

It could be that comic writers are too deeply into humor to smile; but it could also be that smile-impairment drives us into comic writing.

All I know is—and I know this for sure, because there have been so many times I've wished it weren't true: I can't smile, even at a pretty woman, even at a child, unless there is some small element of humor involved.

I can smile at a dog. Well, not smile exactly, but a dog doesn't register a smile, a dog registers friendly eyes, and I have those, for a dog. Because a dog is funny. A dog is this little *animal*, descended from a wolf, that walks around in people's houses. I see a dog and I feel my face getting naturally friendly, because a dog and I, I believe, have a similar deep-set confusion about why it is that we are walking around in people's houses. "I wouldn't rip out your throat, not *yours*, anyway" a dog is bred to convey. "I didn't *mean* to nearly kill my mother" is my comparable message.

3. The Old Switcheroo. It's not funny when a man pulls a knife on a

woman. When a woman cuts off a man's penis, it is. I'm not complaining, I'm just saying.

4. Flow. Many people have the misconception that humor derives from the Latin *humus*, meaning "dirt." In fact, both *humus* and *human* (I am not making this up*) derive from the Indo-European root *dhghem*. *Humor*, like *humid* and *humph*, is from *umer*, meaning "fluid." Hence we say, "He has that *dry* sense of humor" when we mean, "He isn't really very funny, is he?"

5. The kicker. Uplift, in a sense. Vestigial form of the Happy Ending. "There are no jokes in heaven," said Mark Twain. Because no one needs them there.

6. A good, solid grounding in despair. It is my job to lift up your heart, yes, but only if it is down where it ought to be.

7. Inevitability. You can't be *trying* to get hit in the face with a pie. Well, sure, a virtuoso on the cusp between uproarious and flatline like my friends Ian Frazier and Veronica Geng (who agreed at one point in their careers that they were trying to be as *unfunny* as possible, without quite— remember *The Gong Show*?—getting gonged) might, just to prove it could be done, write something funny about someone who goes about trying to get hit in the face with a pie, but there would have to be *motivation* there, and the protagonist would have to *fail* to get hit by a pie, except perhaps in some way that is *worse* than *not* getting hit in the face by a pie—like the ballplayer in Philip Roth's *The Great American Novel* who is so eager to be given a colorful nickname that his teammates start calling him Nickname. "You don't *have* to do that," my mother used to say when we children were doing something that was driving her crazy. "You're just trying yourself." Sometimes she would add, "to get on my nerves," but the issue wasn't solely her suffering, it was also the whole quandary of necessity, compulsion, willfulness, intent. "You won't *let* me be sweet to you. You're just *determined* to make me yell at you."

8. Self-loathing. Just don't take it too personally.

Those are the eight principles upon which I have based my life, or my life has based me. "Has your sense of humor ever failed you?" an inter-

---

*Another key humorous technique is, of course, the Handy Catchphrase. This one, "I am not making this up," is my friend Dave Barry's. I *think* I made it up and he stole—popularized—it. Now I have no way of telling whether I am making things up or not. Dave actually does have a nice smile. Maybe he is an imposter, and I write his stuff.

viewer asked me once. And I'm afraid I let down the side. I gave her an incredulous look and said, "Yes. Of course. For God's sake."

I was tired. But that was no excuse. I was in Ohio. Not much of an excuse. I have no interest in being loathed by other people, thanks, but I do want them to acknowledge the grounds for my sefflo, not just blithely assume that because I'm being funny, I'm cheerful—come on! Still, I guess I should have given her a straight-faced look and said, "Only once. When they amputated my feet. I loved my feet, and there was nothing wrong with them, really. But that was the state of medical thinking in those days." And then, you know, come up with the lift at the end.

But as I say, I was tired, and in Ohio, and I had to catch a plane to Los Angeles to be interviewed further. So I responded not as a humorist but as a *human being*. Presented my guileless interviewer with the all-too-vulnerable face behind the shooby-doop.

She was shaken. And it was my fault.

Do we really need yet another human being? I swore at that moment I would never break character again. Until now.

As I mentioned before, I am fifty-five, about the age when humorists stop being funny. When Robert Benchley, my boyhood humorist hero, was fifty-four, he announced that he was officially ending his career as a writer, to concentrate on being an unhappy movie actor. "I don't think I write funny anymore," he said. The *New York Herald Tribune* editorialized: "Many of our writers, once regarded as excellent humorists, live to a great age under the amiable but often pathetic delusion that their powers to create laughs are in no way dimmed by the passing years. They are not critical enough to be bored with themselves. Mr. Benchley may be wrong, but his example is salutary." Two years later, he was dead. And he wasn't wrong, by the way. Every morning I wake up and wonder, Has it happened yet? The only thing that keeps me going is my drive to rehabilitate the spicy limerick.

I like spicy limericks, but can hardly condone them if the only roles for women in them are "an old whore from Pawtucket" sort of thing. What the spicy limerick needs is strong female characters.

> *After weeks of loitering palely*
> *As a swain serenaded her, Zalie*
> *Said, "Won't you quit plucking*
> *That (hint, hint) fucking*
> *(hint, hint, hint) ukulele?"*

Of course Benchley was more popular than I am, and more devoted to drinking. Once I told Heywood Hale Broun, son of Benchley's friend Heywood Broun, that in applying for a college scholarship back in 1959 I had declared my ambition to become "a humorist and bon vivant like the late Robert Benchley."

"Bon vivant," said Broun. "That's a nice term for an old soak."

As Benchley himself might have written, there's a joke in there somewhere—bon vivant, bad liver—but let it go. That was his way of eating the joke and having it too. Benchley always had better sense than to write about humor, except when he said that a popular book entitled *Enjoyment of Laughter* "has got humor down, and broken its arm."

James Thurber, another of my early heroes but not so pure a one as Benchley, allowed himself to write that "humor, as Emily Dickinson said of hope, is a feathered thing that lives within the soul." Feh.

Can a humorist of fifty-five get to the bottom of humor and himself? It sounds indecent, I know.

While the illicit couple sprawl naked . . .

That's a line from the tabloid story in which Richard Morris, intimate aide to President Clinton, was exposed as having lain with a prostitute while chatting on the phone with the leader of the free world.

Humor and me, we're an illicit couple. Not strictly professional, not strictly romantic. Co-dependents, maybe.

Maybe the time has come to tell on Humor before she can tell on me. Come clean. And as my mother used to say, "I don't care if it harelips Belgium."

She used to say that, but she would have cared, audibly, if she had heard of even one lip-impaired Walloon. The pathetic fallacy was made for my mother. She could feel sorry for animals, vegetables, minerals. "Aww, that little cinder block is lying there all alone. All its friends got picked to help build somebody's house, and it got left out." She was extremely sensitive to the issue of people being left out.

"Abandoned. Betrayed. She felt betrayed and abandoned by her parents," says Susan, "and that's what she anticipated we would do to her."

She couldn't stand to listen to classical music (except for lullabies) because of "all that churning," as she put it, and she hated it when we children squirmed (or "squirmled," to use a word of hers that just now made me go briefly rigid when I typed it), but she was always "on the go" as she put it, herself. When she wasn't keeping strenuous, resentful house, she was running all over town—her "coattails popping," as she would say— helping people. She would go to the nursing home and fix Miss Maybelle's hair, for instance. She made me go along with her once. Miss Maybelle was her Sunday school class's project. Miss Maybelle was about 104 years old, bedridden, smelly, skeletal, out of her mind, liable at any moment to look over at me and say, "Come give Miss Maybelle some sugar, honey." Jesus of Nazareth, given a choice between washing a leper's feet and fixing Miss Maybelle's hair (or even watching his mother fix Miss Maybelle's hair), would have made a beeline to the leper. We didn't know any lepers, but if we had, Louise would have seen to them.

First and foremost, Louise was an orphan. Her mother died before she was two, her father when she was seven. Before Aunt Pearl took charge of her she bounced around from relative to relative, none of whom really wanted her, she felt. She overheard some of them saying so. She could identify with that cinder block. And with Miss Maybelle.

Who was ever man enough to empathize with Louise? When I was a boy, we supported a Korean war orphan who would send us cards saying things like, "I had a very nice Easter yesterday. I ate a boiled egg. I praised His coming to life again. Bye, Lee Jung Sook." She wasn't anywhere near as poignant as my mother.

When little Louise had a button missing or something else wrong with her clothes, Aunt Pearl would say, "It'll never be noticed on a galloping horse." Aunt Pearl made her wear long johns, in Florida, and an asafetida bag around her neck to ward off germs. Asafetida stank. Louise would hang it on a nail behind a billboard on the way to school and pick it up on the way home. When Aunt Pearl caught her playing outside with neighborhood kids, she would make her come in and sweep. In high school, Louise got a ride home one day with two football players in a coupe, and Aunt Pearl gave her holy Ned because her limbs *had to have* touched theirs. Louise got invited to the senior prom but Aunt Pearl wouldn't let her go. She wasn't allowed to date until after she graduated.

And Aunt Pearl was a cupcake compared to Louise's stepmother. My mother actually had a wicked stepmother. "I just want to get you children raised," Louise used to say, "and then I want to die."

Sense of humor ever fail me? Are you kidding?

CHAPTER 11 / Attitude

Let the clown die! Let the clown die!
—A CHANT SENT UP BY PRO-DEATH DEMONSTRATORS OUTSIDE
THE PRISON WHERE MASS MURDERER JOHN WAYNE GACY JR.,
WHO HAD BEEN KNOWN FOR DRESSING UP AS A CLOWN,
WAS ABOUT TO BE EXECUTED

Ed Koren, the cartoonist, was out jogging bright and early one morning in New York City. He passed a young man breaking into a parked car. Nothing out of the ordinary about that, but it was such a nice morning that Koren was moved to shout, "Hey!," as he went by, and even to make glancing eye contact with the young man. Who went on about his business. Koren, irritated, jogged on, but when he came over the next hill he saw a police car. He waved it down. The cops actually took an interest, responded over the hill and nabbed the young man red-handed. When Koren jogged back to see, the culprit gave him a look of outrage.

"Why ME?" he cried.

Little do we know.

But I accept the burden. Now, however, I am determined to stop being nice about it.

A while back, *Newsweek* actually did a cover story on niceness: "Being bad isn't cool anymore; now is a good time to be good." In music, Hootie and the Blowfish and Coolio up, Pearl Jam and Snoop Doggy-Dogg down. In kiddie-show ratings, a bunch of smiling bananas from Australia up, the violent Power Rangers down.

Well, does anyone honestly believe that people will be asking each other years from now who was their favorite Blowfish? As for the kiddie shows, the bananas can't possibly be as nice as Barney, that purple dinosaur-blivet, whose little songs of stupid love have surely caused every American three-year-old with any aptitude for acuity at all to become a closet Snoop Doggy-Dogg fan. My parents didn't want me to find out about

83

sex. My daughter and son-in-law live in fear that their babies will find out about Barney.

"Be sweet, now," my mother would tell me when I was little and she wanted me to sit still in some lady's house while she and the lady talked about curtains. Or, "Behave." That's a great one, isn't it? "Behave." What that meant in fact was, "Stop showing any signs of human behavior for a while." Why didn't she just say that? "Negate yourself." That would have been interesting, I could have gotten into that. "Be a zombie now, son." Cool. But no, it had to be "Be sweet."

There was a story in the paper the other day about a man who abducted a seven-year-old girl. While he was fleeing police in a high-speed chase (she told her rescuers later*), he had a gun to her head, telling her, "Behave." *He* was telling *her* that.

Oh, I know, I know, I've been a parent myself. "Be sweet" just means "Please let me forget for a moment or two that I am a parent so I can be a human being." But children don't know that!

I want to be sweet! Maybe nice is the enemy of sweet.

I am myself one of the nicest people in the world, except when someone tells me to have a nice day. When someone tells me to have a nice day, I say, "Thank you, but I picked up some kind of tropical parasite on my last trip abroad, which has already grown to the size of a mature Chihuahua, I'm told, and which may burst out through one of my orifices at any moment. Incidentally, I exude its spores, so if I were you, I wouldn't take a breath for ten to twelve minutes after I leave. That's what the experts recommend, the ones who haven't died horrible, retching deaths in the course of their research into this thing, which . . . Oh, look, sticky buns. I didn't notice those before. Could you wrap up a dozen of those for me? And a bottle of soy sauce. No, on second thought, I'll eat the buns here, and just go ahead and pour the sauce over them. I seem to have these cravings lately. Let me dig out my charge card again, *n'tou'ouaaaa'unh-aunh-h'munh,* oh, rats, now I'm beginning to speak the parasite's native tongue. I try to be a gracious host, but—oh, speaking of tongues, you should see what's happened to mine. See, looghk 'ere baghk inna . . . ."

At all other times, I am one of the nicest people you would ever want to meet, and where has it gotten me? Every single person I can think of

---

*You notice I don't leave you worrying about whether the little girl was saved. Because goddammit, I'm nice! I'm a father! I'm a human being! Okay?

who has gone farther in life than I have is pronouncedly less nice than I am. Martha Stewart? Please. Gennadi A. Zyuganov? Please. The latter would never even have been able to forge the coalition that nominated him for president of Russia if he weren't as mean as a rock-quarry snake, and when Boris Yeltsin beat him in the election, Zyuganov's critics said it was because he had abandoned the class struggle. As for Yeltsin himself, please.

I abandoned the class struggle myself long ago, because I had to admit that capitalism was too rough an eye-gouging, price-gouging competitor. My dream of universal income parity or at least government-supported equal access to video rentals for all Americans regardless of credit rating just couldn't hack it: too nice.

What is the most dominant team in sports? The Chicago Bulls. Are they nice? Michael Jordan is so competitive that he tends, I am told, to win more money from his security guys on the golf course than they make for protecting him. The only Bull who has ever been called nice is the center, Luc Longley, who is widely regarded as the team's weak link. Of Longley, the Bulls' Dennis Rodman—who is himself such a virtuoso of the flagrant foul that he gets away with flaming transvestitism—says condescendingly, "He wants to burst out and be a mean and vicious center in this league, but he can't. It's not in his nature."

Ah, nature. Do you know why I will almost certainly never achieve my lifelong dream of making the Baseball Hall of Fame? No, not because my father never played catch with me so far as I can remember. Because I lack, in honest, hale, masculine competition, a killer instinct. In Little League, I once took such pity on an enormously fat boy who had hit a little dribbler to me at third base that some demon took hold of me (perhaps my mother's voice murmured, "Aww, look at that little enormously fat boy's little dribbler there, poor little thing") and I couldn't pull the trigger on my throw to first. The fat boy ran, and ran, and ran, and paused to catch his breath, and ran some more, and my teammates were screaming at me. . . . By the time the fat boy reached first safely, his entire family was sobbing and hugging each other. And there I stood.

Ring Lardner once said that it was embarrassing to say you're a humorist: "It's like calling yourself a great third baseman." In fact, it's calling yourself a failed third baseman. The high point of my high school baseball career was when Emory Webb, our first baseman, was named to a city-wide all-star team. Webb was a nifty glove man who occasionally hit long home runs, but he also struck out a lot and had an embarrassing batting average. On hearing that he was going to be written up as an all-star, he grabbed our scorekeeper. "I want you to go through the books and get all my stats together," he said, "and—"

"And change them," I said.

There was my killer instinct. As I look back on it now, one of my inspirations had been a boy named Ferris who joined my fourth-grade class in the middle of the year. Transferred from a Catholic school, some said. He might almost have been a monk. Close-cropped hair, absolute silence and a stooped, meditative posture. He would sit at his desk arranging his books in an unnaturally neat stack. We all sensed, I believe—even the girls—that he was a cataclysm waiting to happen.

His second day, we were each supposed to ask the class a science question. How is the mollusk a friend to man?, that sort of thing.

It came Ferris's turn. He made his way slowly, almost ceremoniously to the front of the room. He raised his head almost high enough to make eye contact with his audience. Then he asked his question.

"Now whut . . . pwanet . . . has weengs . . . awound it?"

Whenever people blather about the innocence of youth, I remember with what vicious delight every child I have ever known has pounced on naiveté revealed by another child.

Ferris's question was followed by a long moment of delicious, horrified silence. And then the class erupted. People actually fell out of their desks. Girls tittered, boys guffawed. Even our teacher was unable to suppress her natural reaction. She shook. A couple of boys threw erasers.

Ferris transferred to another school.

And how had I reacted to his question? On several levels. On one level, the level of niceness, I wished that God would give Ferris wings so he could fly over our heads and out the window, or at least that I would have the decency to cry out, "Saturn! Saturn! It's a good question!" Mark Twain wrote, "Let your secret sympathies and your compassion be always with the underdog in the fight—this is magnanimity."

But, Twain added, "bet on the other one—this is business."

I whooped at Ferris.

I also turned Ferris's question over and over in my mind. I turn it over to this day. "Now whut . . . pwanet . . ." What made it so explosive? That old-fashioned formal "now" at the beginning, as in "Now when Jesus was born in Bethlehem of Judaea in the days of Herod the king, behold . . . ," was the exquisite touch. Somewhere in my developing lingo-cerebral wheelhouse, perhaps "where the tip of the tongue meets the back of the mind" (to misquote Seamus Heaney, who had it "where the back of the throat . . ."), it registered that if I could ever get that big a laugh, on purpose, without causing erasers to be thrown at me, I could make my way in the world. What if I had saved my second-grade pants-wetting situation with a quip? Turned it right around and made it work for me—it could have been *better* than Ferris. Just as unsightly adolescents shave off patches of hair and put studs in their noses to make it appear that they *mean* to be ugly, I began to cultivate my comic potential.

"What was the big break in your career?" feature-story interviewers have asked me briskly, having gotten a perfectly straightforward answer to that question just the day before from Werner Klemperer, in town to appear as the Wazir in a dinner-theater production of *Kismet*. And I have had to let them down by saying something to the effect that I haven't careered so much as careened, only more slowly than that word has come to imply, and that I am just lucky not to have broken more of the things I've run into.

I did, however, have the great good fortune of having Ann Lewis as my tenth-grade English teacher. She took note of my peculiarities (I would choose the most hackneyed theme topic, for instance, "What I Did Last Summer" or "The Most Unforgettable Character I Have Ever Met," and wind up writing about how strange the pencil I was using had begun to seem to me) and suggested I consider becoming a writer. By the time I broke up the locker room at Emory Webb's expense (and let me say to his credit, as well as mine, that he laughed too), Miss Lewis had given me Benchley and Thurber and Perelman and White to read and inspired me to be a humorist. She was the only person I was ever likely to meet in Decatur who subscribed to *The New Yorker*. She was also advisor to the school paper, *The Scribbler,* for which I became a humor columnist, making fun of more popular students. That had made me so popular that I was nominated for president of the student council. I was too much my father's son to be a class clown, but just barely.

Before my big campaign speech I was in the boys' room putting on a tie. One of the other candidates was doing deep knee bends. I asked him why.

"So my calves will be big," he said.

"But you're wearing long pants," I said.

"I'll know," he said.

In my speech, I attacked him on that issue. I pulled up my pants and showed the school my honest, unpumped calves. I went on in that vein, more and more farcically. The speech went over big.

My father, who attended, gave me an odd look afterward. He was chairman of the board of education. I lost that election handily. Somehow, though, I did get elected president of the senior class. My administration didn't accomplish anything, and I was never president of anything again, and now I am a humorist.

On my forty-eighth birthday, I made a speech in Columbus, Ohio, under the auspices of the Thurber House foundation, and spent the night in James Thurber's actual boyhood house, now a museum. The bed didn't fall nor did a ghost get in, but I couldn't get to sleep so I wandered downstairs and wrote Ann Lewis a letter on Thurber's old typewriter.

And today that Little League fat boy whom I allowed to reach base for perhaps the only time in his life—he gave me a "You pussy" look when he finally got over his astonishment—probably makes ten times what I do. My coach never forgave me, and no doubt passed the word along through the coaching grapevine, because every single coach or manager I have ever met since then has looked at me askance.

One of those was Leo Durocher, the late baseball manager who will go down in history as having said "Nice guys finish last." When Durocher was manager of the Cubs, I approached him for a routine interview. It was a lovely spring-training day in Scottsdale, Arizona. Durocher gave me one look, curled his famous lip, cursed inventively, and stalked off, saying over his shoulder, "And you know why, too."

The Little League thing was the only explanation.

According to anthropologist Lyall Watson, the three rules for the game of genetic survival are BE NASTY TO OUTSIDERS, BE NICE TO INSIDERS, CHEAT WHENEVER POSSIBLE. I have never mastered these rules. I have a tendency to do almost the opposite. Why? The switcheroo? Or because I can't keep straight who the outsiders are. When it comes to gender, for instance.

Girls are supposed to be made of "sugar and spice and everything nice," right? They complain that we boys aren't nice enough, don't they? And we try to be nice, so they'll let us kiss them. It doesn't come naturally to us, because whereas (let's say) girls are relatively nice people, sort of, boys are hardened by the necessity of dealing with other boys—who are not trying to be nice to us, because they don't want us to let them kiss us. So when we are trying to be nice we are flying blind—but we do try to be nice, don't we?

And yet—last night I asked a woman what *nice* meant to her.

"If we say someone is a nice man," she said, "it means we're not interested in him."

Even the word *nice* has a checkered past. It comes from the Latin for "ignorant" by way of the Old French for "simpleminded, stupid" and the Middle English for "foolish, wanton." In its earliest usage in English it could mean "lewd, dissolute" as well as "coy, diffident"; "trivial" as well as "agreeable"; "lacking vigor" as well as "requiring, marked by, or capable of delicate discrimination." According to the *Oxford English Dictionary*, it is often impossible to tell what writers as late as the seventeenth century meant by *nice*.

The other night a friend of mine told me a story about a mutual friend of ours, let us call him Frog. Frog was not having a nice night when my friend ran into him at a party at some nice people's house.

Frog came up to my friend and confided to him, loudly, "I may need a ride home. My date is getting madder and madder at me. Because I keep calling her Marcy." Which is his previous girlfriend's name.

"She says to me, 'Why do you keep doing that?' " said Frog. He shrugged. "I told her, I said—"

And at that point in his loud conversation with my friend, Frog did a terrible thing. I, myself, nice as I am, have done some terrible things—in all innocence, usually—at parties, but never anything quite this terrible.

What Frog did was, as he was about to tell my friend what he had told his date, he flung his arms wide in a gesture of expansive bemusement, and he was holding a lit cigar in one hand, and a man happened to be walking by with a baby in his arms, and the lit end of Frog's cigar hit the baby squarely in the cheek.

Another friend of mine threw up on a stranger's baby once, in a bus, and that was pretty bad, but this, I think you will agree even if you aren't as nice as I am, was worse.

On the baby's part, and its father's part, a moment of horrified silence followed. Then the baby bellowed. With that the whole party, except for the baby, fell silent as everyone turned to look. An ugly smudge on the baby's face, and wisps of smoke that suggested the baby might be on fire. The father reacted quickly. He leapt, holding the baby, into the swimming pool.

What, you are wondering, was Frog's reaction? Well, the nice thing for him to do . . .

Would have been what? Frog did look, along with everyone else, in the baby's direction, as the father came clambering out of the pool. Frog noted, along with everyone else, that the baby had suffered no serious damage. No doubt the baby was surprised that life could be like this, but then, babies have a lot to learn. And one of the things that everyone learns eventually is this:

Sometimes there is no nice thing to do.

So what Frog did was, he picked up where he left off.

"I told her," he said, " 'If you'll pay for the goddamn psychotherapy, maybe we can get to the bottom of it.' "

CHAPTER 12 / **The Bottom, Ontogenetically**

I don't know just what you heard,
But "Come on, Baby" are my favorite words.   —LYLE LOVETT

I may be a kind of Everyman, at least on the surface. A close friend once told me, "You look more like more people—I mean, I see more people on the street that I think are you, at first—than anybody else I know." Occasionally I, myself, see someone coming down the sidewalk toward me and I think, "That looks like . . . It can't be."

Strangers have told me they thought for a moment I was Dan Reeves, the football coach; Sydney Pollack, the director; Randy Newman, the singer-songwriter; Bill Moyers, the philosophy vicar; and (it was dark) Charles Nelson Reilly, the TV personality. I have given some thought to all these people's faces, and the only characteristic I can see that we might share (except Pollack, maybe) is a kind of squinched-up, distant-looking quality.

Once, after making a speech, I was described in a student newspaper as having "features too small for [my] face," but that can't be true of my nose. Years ago in Minneapolis a photographer looked through her lens at me for some time and then put down her camera. "I don't see anything," she said. "I thought there'd be more texture." I'm more wrinkled now, but still you probably have to get to know me before you are likely to recognize me.

During my first year or so as a writer at *Sports Illustrated*, in the late sixties, certain people around the office blithely informed me that they had trouble telling me and Billy Reed, another writer, apart—of course we were both white Southerners and wore glasses. I have been told that both Bill Murray, the actor, and my ex–brother-in-law Johnny Pearson, the lawyer—who look no more like each other than Jerry of "Tom and Jerry" and Mickey Mouse—look enough like me to be my brother. People assuring me of their familiarity with my work have complimented me on things

91

actually written by Garrison Keillor, Harry Crews, Lewis Grizzard and, perhaps least inevitably, Bernard Malamud. My personal physician, Dr. Bruce Yaffe, claims to have another patient who looks so much like me that for years he kept trying to get us both to come out to dinner with him at the same time, to prove to his satisfaction that we were two different people. Only the other day, after a rectal exam, did he tell me he had managed to draw between us some subtle distinction. (I didn't ask.)

And yet, when I feel like myself, I feel different from everybody else. Of course maybe that's the one thing I have in common with everybody else. (If only such a feeling weren't so hard to organize around!) That, and the fact that I was born of woman. But with what a twist in my case.

I don't know how my egg-half felt—just a plump, round target hanging out, humming "Someday my prince will come" and waiting for a bullet with my name on it? Or maybe egging a certain bullet on? I like eggs, but it's hard for me to imagine I am one. Whereas I actually dreamed that I was a sperm cell last night, and it was cool. Not winking, not worrying, just going like a son of a gun. Might be a children's book in it. No, I guess not. Anyway I couldn't keep it up, so to speak, *forever*. Second thoughts kept flooding in. I kept catching myself, looking over my shoulder. It was like being a rat in a cathedral. What was I doing here? Was I going about it right, was I missing something? *Où est le fromage sacré, enfin?*

Then, glom.

To what can we compare that first wild, stuck instant of union? Landing on another planet? Maybe from the egg's perspective, it would be an alien landing on oneself. Here's an actual headline from *The Times* of London:

PILOT WHO LANDED PLANE
ON WIFE WILL QUIT FLYING

More precisely, the husband in question had crash-landed his one-seater microlight plane, which he had built himself, and which he flew as a hobby; and his wife—trying, I dare say, to be a part of his life—had been struck by some debris from the impact. (It comes to me with a jolt that my sympathies *should* lie, of course, with the wife.) "I could hear my wife shouting," he is quoted as saying, "so I knew she was all right. She was lying on the ground and shouting. She actually seemed more cross than anything."

If such relatively mundane air travel can lead to such consternation, imagine what we can get into when we start landing spaceships on Martians or their spouses.

This is for sure: every person, from the ordinary citizen who photographs strange, glowing objects in the sky to the scientists who recently found what appear to be the remains of 3.6-million-year-old Martian microorganisms in an Antarctic rock—every last person who has come forward with one more piece, however small, of the vast puzzle whose solution someday will surely enable us to establish contact with life on Mars—is crazy.

Don't you want to give each such person a good shake and say, "Did you have any earthly idea what the last *Earth* being you listened, really listened, to—if he or she differed from you by so much as gender, generation, creed or political affiliation—was going on about? I thought not. Do you even have any inkling of what I am trying to get through your head now? I thought not. And you expect to communicate with *Mars*?"

If Mars does harbor sentient beings, they may well be so elementally out of synch with our perceptions, and vice versa, that for all we know there is one tapping away with his or her *thorpylts* (sensory filaments) right now on what he or she takes to be the *pharyb* (central nervous-system node) of Supreme Network Commander James Earl Jones but is, in fact, say, some little valve on some little gizmo connected to, say, the solid-waste-disposal system several hundred feet beneath, say, Denver.

If Martians insist on getting in touch with us, well, we'll see. But what's the hurry?

Because I know what's going to happen. As soon as we do get involved with Martians, that guy John Gray, Ph.D., is going to come out with a book entitled *Earthlings Are from Mars or Venus, Martians Are from Washington.* (Or *Montana*, or wherever.) And I'm going to be yelling, "Wait a minute! I didn't get the men-and-women thing straight yet!"

As soon as I heard of Gray's book, *Men Are from Mars, Women Are from Venus,* I thought to myself, Well, he's probably got something there. Basically, guys are like Stephen Seagal and women are like your mama. Of course not even Stephen Seagal is actually like Stephen Seagal, and I am willing to stipulate that there will never be anyone, for better or worse, like your mama.

According to Gray, a man has to translate what a woman says into his language, and vice versa.

In other words, I guess, when a woman says, "You heartless pig, you don't love me and you never did, and if you dare try to make me feel better I'll come upside your head with this tacky candelabra your sister gave us," men should realize that what she means is, "You heartless pig, I need your support very much right now, so please give me a hug and listen to me rant and rave at you for another couple of hours."

When a man says, "Umf," women should realize that what he means is, "I'm watching the Steelers and the Packers in sudden-death overtime right now, you wonderful all-around human being who does so much to fill my life with sunshine, but I would enjoy it all the more if you would cuddle up against me here and seethe as I explain all the nuances of offensive and defensive alignments so we can share this moment together."

Meanwhile, both parties are thinking to themselves, Why should I bend over backward to bear in mind that he/she is from a different planet, when all he/she does is treat me like I'm from another planet?

Now. We want to introduce actual Martians into this mix?

For one thing, if we are going to follow the principles laid down by John Gray, Ph.D., we have to assume that everyone from Mars is a man. Which means that women are going to be accusing men of always taking the Martians' side. It's one more example of pervasive sexism, that we didn't get in touch with life on Venus first. Even if the first Martian to get in touch with us is a woman, or what passes for a woman on Mars, women on our planet aren't going to like her, because her first message is going to be "How 'bout them Forty-niners? Want to fuck?"

And Earth men are going to be telling Earth women, "Well, what Ms. M'feldrylia here probably means is, 'Where did you find those lovely curtains? Let's sit down and have a good, long gossip.' " And Earth women aren't going to be buying it. And they're going to be right. Women are always right when feelings are involved, and feelings are always involved as soon as a woman sets foot in a room.

The tragedy of it all is that Earth men aren't going to like M'feldrylia much either, because for one thing, her appearance (which is what men notoriously judge women by) is that of, say, gelatinous celery with oddly distributed luminous tufts of what may or may not be hair; and for another thing, she is going to be dead set on *communicating*. About Mars-Earth relationships. In fact, when she opens her mouth (if she has a mouth), nothing may come out, in human terms, but a kind of vapor that surrounds your head, going *fzzzt-bzzt, fzzzt-bzzt*, until you think of an appropriate response. Not because she is what passes on Mars for a woman, but because, let's face it, she is from Mars.

And also because she is, let's not forget, the type of Martian who gets sent out to make contact with other planets. Are the people we send out to make contact with other planets going to be the type of people with whom anyone would enjoy chewing the fat? No, they're going to be highly specialized space cadets, who if they were normal Earth people would be home watching television. M'feldrylia is probably someone who won't hit it off with anyone on Earth except Newt Gingrich. Okay, that's a cheap joke. But she may not think it's a joke at all. She may think it's sweet.

She may, however, be much more highly evolved than Earth people.* She may be capable of passing effortlessly through reinforced-concrete walls, jumping back and forth in time by laying her finger (if she has fingers) aside of her nose (if she has one), and calculating the exact chemical composition of any form of matter in her head (if she has a head), without pen or pencil. She may, therefore, regard Earth people as quaint. To her, anything that Microsoft has in development may be folk art. Whatever our most sophisticated thinkers and statesmen put forward to her may sound like "Mars person speak with forked tongue." She may, in fact, have a forked larynx, if she has to bother with having an actual physical larynx at all. And just wait till the pope asks her what her position is on Adam, Eve and original sin. Earth, to her, may be all third world. We, to her, may be, at best, like prairie dogs to Japanese tourists. I heard a story the other day that bears on the difficulty of communicating between different forms of life.

The Lone Ranger and Tonto are captured by hostile Indians. Tonto's first reaction is to point to the Lone Ranger and say, "Kemo sabe!" And then to join in the general laughter. "Kemo sabe!" cry all the Native Americans as one. "Kemo sabe! Hooo-ha!" They are taking the Lone Ranger's hat away from him and tossing it around and pelting him with bits of buffalo dung.

---

*We always assume, about beings from other planets, that this will be the case. But what if they manage to land on us and yet turn out to be *dumber* than we are? They're eager to absorb all our advanced knowledge ("What do you call that thing again? A whale? Whool? That thing—there goes a bunch of them, on the bottom of that transportation thing. Oh, right, *wheel*. There goes some more of 'em! And they go *uphill*? Can I eat one?"), but they can't seem to *get* it. That's all we need.

The chief steps forward. He speaks some English. "How 'bout them braves?" he chuckles.

The blood is draining from the Lone Ranger's face. He looks around for Tonto, spots him exchanging high fives.

"Uhh . . . ," says the Lone Ranger. "I always just assumed . . . What does *Kemo sabe* mean?"

"Means 'Buffalo-dung-for-brains,'" says the chief. "We give you two requests, and let you live two days. Then we burn you at the stake."

The Lone Ranger pulls himself together. He is, after all, who he is. "All right," he says. "My first request . . ."

And he calls Silver over to him and whispers something in his trusted mount's ear.

Whereupon Silver runs off like a scalded dog.

"Whoooo-ha!" cry out the hostiles in utter hilarity. "Kemo sabe! Hi-yo, Silver! Ah-ha-ha-ha!"

But suddenly the laughter is cut short. Because here comes a thunder of hooves—Silver reappears. And on his back, lightly beaded with perspiration and wearing a loose gingham gown that clings to her damp bosom and thighs, is the most voluptuous woman ever seen around there.

"Hmmm," says the chief. "Lone Ranger a great warrior. Train horse well. Tonight, Lone Ranger take Twisted Snake's wickiup." (Twisted Snake doesn't care for that idea one bit, but that's a side issue, tribal politics; he and the chief have never seen eye to eye.)

The Lone Ranger retires to the wickiup with the woman, and the next morning he comes out looking refreshed, on one level, but still clearly aware that he is in a jam. The woman appears in a moment, looking radiant. (Her name is Gwyneth Louise and she is not about to stay cooped up in a wickiup when the punch line is about to be delivered, but that, too, is a side issue.)

"Lone Ranger look refreshed on one level," says the chief. "Heh-heh. But we still burn you at the stake. One more day. One more request."

The masked man calls Silver over to him again. Again he puts his lips close to the great horse's ear.

"Dammit, Silver," he whispers, "I said *posse*."

CHAPTER 13 / Going Down

"She'll do it."

"Yeah, but she'll resent it."

"Well, maybe she likes resenting it."

"Yeah, but that's what she really hates."

"What? Liking it? Liking resenting it?"

"Yeah."

"Damn."
— A CONVERSATION OVERHEARD

I'll bet the womb is not all it's cracked up to be," my friend Lois once mused aloud. Apropos of I don't know what. She was watching her husband, my friend Roland, and me play tennis. I couldn't concentrate after that.

Her point was that you're upside down, and for the last couple of months you're extremely cramped. As the mother of two, she spoke with a certain authority. It's undoubtedly false nostalgia when I am tempted to believe that I was cozy there, in my element, an unshelled pea, an unshot cartridge.

Though when I learned to scuba dive . . .

There are some people who see nothing strange about breathing underwater. I am speaking of people, now, not of fish, though I will soon be speaking of fish and of how I acquired a whole new perspective on . . .

Sharks, even!

There I am, kneeling on the bottom, breathing, underwater, and I notice that the Japanese man kneeling with me is staring in my direction as if I were some kind of startling sea creature myself, and I look over my shoulder, and there are seven sharks! Lined up!

Actual sharks! But we'll get into sharks later. Don't hold your breath.

Excuse me, I am addressing myself there: "Don't hold your breath." Call me a stick-in-the-mud, but my instinct, underwater, has always been to hold my breath. Because I am a person. But I learned that if I hold my breath scuba-diving I will get a reverse block and my teeth will explode, or at least I will start seeing pink water in front of my eyes, unless I am at thirty feet, at which depth blood looks green. Deeper, it looks brown. Is what I'm told.

You can't smile.

Well, *you* can smile, because you are not underwater at the moment. Or, even if you are, diving is probably second nature to you by now and therefore you don't have any problem with the fact that if you smile underwater, water gets in your mask and you find yourself breathing water—colored water, maybe—underwater.

Is this why fish don't smile?

No. Fish don't wear masks. Furthermore, fish breathe water as a matter of course.

This was down off Nassau, I should mention. I wasn't smiling. And it was probably fortunate that things—sharks, for instance—look larger and closer underwater. Because, therefore, you can keep telling yourself, "This thing [shark, for instance] is not as large [sixty-four feet long] or as close [three eighths of an inch away] as it appears."

Until it actually brushes you on its way past. A shark—a bull shark—brushed me.

And then it hits you: these sharks are ignoring me.

Last night I dreamed that I was bubbling. Lying there, in the darkness, bubbling. And wondering what my buoyancy was.

Sharks!

Take a deep breath. I can do that, now, without embarrassing myself by exhausting my entire tank in one fell fwooooop. Because I am not underwater, now. Right? Right.

Okay.

There are some people who see nothing strange about learning to breathe underwater. I am not one of them. For one thing, I am a person who suffers not from dyslexia but rather from dysnearlyeverythingelsia.

Reading, I'm good at. However, I found the written portion of the PADI certification test unexpectedly challenging. I feel most comfortable with a multiple-choice test when at least one of the choices on each question is preposterous, or positively buoyant—it floats to the top and away from consideration. For instance:

Of the few problems that do occur under water, check those that are most likely:

a. entanglement
b. eel attack
c. running out of air
d. regulator malfunction

There, "eel attack" is obviously out of the question. Isn't it? Of course it is. In Hollywood films, eel attack is all too frequent. But not in real life, I was assured. Of course in real life, people don't breathe underwater. Or at least . . .

Running out of air?

Far too few questions on the written test enabled me to reject "eel attack" or "running out of air" out of hand. However, I applied myself vigorously to that test, and made a ninety.

"Pretty good," said my instructor, Kevin Ogilvie-White. "Only one person has done better."

"Who was that?" I asked.

"Brooke Shields," he said.

And they expected me to believe that this was real life.

One of the first questions Kevin asked me during in-the-water instruction was, "Are you naked?"

This struck me as curious, since I felt, if anything, overdressed. The last time I'd checked, I was wearing not only several bulky devices with gauges on them but also a wet suit, in which I felt that I probably looked like George Reeves in a Superman costume. In the old black-and-white TV Superman, George Reeves looked like a flying sausage. It seemed to me highly unlikely that I would ever be able to peel this suit off, not to mention that anyone could imagine that any part of it had slipped off into the water.

I was reminded of that moment when Huck Finn has swum from his and Jim's raft to a big commercial one, to eavesdrop on raftsmen and find out where on the river they have drifted to. He's hiding behind some bundles of shingles when a raftsman approaches. "He come rummaging around in the dark . . . where I was, and put his hand on me. I was warm and soft and naked; so he says 'Ouch!' and jumped back." An interesting passage. The *raftsman* says "Ouch." Huck is of course a severely abused child—his father beats him viciously. And Huck is extraordinarily matter-of-fact about it. He wouldn't be funny if he weren't. Sam Clemens's father didn't beat him so far as we know, but he never showed his children a single sign of affection, never touched them at all. My father taught me to swim, in an absent sort of way. He preferred doing things like tearing out a wall in the house, and he'd have to stop and wash all the plaster off before taking me down to the pool and stand there while I paddled to him.

Anyway, "Are you naked?" seemed an awfully personal question. Had Kevin been so bold with Brooke Shields?

Then I realized that Kevin, who is English, was saying, "Are you knackered?" Was I tired. That was the least of my concerns.

I understand that most people who learn to breathe underwater begin to do so in a swimming pool. Since this was a three-day immersion course and Kevin naturally assumed that I wanted to hurry on ahead to the point of hanging out with sharks, I began in a cove. And the next thing I knew, I was going off the end of a boat—thinking, What color is blood at what depth? and reminding myself involuntarily of the most interesting and least useful things that I had learned: "Manta rays like being ridden on, turtles don't," and "In the unlikely event that you do get entangled in a plant, remain calm" and "Most accidents involve semi-drowning on the surface."

Semi-drowning?

One thing that troubled me was that I couldn't gasp. It's not that I like to gasp, but I like to feel that I can gasp, if the situation calls for it. And this situation—jumping off the end of a boat and then floating, more or less, in choppy water at eye level—seemed to. Call for it. And in the coils of all that equipment and water . . .

I was indicating to Kevin as coolly as possible that I would like to take a moment to get back up on the boat and gasp a few times and maybe scream just briefly at the top of my lungs—do anything at the top of my lungs, at the top of anything—when vwoooooooooooom. . . .

Weee-ooo, weee-oooooooo.

That's just theme music. Here's what it sounds like, as best I can put it into writing:

BRORbrorbryl . . . sschyuuuuu . . .

BRORbrorbryl . . . sschyuuuuu . . .

I was breathing underwater.

Maybe being born is a lot like learning to scuba dive, only backward. And with no instructions. No Japanese men on vacation in there with you—God help them if they are, in the womb it's every man for himself. (I wonder if the average mother, in fact, is tempted at some point during a long labor to think, "Forget the baby! Save me!" Only human. We are not always nice, male or female. A woman told me once that she never really forgave her husband, deep down inside, for the pain of her son's delivery.) And no fish. Unless you are twins, there's no company at all, just union with the Mom. Increasingly cramped union. Then . . .

There is that moment when we go from nothing we can imagine afterward to nothing we could have imagined before.

Humor, we have noted, comes from the Latin for "fluid." Perhaps the primal bit of dry humor is that first astonishing breath you take out of water. Only in my case it was more complicated.

My mother's mom died before my mother was two years old.

CHAPTER 14 / An End of Something: I Am Born

I have always had a problem with innocence. Ronald Reagan's, for instance. It's crazy for a president of the United States to get away with coming off as innocent. Pretty soon everybody is feeling innocent. Conservative and innocent. It won't wash. If you don't believe in original sin, you ain't conservative, friend.

But you say to me, "Isn't supply-side economics a romantic notion?"

Yes. A romantic notion the rich can get richer behind. You can call that innocence if you like. I call it knowing from the cradle what side your bread is buttered on.

I was born to parents who just barely had their hard-working heads up out of the Depression. *They* were innocent in many respects—and I'll say this for me, I tried to protect that. I remember once when I was seven or eight, some of us boys were playing on a clay bank just down the street from my house and James Henry, who was standing on top of the bank, and was bigger than the rest of us, took it upon himself to pee down onto Tommy's head.

Tommy was understandably outraged, but stood no chance of beating up James Henry, so he started running toward the nearest authority figure—which would be my mother, since my house was handy. He ran into my front door yelling, and I was right behind him, trying to get there ahead of him, trying to prevent him from corrupting my mother.

But he got to her first. "Miz Blount! Miz Blount! James Henry peed on my head!" he cried.

And I jumped in, trying to cushion the blow, at least to the extent of translating for my mother a term I assumed to be too vulgar for her to have heard: "*Pee* means 'tinkle.' "

My family said *tinkle*. For bowel movements, it was something even worse. *Big potty.* Okay? Are you satisfied? Everybody else in the neighborhood said *comic book, hunky bar* and *fart.* We said *funny book, Eskimo Pie* and *little bad smell.* Partly a matter of euphemism, partly a matter of not being in touch with the vernacular. I didn't have the meaning of *fart* straight until I misused it once in the fourth grade and a kid in my class (who was rumored a number of years later to be involved in gunrunning) looked at me as if I were some kind of Martian.* Undoubtedly such experiences heightened the sensitivity to language that has gotten me where I am today (sitting, stark naked, in the middle of yet another sentence that needs some punching up, what the heck, I'll go back and stick in "stark naked"), but—to my astonishment—my mother seemed to know what *pee* meant, in fact. She suggested to Tommy that he go home and clean up—he probably wasn't much wetter or nastier on top of his head than anywhere else, since we had been sweating and rolling in the red Georgia clay—and not to play with people like James Henry anymore.

Easy for her to say. I already realized that everybody, to some extent, was like James Henry. That even everybody else's *parents*, but mine, were like James Henry. But I knew we had higher standards in our family, *intrinsically*. Which meant that it must have been only after leaving the womb—or, okay, while leaving—that I had begun to go wrong.

When my first grandson, Jesse, was born, the first thing he did was to protest the imposition and the second was to give his mother, my daughter Ennis, a look. A look like, "Where did *you* come from?"

Did his mother respond to that look by putting him on the defensive? Did she give him a look back like, "Little do you know. You just don't know. And if you did, you wouldn't care. Not really."

No. She's a social worker. She and my son-in-law, David, whose work is in organic produce, are teaching Jesse Roy about being happy and being sad, and here's what they have told him: "Happy is what you come back to."

She gave little old Jesse Roy a look back like, "You were a snap."

Not me. I'm proud to say I helped raise a child whose little boy entered the world with natural dispatch. But I came hard. October 4, 1941, two months before Pearl Harbor. My first act in life was to nearly kill my mother.

---

*"I didn't know what *fart* meant until I was fifteen," Susan says. "And then I had to ask."

In the circles I grew up in (white Methodist middle-class in Decatur, Georgia, just outside Atlanta), near matricide was a common offense—but among *older* children, and *figuratively*. A young person, having gone off to college, would go along with colored people on a Freedom Ride, say, or would stay out all night with someone without being married, or— theoretically, but more or less equivalently—would wake up one morning metamorphosed into an enormous insect; and whatever else the maternal community would say about it, they would be sure to say this: "Of course it nearly killed Mary Frances." Mary Frances being the young person's mama.

But I nearly killed mine right off the bat, and *literally*. As if her life weren't unbearable enough already.

What can my motive have been?

Maybe I just wasn't paying enough attention to what was going on around me. "You look like you're a thousand miles away," women have often told me, and I have responded, like Dagwood to Blondie when she's trying to wake him up to tell him she hears something (my mother dug that strip): "Fnf?" Women expect you to be listening immediately when they start telling you something, and to answer right away as soon as they've finished. But, gender aside, it is the lot of a creative person, surely, to be in a fog. To be off in one's head somewhere, meanwhile bumping into people, dropping things, stepping on a baby on the beach.

I can't let myself off that easy. Maybe at my nativity I was being per-verse. "Just trying yourself," as my mother used to put it. What would I have been doing, when my mother said I was trying myself? Fidgeting? Making one of those annoying little noises that children make over and over and over and over and ooover and ooover? Hey, I know, children will drive you insane.

Anyway, it's not funny to try yourself—unless you're a judge. Pigmeat Markham in his "Here come the judge" routine: "I'm in a evil mood this mawnin'. I'm liable to give *myself* thirty days."

When I was older, Susan and I would be sulking and picking on each other in the backseat of the car, and my mother, in the front seat, would commence to fume—and I mean the heat was coming from deep down inside—and say, "You children ruin everything we try to do."

As my mother went through labor, I was no doubt being stubbornly unforthcoming—or, I guess the correct term is, withholding. Males do that to women. Hang back from calling on the phone, from chatting at breakfast, from saying "I love you" between anniversaries, from sharing feelings. (Can you share a feeling, really? I don't know. You can share where your feelings overlap.)

Anyway, I wouldn't be at all surprised if my mother was fuming because my father was just frowning, concentrating on driving, and wishing he could have a little *peace* so he could think about business. I feel for him. But that was a form of withholding. I'm trying in this book not to withhold, though of course there's the other side of it. The "I don't believe I'd've told that" side.

Women do sometimes withhold from men. I got on the New York subway once and sat down next to a couple who were arguing. This couple was dressed in black leather, and they seemed to have lizards tattooed all over their bodies. I say seemed, because all you could see for sure was a lizard's tail at the wrist here, a lizard's front quarters at the neck there, and so on, but the impression given was, there were lots of lizards where those were coming from or going to.

This couple's argument, though, was one that many couples without lizards tattooed all over themselves have.

"You don't share your life with me," the man was saying.

"What do you mean? What don't I share?" the woman replied.

"I tell you about everything I do, but I have to find out what you do from other people."

"What? What didn't I tell you?"

There was a pause. Then the man said, "How about Francesco?"

"Francesco? Oh. Well, I thought you knew about Francesco. He's a very nice man, and when I first came to the city he gave a party for me, and—"

"*See!*" cried the man. "*That's exactly what I'm talking about. I pick a name from the AIR! WHO THE HELL IS FRANCESCO!?!?*"

But that's just anecdotal, and besides, that was male exasperation talking—that doesn't qualify as a feeling, by women's standards, which, let's face it, are the standards by which feelings are judged and undoubtedly a good thing too. If men were the judges of feelings, the Saul Rogovin standard would obtain. Saul Rogovin is a man who, in 1952, pitched an entire sixteen-inning game for the Chicago White Sox. Forty-two years later, a *New York Daily News* reporter asked him what it felt like.

"How did it feel?" Rogovin responded. "I can't tell you. I was a pro, and a pro isn't supposed to talk about something like that."

When a woman withholds, a man is expected to realize, it's in reaction to men's withholding of sweetness. Or perhaps to men's coming off as needy. Girls grow up making distinctly emotive sounds and giving each other hugs and saying to each other (whether they mean it or not), "Oh, I like your dress. Where did you get it?" Boys grow up grunting and frogging each other on the arm and saying (whether they mean it or not), "Where'd you get that shirt? It looks like a dead dog threw up pizza on it." It is hard for boys to shift gears.

Creative boys, because we are so often in a fog and bumping into things and so on, do develop, over the years, a good second move. We catch ourselves. For instance, I have never put my full weight down on a baby on the beach. But how was I supposed to have that second move at *birth*?

Was I just not paying sufficient attention at birth? Was my mind somewhere else? Maybe my head was just too big. Today, even with a haircut, I wear a size seven-and-a-half hat. My mother was always vague as to the details (which was okay with me), except to let drop from time to time that the doctors didn't think they would ever stop her bleeding. That's how much she loved me. I believed her.

"You know, I nearly bled to death having you, son." I'm trying to picture what my mother is doing when she lays this on me. Maybe we're in our den on Clarion Avenue in Decatur, and I'm playing Superman fighting with several people at once, and she is scrubbing some domestic surface with Bab-O. Or maybe we were in my parents' bedroom and she was putting lotion on her hands.

Bab-O and Jergens. Gritty-sudsy cleanser and icky lotion to counteract the effects. Crepe de chine. "Look at these hands. Who could love these hands?" she would ask me. Jeez, I didn't know what to say, I was just a kid. I guess her hands were work-worn (and one of her fingers was crooked— she broke it fixing the cocking lever on my Red Ryder BB gun), but what was not to love?

She was tender. But with a catch. Crepe de chine. On what would have been Mother's seventy-eighth birthday, had she lived twelve years longer, I was talking to Susan on the phone. She was telling me about the bats in her attic. She had found them hanging upside down, suckling baby bats. At night, Susan would hear them fluttering, a sound "like tissue paper tearing." Soft, but edgy. A flicker of our mother.

"I work my fingers to the bone," she often reminded us. She was an upwardly mobile middle-class white lady, highly regarded in the community, and the prettiest woman I knew. Before I started school she taught me to read, phonetically—to sound out the words. Mmmm. That's where my vocation comes from, sure as anything.

"You taught me language," says Caliban, "and my profit on't/Is I know how to curse." I like to curse.

As I've mentioned, the only curse word my mother used was *hell*, and that only because she was brought up to believe in that place. When she called me an infidel, I realized that she thought I was going there. When I was a child I loved reading about the Crusaders, who slew the infidel, but by the time my mother called me one I had the advantage of a college education, and had even written for my own pleasure a bit of verse entitled "Crusader":

> *So the infidel,*
> *Though anyone can see they're cursed,*
> *Don't believe in Christian Hell?*
> *He sends them there, but first,*
> *If they're buxom,*
> *He fuxom.*

But even then, in college, I was regarded as a straight arrow—belonged to the Student Christian Association, didn't drink—and as teenagers Susan and I were certainly nice, even by fifties standards. We didn't get into trouble to speak of and we got good grades. Okay, I failed to pick up after myself and I developed, belatedly, a penchant for heavy petting.

And I did bring indelible disgrace on the family once, in the eighth grade. Thirty-odd years later I was on a radio talk show in some far-flung city (Portland, Oregon?), decrying the Senate Judiciary Committee's treatment of Anita Hill and belittling Clarence Thomas (which had nothing to do with the book I was supposed to be promoting—I will say this for myself, I am terrible at marketing), when the guy in the booth who was screening phone calls held up a card that said, "Ann—cheated with him in school."

Hey, great, we may make news here, I thought. We broke for a commercial. Then we came back and the caller on the air was Ann Bloedorn, who had cheated in school not with Clarence Thomas but with me.

Ann sat in front of me, alphabetically. During a test she looked over her shoulder to ask for one of the answers, and I, always happy to share my erudition, gave it to her. And Miss Head—who had reputedly been a marine in Korea—descended upon us as if we were Chinese Communists. On the next report card, I had an F in conduct. With an asterisk next to it, referring to a handwritten footnote that said simply, "Cheating."

In ink.

I don't remember what my punishment was, other than a profound sense of having ripped my mother's heart right out of her body. When I got a U (for Unsatisfactory) in conduct in the third grade, for talking, she wouldn't let me go see the final episode of the *Superman* serial that had been showing every Saturday for months at the Decatur theater. I never did find out how Supe got out of whoever's clutches he was in.

Anyway, when I realized it was Ann Bloedorn who was calling, my immediate reaction was a kind of delight. Here I was being exposed on the radio for the worst thing I had ever done in school, worse, no doubt, than anything my mother ever did, worse probably than anything Clarence Thomas ever did in the eighth grade—my permanent record coming back to haunt me—and I didn't care. I wished I were before the Senate Judiciary Committee, and my mother were there, and I could turn to her in the gallery and say, "Mom! It wasn't that bad!"

From time to time I run into somebody I knew in high school, or the wife of somebody I knew in high school, and he or she says, "Remember that time we put cherry bombs in the boys' room toilets?" or "Ted told me about the time you and he stole a mummy from the museum at Emory." I always say, "Oh, yeah, heh-heh, those were the days," because it gratifies me to have become someone who would presumably have played such tricks, but the truth is (and would I lie, now, when the mummy-stealing escapade might make this book the next *Tom Sawyer*?), I never did anything that high-spirited. It would have killed my mother. Ann, however, remembered the cheating incident exactly as I did.

"The worst thing about it," Ann said on the radio, "was my mother said, 'You cheated with Roy Blount?' " What Mrs. Bloedorn must have meant was, "You cheated with Louise and Roy Blount's son?"

I grew up with the feeling, which I retain to this day, that everything I do is probably in some sense profoundly wrong.

Woody Allen once told an interviewer that being funny "is always a second choice." The first choice, I guess, is being . . . sweet. Or happy, or something.

When I was a child and had a friend over, my mother would say, "Now you children run outside and eat on the steps, so the grown-ups can enjoy supper at the table," and when the friend would look unsettled she would say, "I'm just teasing. Maybe y'all don't tease as much at your house as we do."

When my mother was a child, she felt genuinely shunned.

What was the tone in which she told me how close I came to killing her? Seems like it was almost wistful, somehow. Almost flirty, too. When I was a little bitty kid, I called her Sugar, because my father did. I don't remember doing that, I just remember her bemoaning, for many years, the fact that I had ceased to.

"You used to call me Sugar," she'd say. What was I supposed to say to that? I remember giving her a big, sudden kiss on the cheek in church once when I was, I don't know, kind of old to be doing that, and then suddenly thinking to myself, Hm, that's weird. It seemed to startle her, even. That may have been the last time I kissed her spontaneously.

When I was in high school, she got it into her head that I didn't want to be seen with her. Once we happened to be walking past school together, after classes, when girlfriends and boyfriends were lingering out front, and she suddenly sped up and opened up a lead of several strides, the very picture of a woman scorned. That *was* embarrassing. I lurched into an awkward gait, trying to catch up with her—and she could *motor* when she was steamed.

One reason I never resolved my Oedipus complex, I think, is that I may have had for my father the fellow feeling of one frustrated suitor for another. Fellow feeling mixed with *why didn't you just once say to her*, "Hey, come on, Sugar, give the kid a break"?

"Lighten up," he might have told her with a wink and a little pat. But God knows I can't imagine anybody telling my mother to lighten up. He'd've drawn back a nub.

My mother loved me to pieces, as she often said, and I'm still trying to put them together.

CHAPTER 15

Back, Back, Back to Where We Once Belonged

We put on our clothes, she and I, and walked out into a town flooded ankle-deep with white, buoyant stones. Birth should have been like that. —FROM A WORK BY DENIS JOHNSON

I remember lying on the floor in my aunt Willie's house in Jacksonville, when I was maybe eight or nine, thumbing through a *Life* magazine and coming upon the first photographs ever made of a human fetus inside the womb. I was studying them with understandable interest, I thought, when my mother looked at me with fire in her eye and said, "I see what you're looking at."

Hey, it wasn't girlie pictures in *Nugget*, it was scientific pictures in *Life*. If I'd thought there was anything wrong with them, I wouldn't have looked at them in front of my mother.

I also remember looking at pictures in *Life* of dead bodies found in Nazi camps. Nobody explained those to me either, but who could? Jews to me were people in the Bible and Jack Benny, and the only reason I knew Benny was Jewish was because some visitor in our home said, "All you ever hear on the radio is Jews," and started naming them. I glanced up and happened to catch my mother's eye and she gave me a conspiratorial "we-don't-say-that" look and changed the subject in the middle of our guest's recitation.

We didn't throw people out of the house for complaining about how many Jews there were on television (though I guess we would have if anybody had said anything anti-Semitic about Jesus), but we loved Jack Benny, and Rochester, and Mary, and dumb Irishman Dennis Day, and Phil Harris (who drank, but my parents didn't seem to hold it against him, he also sang "That's What I Like About the South"), and Mel Blanc's Mr. Kitzel, who said, "Hoo-hooo, Meester Beenie," and his Mexican, Sy, who only said, "*Sí*," and Sheldon Leonard's racetrack tout: "Hey, Bud."

Why would anybody want to kill Jack Benny? I actually saw Jack Benny face-to-face once in the press box during a California Angels game and was struck dumb. He looked disappointed. Not because he knew who I was and would have liked to meet me, but because he assumed, reasonably, that anybody would like to meet him. I still feel bad that I somehow couldn't bring myself to say to Jack Benny what popped into my head: "Hoo-hoooo, Meester Beenie."

(Years later I was watching another Angels game, during spring training, when who should suddenly pop into the Palm Springs ballpark press box but Sonny Bono. "Am I in the right place?" he said. He was mayor of Palm Springs at the time. Him, I knew what to say to. "No," I said, and he left. How did I know he would go and get elected to Congress! That's all anybody should have needed to know about the Republican Revolution of 1994: Representative Sonny Bono! But, then, maybe all anybody needs to know about me—here comes some sefflo—is that I am better at dismissal than at paying tribute.)

People talk about living under the shadow of the Bomb, in the fifties. I lived under the shadows of Jesus and my mother. Having the power to betray the one and kill the other, and dreading some horrible accident that might unleash that power, was a scarier nuclear secret than anything to do with the Bomb. In school we had hiding-under-the-desk exercises and were issued dog tags—the notch at one end, it was said, was so the tag could be wedged between our teeth to keep our corpses from bloating. We boys thought the notch thing was cool. McCarthyism went right by me; nobody I knew ever talked about anything like that.

People I know in New York grew up in the throes of strenuous politics. Not me. My parents voted for Eisenhower in 1952 and said not to talk about it. About voting for Ike! To be sure the South was so solidly Democratic that pointy-headed intellectual Adlai Stevenson carried Georgia in '52 and '56 by more than two to one, but it wasn't as though my father was involved in local business at the time, so that he had to worry about the alienation of any customers within the reach of my voice. He was a zone manager for Packard Motor Car Company. Friends of mine in New York who grew up going to Communist summer camp have a hard time getting a handle on the politics of my childhood. So do I.

We didn't talk about politics, or music, or art, or literature, or even movies. Our forms of culture—food and my parents' bridge club aside—were religion and comedy.

Our religion was Methodism. Emotionally hairy Methodism, on my mother's part at least, but still it didn't touch those photographs—okay, Jesus died for our sins, what did those people die for?

The only thing in the newspaper that had much of an influence on our family life was the funnies. My Southern mother, Louise, was not at all ethnically self-conscious about identifying herself with Loweezy, Snuffy Smith's hard-pressed hillbilly wife,* or even with Dogpatch characters. When she couldn't find her glasses she called herself Weakeyes Yokum, and when somebody was at pains to explain something to her that she didn't want to understand, she would quote Pappy Yokum: "As any fool can plainly see. Ah see."

From the radio we soaked up Jack Benny, Red Skelton, the Great Gildersleeve, Fibber McGee and Molly. "Tain't funny, McGee," my mother would say when we kidded about something that somehow touched upon her central misery. It wasn't entirely shtick but it was shtick enough to get us through the moment.

Those photographs, though, were real, like a dirty dream. There I did feel that I was wrong to look—I feel wrong even talking about it now—but I looked. The people were naked. Which meant, Don't ask.

Paintings of the Crucifixion had a similar charge, but they came with sacred interpretation. The upshot, though grave, was *good*, and Jesus in his modesty always wore a pelvic wrap. I doubt I had seen depictions of naked adults before, and here they were dead in piles. I knew they were the enemy's fault, that we had come to the camp as good guys, but there was no way to feel good about those pictures. They were stronger than religion to me, which was saying a lot at that time. Since there was nothing Methodist or homey or funny to say about them, we didn't say anything. We didn't discuss my mother's childhood, either. And we *needed* to. I am wary of drawing too close a parallel between those pictures and the star over Bethlehem, but I do believe they helped draw me to a place where I don't feel entirely at home but do feel more at home in some ways than I did at home: to New York.

*Mother would not have countenanced an anecdote I've since heard about Fred Lasswell, the creator of Snuffy and Loweezy. Lasswell, who hails from the Ozarks and has a booming voice, is in a restaurant with a group of cartoonists, telling highly entertaining stories in which a certain epithet recurs frequently. At length a crusty gentleman at the next table taps him on his shoulder and says, "Sir, you are ruining our dinner. *Must* you use that word?" Lasswell gives him a look, summons the waiter and says, "How can it be, that you have somehow seated us in the non-fucking section?"

I have mentioned the jingle we were often led to sing in Sunday school, "Red and yellow, black and white, they are precious in his sight, Jesus loved the little children of the world," and there being nothing but white children in sight. That helped lead me in time to irreligion and antisegregationism. My children, and most of my oldest white Southern friends' children, have gravitated toward black friends, mixed neighborhoods, social work, break dancing, being the only white player on the basketball court, Peace Corps service in Niger. Except for anti-Republicanism and struggles with feminism, my own politics have stagnated since the civil rights movement.

My favorite Bible stories were Shadrach, Meshach and Abednego in the fiery furnace and, especially, the Crucifixion. My mother shuddered at the thought of the nails in the Savior's hands and feet. She had severe arthritis in hers. As she labored on, as she often reminded us, "my hands and knees" to keep spic and span the house that the rest of the family persisted in dirtying, she sang, "I love to tell the story, 'twill be my theme in Glory, to tell the o-o-old story, of Jesus and his love," and, with particular relish, "I come to the garden alone, while the dew is still on the roses, and the voice I hear, falling on my ear, the son of God disclo-o-ses. And he walks with me, and he talks with me, and he tells me I am his own. And the joy we share, as we tarry there, none other has ever known."

Maybe many another man has managed to be that gratifying a companion to a woman over the long haul, but I haven't. At first those roses may be so dewy that I feel like being that Jesus with one hand tied behind my back, for a good long while. But sometimes I have to write a book or watch baseball on television or stare dully out into space. A woman may see any one of those activities as something I am doing *to* her. A bad thing about a writer as a husband is that sometimes when his thinking is most scintillating he could easily be mistaken, from the outside, for a pile of old clothes.

Let's face it, men aren't ideal husbands. And husbands aren't ideal company for women. And writers have more downtime—to all appearances—than the Ugandan phone system. But other people's marriages somehow survive those conditions. Maybe if you're married to me it's even worse because I feel like I *ought* to be that Jesus. Then I resent feeling that way. And then I wonder whether the problem is her expectations or my apprehensions about her expectations. I'm not that Jesus, therefore the two of us are going to descend into pluperfect hell and I won't know whether to shit or wind my watch. I'll just be standing there with my mouth open incurring one ineradicable and unredeemable onus after another.

I wrote a column for *Men's Journal* about pain. Certain scientific studies reported in the *New York Times* had suggested that women respond more dramatically to less pain than men do. And I kind of pussy-footed around the thing, but in the end I said, maybe, just maybe, women have this proprietary thing about pain.

I hoped no women I knew would read it, but then I was at the *Men's Journal* Christmas party and my editor there came up to me as I was talking to an attractive TV producer who was too young for me and he said, "Roy's column this month is about women and pain."

And I thought, Oh, Jesus, I'm in for it, but the TV producer was of *such* a young generation that she said, "Oh yeah. Women use pain. Like, if my boyfriend [there, she had a boyfriend anyway] squeezes my wrist, I'll say it hurts before it hurts, so it won't hurt."

Is it possible that what I do is respond to a guilt trip before it becomes one, so that . . .

No. I don't believe I am even subconsciously that intricate. My mother was crazy, that's all.

Whenever I get interested in a woman, I get the impression that she understands me, and I stop thinking, and then after a while she gives me a despairing look and it hits me, Oh, shit, I'm being myself.

When I was a child, my thinking had not even progressed to that point. I wanted somebody to ease my near matricidal burden in more or less the way I wanted somebody to explain those photographs in *Life*, but who? My father was busy. My mother? She would look at me as if I were getting too close to some terrible thing she knew that was even worse than what I feared. I felt that way a lot as a child.

It it any wonder that I am a humorist?

Film noir was responding to the tensions of the time, but you couldn't prove it by anybody I knew. I remember sitting around with my parents and some friends of theirs, looking at the movie listings to see if there was anything worth going to. *Iron Mistress* was playing. "Well, you can imagine, with that title," my mother said, and that was the end of that. I would have been ten. It was Alan Ladd playing Jim Bowie. The mistress was his knife.

My parents did, however, take me to see *The Snake Pit*. Seven, I would have been, when it came out in 1948—the year my mother got pregnant again and lost her eye. I rented it the other night. Olivia de Havilland (that sweet, motherly lady from *Gone With the Wind*) in a mental hospital, getting crazier and crazier—"When am I real?" she asks someone—until she finds herself, as she says in the voice-over, in what "seemed to me like a deep hole, people down in it like strange animals—like snakes. As if I'd been thrown into a snake pit." The camera pulls back into a long overhead shot and we see de Havilland in the midst of a writhing, moaning, screaming, yammering roomful of madwomen. They're dancing all around her, kicking up their bare feet, casting wild shadows on the walls. I had remembered the bodies (from my dreams, maybe) as naked. They aren't, of course, but still it's not a scene I would have subjected either of my kids to when they were *seven*, media-hardened as they were. For years I wondered what had possessed my parents to take me to it at that age. My father's parents met when they were both working as guards at the Florida Hospital of the Insane in Chattahoochee, but nobody in the family seemed to find that very remarkable. I asked my grandmother once if conditions in the hospital were pretty harsh, thinking I might dig up some semblance of social reform in my background, and she said they sure were—"one of the crazy people got me down one time and banged my head on the floor till I thought I was going to die."

My mother mentioned once or twice (when there was a beer commercial on TV, perhaps) that her father died of the d.t.'s, but she mentioned it in the same ominous tone that she mentioned having nearly given up her life to have me. I never wanted to ask her any more about it, like exactly *where* he died of the d.t.'s.

Those fetus photographs, also, were stronger than church. The fetuses were naked. In this case my mother did furnish some perspective, which, however, was even scarier than the lack of it with regard to the corpses: I got the impression that she didn't approve of fetuses. Of course, in my case she had grounds.

A zoologist told me once that she reached inside a dead pregnant shark she was dissecting, and the fetus bit her.

An unborn human is more complex. In a few months you manage to recapitulate phylogeny, from protozoan (go on, go on) . . . to fish ("You wat'ry folk that know not your felicity"—Anne Bradstreet) . . . to frog (in a mighty small pond) . . . to reptile (uh-oh) . . . to bordering on the big time: mammal. And already you're feeling the weight of something which, at this point, is the last thing you need: history. Anxieties, expectations, unworked-through family issues.

Yet as far as you know, no one has ever been like this before. In my case, nobody ever had been. Because I was getting vibes that caused me already, in the womb, to lean over backward so as not to invite the response, "Well, you *would* think that." For me to be thinking, in the womb, "Right now, the family curse is the last thing I need," would have been like Plato saying, "The unexamined life is not worth living": he *would* think that, he's a philosopher. A politician, if it would help him get elected, would probably say "The unelected life is not worth living." However: what if what you *would* think is right? And if you can't say what you *would* say, what can you say? You've got to come up with something liberal, something original, something funny.

On October 4, 1941, I made my entrance, and bombed. Nearly semi-orphaned myself. I didn't *mean* to be a threatening delivery—but, there you go, that's easy for me to say. Here's what probably happened: I felt that I had to come out quirky, at an unexpected angle. But by that time, *that* was how I *would* come out.

How would I have preferred to see the light of day? Delivered into a litter of puppies. Or with something light to read, for distraction. As it was, I was plucked from someone who was bleeding nearly to death. People talk about being born again, but once was enough for me. You're cramped, outgrowing your situation, feeling a bit too hip, frankly, for the womb— and then your known universe convulses to a soundtrack of agony for hours and WOOM: the Big Time. Somebody slaps your bottom, you're breathing *dry air* all of a sudden, and while you're trying to take that on board, they incidentally whack a little bit off the end of your you-know. I say incidentally, but, hey. The other night I was talking to some women who brought up a recent report that in the early twentieth century, in some quarters *in this country*, clitorectomy was practiced on little girls who wouldn't quit touching themselves.

I felt implicated. Why? I am a liberal, and a humorist. I always feel implicated, and I have to find the switcheroo in there, somewhere, that shifts the onus—the ball is in my court, and if I don't return it with some spin, I die a little. I knew there was nothing *funny* about clitorectomy. But I felt a terrible need to establish that I took this matter, like every matter, defensively but not lying down. I had to say something.

That I, personally, had nothing but the fondest feelings for clitorises? That there was nothing I, personally, would not do for one?

The wise thing would have been to come down foursquare against clitorectomy, with a straight face, and leave it at that. But a humorist, humor aside, has a hard time—and this has been a problem for me in my relationships with women—not only saying the obvious thing, but *appearing* to say the obvious thing. I ventured to observe that, for what it might be worth, throughout most of the twentieth century the great majority of American boys have been welcomed into the world by foreskinectomy.

My female friends pooh-poohed. "Just stings for a minute," one said. "Like snipping off a puppy's tail."

Easy for them to say, but try telling them that.

Why do I always have to raise my consciousness on someone else's behalf? Just because I'm white and male and Southern and so on? I'm human, I feel discriminated against—and I have the added burden of knowing it isn't true.

At any rate, whatever girls may think, there are vulnerable moments in a boy's life. And birth is one of them. There we were. Louise and me. A pretty woman, but try to tell her that. "You nearly killed me, son."

A humorist is born. What could I say? I yelled bloody murder, but any baby does that, I had to come up with an act.

A baby comedian, who works blue? How about these anal thermometers? Can you believe it? In the hospital the baby next to me whispers, "Hey, Bud. Don't ever turn over on your stomach. Pass the word." I don't know what he's talking about. Then, whoot, there it is! What are they testing for, my sexual preference? Take my temperature, please? Remember when you were an embryo? If I'd known then what I know now, I'da stopped at reptile. Get some respect. That's right—you don't see anybody sticking anything up a snake's butt. Or a frog. A frog is ugly, right? I'm cute. So how come a frog is out getting laid already and I'm lucky if fifteen years from now I get to second base? First base, sure, they give you that right away. Hey, this is going to be easy, you're thinking. But then they got this thing called weaning. You know where they got that term? From Get away from me, you little wienie. And they wonder why there are topless bars?

I know one thing. You can study the techniques of comedy all you want, but you will never really *kill* up there unless the switcheroo drive is lodged in the cockles of your heart.

Do you know what the word *mammal*, the word for our biological class, comes from? The word *mammary*. And you know what *mammary* comes from? *Mama*. Which comes from . . . ?

Baby talk. You could look it up. The first baby classified us all.

Some will argue that words are arbitrary. (Right, and it's a coincidence that *mouth* so exercises the mouth, *tongue* and *language* engage the whole range of the tongue, *throat* is so throaty and *nose* so nasal.) Here is all the theory I have, and all the theory I need, as regards the origin of language: *Mama*. In every language from French to Hindi. Lips together as in nursing, *mm*; then apart, an empty sound, *ah*; and again. *Mama*. Then you're given something to glom onto, and your mouth fills with Mama's milk. *Mmmmm*. Means *good*, in any language. *Mmmm*. *Yum. Ommmmm. Me. My. Empathy. Humor. Memoir.*

Check the Indo-European roots section of the *American Heritage Dictionary* (of whose usage panel I am a member):

> *mater-*, Mother. Based ultimately on the baby-talk form *ma-2*, with the kinship term suffix *-ter*. *Material, matter. Matriculated, matrix, matrimony.*
>
> *ma-*, Mother. A linguistic near-universal found in many of the world's languages, often in reduplicated form. *Mamma, mammal, mammilla. Maia*—Greek for "good mother," also for "nurse."
>
> Compare *ma-1*, Good, with derivatives meaning "occurring at a good moment, timely, seasonal, ripe: mature."

Not to mention, if you ask me, *maw mouth milk Mary Madonna marry Marilyn mutual Mallomar M&M mind meat meal mot much munch moo mensch myth mystery mumble* (I have a tendency to mumble—in college my nickname was Rmmm) *melon mellifluous mutuality*. *M* is the difference between *war* and *warm*, *mother* and *other*.

In point of fact, I washed out of breast-feeding. According to my daughter, who majored in psychology at Stanford (which is what my mother would have loved to do at Ole Miss or somewhere homey like that, but she couldn't afford to go to college when she got out of high school in the depths of the Depression), it is because of my failure at nursing that I 1) chew tobacco when I'm writing, 2) sometimes eat and drink too much when I'm not writing, and 3) write. I'm a very oral person in many ways, oral to a fault really, so you'd think I'd have had more of a knack for suckling.

I tried. Mmmmm . . . Colic. Took a long time to find a formula that suited me.

I take you now to the Mississippi Delta. One of the things that I resolved to do when I turned fifty was spend an evening in an honest-to-God Delta juke joint. A juke joint is not dissimilar from the *American Heritage Dictionary* index of Indo-European roots, in that it gets you down into sub-verbal basics. Sort of like the womb. Dark, funky, enfolding (but anything could happen), pervaded by a deep, steady beat.

There I was, one night when I was fifty-one, in Margaret's Blue Diamond Lounge in Clarksdale, Mississippi, listening to a local band play a blues that was more like a throb than a song. I had noticed an empty .38-caliber cartridge on the floor next to my feet, and someone had informed me that the lead guitarist's middle name was Pecan. A man took the chair next to me, introduced himself as Raymond, and confided that he was a drummer and the band wasn't all that it should be, because he had been kicked out of it—not for musical reasons but sociopolitical: one night when they were playing at an all-white dance at a plantation, he had jumped in the hosts' pool.

All around us local patrons were shouting "Show me what you got," and "Gimme something" to the band, which would occasionally get to arguing amongst themselves so intensely that they had to stop playing. But then they'd be back into it again. "Gonna throw a wang dang doodle," asserted the lead singer. I had never heard that assertion made straight.

I was with Polly, an excellent woman to do the Delta with, but we had been arguing, ourselves, because she wanted to have a baby and I was content with my two kids. We had spent the previous night in the room where Bessie Smith died. The Riverside Hotel had passed for a black hospital in 1937, when the greatest of blueswomen was taken there after a terrible car wreck. The myth is that she was turned away from a white hospital. The truth is, it hadn't occurred to anyone that a white hospital would take her in.

"This is Bessie's room," the man who showed us to it had said. "Y'all scared?" Actually, we—*white folks!*—were halfway hoping for a ghost.

In Margaret's, a man at the next table took offense. On a point of etiquette: I hadn't tipped my plastic cup toward him while he was pouring me some of his malt liquor from a quart bottle. To me there are schools of thought on that—some people tip, to catch the flow on the side of the cup and minimize the head, and some people just don't care by along about two o'clock in the morning, which is what time it was. This man cared.

"You ain't right," he said. Not the first time I had been told that, nor in the first context. But I am a white Southern humorist. There is nothing that puts me on my mettle like a challenge from a black Southerner. In the Delta, whence cometh deepest funk.

He had a scar that suggested somebody had just missed stabbing him in the eye. I made a little here's-to-you gesture with my cup. He looked at my raised wrist. "You think I'm going to steal your watch?" he asked. It was a Timex, but he didn't have any watch, advantage to him. But I didn't blink. Then, leaning in closer, he said, "You think I'm telling the truth? Or am I drunk?"

"Both," I said. He heard that. We did a soul shake. He looked over at the musicians who had rejected him. Cut him out of the music. How could they? He looked back at me.

"I got feelings," he said. "I love my mama."

CHAPTER 16 / A Date with Destiny

Ah, you mother of a child—you want his manners to be nice, you want his brain to be quick, you want his back to be straight, you want his hands to be agile—but don't you want his feet to be sturdy and true, well-shaped and graceful? Or those feet of your daughter?

—FROM A BUSTER BROWN SHOE AD IN THE ISSUE OF *LIFE*
THAT CAME OUT THE SAME WEEK I DID

I was born into a phallocentric world. More specifically, into Indianapolis. Right away, two things to explain.

1. As regards *Life*'s assumption that a child is male unless, by afterthought, he's a daughter, I can only say . . .

One time the novelists Mary Lee Settle and Pat Conroy and I were on Memphis television. All of us Southern. Mary Lee proclaimed her resentment that, as a woman and, on top of that, a tall woman, she had spent her life constantly feeling pressure to stoop down. And what made matters worse, ever since the Confederacy lost the War, Southern men were always apologizing.

Conroy and I could only respond, spontaneously and in unison, "We're sorry, Mary Lee."

I can also come on with the vagino-centric . . . or, better put it this way: the fully-realized-female-character limericks:

> *I know a lady, Lucille,*
> *Whose virtues are few and unreal.*
> *She finds William Bennett*
> *A chuckle a minute:*
> *"You mean we can't even steal?"*

121

2. As regards Indianapolis. My mother was from Mississippi and my father from the Florida panhandle, which in effect is Deep South Georgia; they met at Andrew Jackson Senior High School in Jacksonville, Florida; and we moved to Decatur, Georgia (via Columbus, Ohio), before I was two. So I am Southern certainly. But since my father had been transferred from Jacksonville to Indianapolis by his employer, the Libby canned goods company, a year or so before I was born, I am also a Hoosier. Maybe that's why I tended to get sluggish during Georgia summers, which may be one reason I always felt a migratory urge, but the only times I have ever felt Hoosierishness kick in was when I read Booth Tarkington or listened to Herb Shriner (remember him?) as a boy and when Lyndon Johnson, having been annoyed by Senator Birch Bayh, said, "Nobody from Indiana was ever worth a shit." Big Daddy Lyndon always got my back up.

But Indianapolis means that just as there will be those who respond to my assertions by sniffing, "Oh, he *would* say that, he's Southern," there will also be those who sniff, "Oh he *would* say that. He's not really Southern."

Even the year of my birth, 1941, is problematic. A great year in baseball—Ted Williams hit .406, Joe DiMaggio hit in 56 straight games, Mickey Owens dropped (the day after I was born) the third strike. That's relevant because I went on to be a baseball writer. I didn't stick with it long enough to become a *distinguished* baseball writer, which you might say (if you were a baseball writer) parallels my marital history. But then I believe it was Ring Lardner who said there is nothing sadder than an old baseball writer.

A great year, too, in movies—*Citizen Kane*, *The Lady Eve* (which happens to be my favorite good movie), *The Shanghai Gesture* (which happens to be my favorite bad movie). That's relevant, because I went on to write a movie, as I have mentioned, that actually got made. *Larger Than Life*, it was called, about a man, played by Bill Murray, finding his true self through his father's elephant. I wanted to call it *She Followed Me Home*, but everybody said, "Who's going to say, 'Let's go see *She Followed Me Home*'?"

I'm not going to tell you the whole story of the making of that movie, I'm saving that for the night of my Lifetime Achievement Oscar, but, briefly, here is what happened to my Wee St. Francis scene.

Murray's character is frantically trying to find some place to get rid of this elephant he has suddenly (and credibly, believe me) inherited. He is directed to the nearest zoo, which turns out to be a petting zoo, whose proprietor is Wee St. Francis, a saintly old geezer who regrets that he can't take on an elephant because "my mission is small animals."

However, nobody who read for the part could make Wee St. Francis believable as a sincere saintly geezer. So Tracy Walter was cast as a cynical Wee St. Francis.

So I'm watching this scene being shot. Feeling a bit compromised, because I had envisioned a kind of Peaceable Kingdom. There are all these little chicks and ducklings and bunnies running around underfoot, and Tai, who plays the elephant—and a real pleasure to work with, by the way. I'm not just staying this. Tai is not only enormously talented and truly professional, but also in real life an extremely genial animal. But Tai has a problem with this scene. It's . . . I don't want to get into stereotypes and old wives' tales, but you can see, by the way Tai is acting, why people say elephants are afraid of mice. She is sort of kicking out at the baby animals.

Walter is wearing a T-shirt that says "Softly, Nicely" (that's from the script) and a cap in the shape of a dog's face with ears, which is what I had imagined, but he's also dragging on a cigarette and looking hungover, and the little animals are a-scurryin' around and Tai is not liking them at all, and the owl starts hyperventilating.

The owl. You'd think an owl wouldn't lose its cool over being in a movie, but this owl is no trouper. They have to take it out of the scene, it's off to one side being calmed down by the owl wrangler, and then there's a dove that's supposed to land on Murray's shoulder but it lands on his head, and he says, "Who *wrote* this?" and I hedge a little bit by saying, "Joe Eszterhas." When Walter improvisationally throws a handful of birdseed at the dove to shoo it off, the dove is gone, Jackson, the dove wranglers have to chase it way off down the street, so the backup dove is brought in (there is no backup owl), but the backup dove has a big bare spot on its back, no feathers there. When Howard Franklin, the director, says, "Action," somebody says, "We see a guy in a blue shirt!"

There's not supposed to be a guy in a blue shirt in the shot. He's the Humane Society guy, who not only feels compelled to burst in amongst the ducklings and bunnies to keep them from being trampled by the elephant, now he's worried about the bare spot on the dove. The dove's owner explains that it's from a sexual encounter—with, don't get the wrong impression, another dove.

Certainly I reserve the right to tell people that I fought tooth and nail to prevent my conception from being cheapened by the filmmaking process, but just between you and me, my only regret is that the owl didn't faint on camera.

The year of my birth was also the year that *Life* magazine announced the beginning of "the American Century." According to *Life*, a fine Stetson hat cost five dollars, and "the offense unforgivable in either a man or a woman" was halitosis.

Little did I know that by being born that year, I had given up all hope of ever having a generation.

Over the years I have thought of several excuses why I would never be president:

Because (both before and after the Carter administration) I was Southern.

Because I wasn't a war hero.

Because I experimented with marijuana—purely in an attempt to see how much rum raisin ice cream I could eat on it, but if those lab notes ever fell into the wrong hands . . .

Because I may have said indiscreet things on the phone to women.

The election of Bill Clinton proved that none of those excuses were valid. What is valid is that I will never be president because I will never be the right age. George Bush was seventeen years older than me. Clinton five years younger. The presidency skipped me.

I am a Tweener. Born two months before Pearl Harbor—too late to fight and too soon to be a Baby Boomer. I've *always* been middle-aged.

I'm not the only one. When people of my age get together, we—

I say "we," speaking loosely. That's because people my age are not a media-recognized "we." No one cares what we are going through until we've finished going through it, and the Boomers begin to.

If they would listen, we could tell them what's coming. By "we" I mean everyone of an age to have been in high school when I was—from those who were seniors when I was a freshman through those who were freshmen when I was a senior. People born from 1938 (three years after Elvis) through 1944 (two years before Bill Clinton). We heard about hard times from our elders and about psychedelic times from our youngers.

Here's what we say, when we get together and talk about our contributions to history: "We *were* the Beatles." Also Bob Dylan and the Roll- ing Stones. And Janis Joplin. We peaked early. We were Muhammad Ali, Stokely Carmichael, Mario Savio, Huey Newton, Jane Fonda (stretching things a bit, she was born at the very end of 1937), H. Rap Brown, Joan Baez. We were role models for the Boomers. And then we were Richard Pryor and Lily Tomlin: role models for *Saturday Night Live.*

No wonder none of us are president, you may be saying. But actually, only a few of us were the people I have just mentioned. Furthermore, most of us—unlike the Boomers—had no chance to emulate those people. We were in puberty when rock and roll was just getting under way, so our teen-love songs tended to be about getting in trouble for making out. (Remember "Silhouettes"?) When John Kennedy was shot, we were already in the straight-job market, so we couldn't throw ourselves into disillusion. While the Youth Culture was having Human Be-ins, we were having babies.

In short, some of us set the mold, but hardly any of us are examples of what it molded. And now we're moldy. Boomers have been through a lot, but they've been through all of it on a groove. We, on the other hand, have always been untracked.

Here's another thing we say when we get together: we know what life was like before rock and roll: I played some 50s hits for my children once—"Volare," "Shrimpboats Are A'Comin' "—and they said, "What did the young people listen to?"

We came *before* the domination of culture by television: we can iden- tify only three or four sitcom theme songs.

Before controlled substances: Some years ago I had a Boomer woman over. I didn't think of her as all that much younger than I was. My college- age daughter was there, living with me for the summer. Shortly after my daughter went out somewhere, the Boomer woman asked, "Does your daughter have any drugs?"

("I certainly hope not," was my reply. "Incidentally, I'm afraid I don't either.")

Before desegregation and the women's movement and gay lib.

And furthermore, we know what it was like adjusting—personally and as parents—to these developments. I believe it was Dave Hickey who once said that, as opposed to New Yorkers in New York, he preferred talking to Texans in New York. "At least," he said, "they've been two places."

We Tweeners have been two places. Often at once.

And now we are in a position to tell Boomers what it is like when presidents start becoming younger than oneself.

Let me say that we have been placed in this position rather prematurely. One of us could have been president: Bill Bradley, Paul Tsongas, Tom Harkin, Jerry Brown, Jesse Jackson, Phil Gramm, Lamar Alexander, Dick Gephardt, Sam Nunn, Pat Schroeder, Pat Buchanan . . .

But no. Bill Clinton is five years younger than I am. Hey, I voted for him, thinking Hope. (There being no such town as Fingers Crossing, Arkansas.) But still. When he was a young blade I was a daddy. What does he know about life?

At any rate, what does he know about middle age? You know you are middle-aged when:

You're on the phone arranging to meet someone you don't know and you say, "I have brown hair . . . ," and someone who lives with you laughs.

You give younger people advice and they say, sagely, "Yes, that was true for your generation."

A guess-your-age person at the fair guesses that you're younger than you are and you can't decide whether it's good that you're older than you look or not.

You realize why old people have such irregular tennis strokes and hold their heads at odd angles. Bifocals.

You begin to wish people would speak up—but not be SO LOUD.

I'll say this about middle age: it is full of fantastic surprises. You find yourself saying, "I'm fifty-five." And thinking, What? I'm what?

You're middle-aged. But for every generation, there are consolations. Maybe no one in my age group will ever be president, but at least we can say that none of these guys who have been president was any of us.

But no one will be listening. Because we are a "we" only to us.

So. If I'm so inevitable, why was I wedged into this narrow chink of nonsignificance?

Maybe we can find a clue in the stars.

Like my father (John Lennon and he had the same birthday), and my father's father, and like Graham Greene, Oscar Wilde and Jimmy Carter, I am a Libra. A balancer. On the other hand . . .

A beautiful woman I was in love with believed that astrology was a science. There may be something to it, I would tell her, but it's not a *science*. She had our charts done. I had to call my sister, who has my baby book, to find out what hour and minute I was born. I was revealed as a Libra on every count: my moon, my Venus and so on. All of it, apparently, matched perfectly with this beautiful woman. Was I going to argue with that?

If I had been an Aries, and a rationalist, I guess I would have put my foot down and declared, "Astrology is not a science and therefore it is hooey and the hell with it." Being a Libra, I said, "Well, there may be something to it, and I'm not saying that science and truth are synonymous or anything, but astrology isn't a *science*." She said it was, just because. I stopped trying to reason with her, and stewed, and tried to tell myself this was nothing to be angry about.

We broke up. The last thing she wrote me was that I'd shaken her faith in astrology. Not by my arguments against it, but by getting so angry at her.

Forget the zodiac. Let's look at October fourth in world history.

A heavy date, it turns out. The first complete English translation of the Bible published, 1535; President Rutherford B. Hayes born, 1822; Edward Stratemeyer (creator of the Rover Boys, the Hardy Boys, Nancy Drew and the Bobbsey Twins) born, 1862; the first known published story that is indubitably by Mark Twain appears, 1862; Damon Runyon born, 1884; Mormons in Utah renounce polygamy, 1890; Buster Keaton born, 1895; Charlton Heston born, 1924; Al Jolson premieres the first full-length talking motion picture, 1927; The Boswell Sisters record a song called "Rock and Roll," 1934; Flann O'Brien's first "Cruiskeen Lawn" column appears in the *Irish Times*, bylined Myles na gCopaleen* (the man's real name, of course, was Brian O'Nolan), 1941!; Susan Sarandon born, 1946; the great comic strip *Pogo* first appears, 1948; the Brooklyn Dodgers win their first World Series, 1955; the Soviet Union launches *Sputnik*, the first man-made space satellite, 1957; the TV series *Leave It to Beaver* is first aired, 1957; Janis Joplin dies, 1970; two men chase, punch and kick Dan Rather while demanding of him, "Kenneth, what is the frequency?" and then run off, 1986.

Well, I have read all the Bobbsey Twins and Hardy Boys books and some of the Bible. I am a deep-dyed enthusiast of Mark Twain, Buster Keaton, Flann O'Brien and *Pogo*. I have worked in talking motion pictures. The Hayes-Tilden Compromise, which put Rutherford in office, had

---

*Myles, though he does not use the Jr., is a junior: a frequent character in the columns is the elderly "Myles na gCopaleen, the da."

profound illiberal consequences for my home region, the South. Some of my food poems are now displayed in Threadgill's, the Austin, Texas, joint where Janis Joplin got her start singing "Silver Threads and Golden Needles." My family life in Decatur, Georgia, in the fifties was a good deal—aside from the curse—like *Leave It to Beaver*.

What jumps out at me, though, is the Rather affair. Eleven years after it happened, a man with certain out-of-the-mainstream ideas about the communications industry claimed to have been one of the two assailants, but . . . he had a *confederate*? Two men, ordinary-looking men actually, meet in a bar and one of the men—after taking the measure of the other with a few oblique observations such as, "Has it ever struck you that Dan Rather is, ah . . . , Kenneth?" and noting a cautious flicker of recognition in the other man's eyes, the first man says to the other:

"And of course, if he is Kenneth, he—"

"Would have the frequency!" cries the second man. "And if we can find him in the street and chase, punch and kick him—"

"But we'll have to work fast!"

I've been almost arrested twice, both times in connection with golf tournaments. At the Masters in Augusta, Georgia, one year, I had a car wreck and neglected to go to court for it (I was busy interviewing an old man on a bike with PRAYER on the mudflap, Palm Sunday fronds on the back, and his name, HOKE, on the side, who when asked whether he took an interest in the Masters said, "Oh yes. You got to have some recreation or your mind'll just go . . . plunk") until a warrant was out for me, and at some tournament in Florida I was with Reggie Jackson, doing a story for *Rolling Stone*, and I responded to being punched by a golf P.R. guy by shoving him all the way across the hospitality tent, and he called the cops. The only time I've ever been punched, as an adult, was by a golf P.R. guy. Does that make any sense? What was the *purpose*?

Have I been put here on earth to establish that nothing makes any sense?

Or . . . maybe, just maybe . . . to find some unified theory of everything that no one has found before.

Just a minute ago, right after the next-to-last paragraph, I had a thing happen that I had never known to happen before. I reached for my drink and it had a film over the top of it. When I touched the film, I found that I could peel it off, and roll it into a little ball.

A *sign*? What was it J. Alfred Prufrock said?

To have squeezed the universe into a ball
To roll it toward some overwhelming question . . .
If one, settling a pillow by her head,
*   Should say: "That is not what I meant at all. . . ."*

On reflection it comes to me that some of the rubber cement I used earlier to glue a stamp onto a postcard got off onto the ice from my fingers when I made my drink. Apparently, what will happen when that happens is that the rubber cement will spread out and form a film over the top of the drink, and when you poke at the film to try to see what in the world it is, it will peel off and roll into a little ball.

That's the only thing I can figure. I had to use rubber cement on the stamp because it was one of several stamps that I'd been keeping in my wallet and somehow or another they all got stuck together and I had to soak them apart. The postcard was to my elder grandson, Jesse. He can't read, but we have a joke that I keep reminding him of by postcard. He was in the car when his mother stopped at the developing place to pick up some snapshots, and she showed him one with a picture of me on it, and he said, "Papa!" Then an old white-haired derelict walked by and he said, "Two Papas!" So when I see him I say, "Two Papas!" and laugh, and he laughs, and we slap our thighs. I taught him that. It took him a while to get the thigh slap down. I send him postcards that say, "Two Papas!" and he pretends to read them aloud and laughs and slaps his thigh. I don't really look that old. Though I am getting white-headed. Can you imagine that? I'm getting white-headed.

I never knew that would happen—rubber cement form a film over a drink. I don't usually drink when I'm writing, but it's late at night and I'm doing it now. I hope it was rubber cement, because if it was some kind of drastic bacterial film, I'm a dead man. I guess if that were possible, though, it would have happened by now.

Talk about your famous last words.

CHAPTER 17 / **The Next Morning**

He knew, he alone knew her when she let herself go, when she herself was not sure whether she was wildly gay or wildly sad, but one and the other. But that did not mean that he knew her. Far from it. It only meant that he was closer to her when he was close, but . . . maybe farther away than anyone else when he was not close. . . . "Oh, I'm a son of a bitch," he said.

—JOHN O'HARA, *APPOINTMENT IN SAMARRA*

It was rubber cement. But why was I drinking?

I was remembering getting angry at women I loved.

I haven't hit them. You can't hit women. I accept that. I don't *want* to hit women.

Now tell me this: is there anything women can't do? Women have hit me. Scratched me. One *urged* me to hit her, because she had slept with someone else, but I wouldn't. You can't hit women—and you can't get any credit for not hitting women. You can't even explain why you don't hit women, without sounding, okay, being, sexist—like the man in *Their Eyes Were Watching God* who says, "beatin' women is just like steppin' on baby chickens. . . . Tain't no place on uh woman tuh hit."

I do yell—have yelled, anyway—at women. You shouldn't yell at baby chickens either. I'm not saying that a woman is in any way reducible to a baby chicken, I am just saying that women are like baby chickens in this sense: it does just as much good, in my experience, to yell at women—okay, let's put it this way, to yell at loved ones—as it does to yell at baby chickens.

But what are you going to do, other than yell, when somebody, male or female, keeps on *saying the same thing over and over—like the cavalry riding round and round past the same bunch of cactus—instead of advancing with me to a teetery but interesting and eminently reasonable middle-ground area of discussion that I have painstakingly if*

130

obnoxiously set up. . . . Because without that middle ground, where are we?

Certainly my father never lifted a hand, as they say, to my mother, but I woke up once in the middle of the night, when I was maybe eight or nine, to the sound of my mother yelling at my father, in their bedroom downstairs. Maybe that's when my fate, of being a humorist, was sealed. Or at least my fate of using too many italics.

It was horrible. My grandmother, who didn't have the sense that God gave a goose, but whom my father loved nonetheless, had evidently told my mother that my father sure was good to stick by her when she had her cancerous eye removed. *"What kind of man* wouldn't *stick by me?"* my mother was yelling. My father was trying to tell her, in a pained voice, that he'd never had any intention of not sticking by her, which I think, if you knew my father, you would believe was as true as anything on God's green earth—constitutional staunchness aside, he'd have been scared to death not to stick by her, and I don't blame him—but I guess he didn't know how to say it right, and she just kept on yelling.

One of my best friends, the poet Jim Seay, is one-eyed, and therefore has an eye for that sort of thing, and he says he didn't realize that my mother was a fellow wearer of a glass one till I happened to mention it, but she was certain that everybody was as painfully aware of it as she was. I know, it's too much for me to expect, that my mother would have sat down with Jim and compared glass-eye notes, but it sure might have cleared— well, I was going to say "cleared the air," but my mother was never one for clearing the air. Come to think of it, clearing the air may be a male concept, biting off the matter with a smile: "There, now, we've cleared that up, let's go grab a bite to eat and forget about this whole cultural hegemony business. Huh? Huh? How 'bout it?"

My friend Lamar Alexander, who is probably running for president somewhere even as you read this, had to quit football his freshman year in high school because he got kicked in the right eye, which was damaged in such a way that when he elevates his gaze, his left eye goes up but his right one stays straight ahead. "I can do trigonometry with my eyes," he said. When he told me that on his campaign plane in 1996, I was tempted to take it as a right-left metaphor—his party affiliation doesn't jibe with his progressive instinct—but no, that was just me imposing my politics, such as they are.

At any rate, everywhere I go I am reminded of my poor monocular mother. (Once I was happily getting drunk with three poets when I realized they had three eyes among them.) When my mother accompanied my father to his fortieth high school reunion (he was a year ahead of her at Andrew Jackson High in Jacksonville), Cory Delmar, whom she'd had a crush on, actually noticed her, and came over to where she was sitting. "And I looked up, and, of course, my right eye doesn't move up along with the good one. . . . Cory could tell."

Susan once heard my father entreating my mother, "You've got to put that behind you."

Her being deformed, as she saw it. Her being an orphan. Her insistence that nobody loved her.

How are you going to argue with that? Especially when it comes out as fury. The *conviction* of the woman. I get so mad when, after I have stated a judiciously reasoned opinion, a woman's response is, "Oh, you know everything, you're always right and I'm always wrong." How can she say such a *childish* thing, when surely she realizes that I will never get over the notion that on the deepest, subrational level—a level to which my hat is always off—*she* is always right.

That night when my mother was yelling at my father, I sprang from my bed, got down on my knees like a Norman Rockwell tyke and prayed as hard as any Methodist boy could that she would quit. And she did. If I were still religious and a betting man, I'd bet that God said along with me, *Whew*.

God means *good*. There is such a thing as good. My mother's fried chicken was good. The summer I was nineteen my Grantland Rice Memorial Scholarship got me a job with the now defunct New York racing paper, the *Morning Telegraph*. Sol Rosen, the avuncular managing editor of that paper, and his wife and their son, who was only a couple of years older than I was, took me to dinner, an Italian place in Greenwich Village. It was the first time I'd seen antipasto. I ate it and lasagna (which I had had at one of the two Italian restaurants then in Atlanta) with something Italian that came to me by nature and nurture: gusto. Sol smiled as I smacked my lips and asked me what my favorite meal was.

"My mother's fried chicken," I said. All three of them smiled at me in a way that I knew was—not condescending or patronizing, they were nice folks, but . . .

It struck me, what a Norman Rockwellishly Southern statement I had made, which bothered me, especially because one of the people smiling at me was so close to my age. But I thought a moment, and I didn't care. Because I knew my statement was true. I *like* it when I'm able to make a statement that I know to be true. Especially when it favors my mother. I *wanted* to be a good son to my mother.

Now, thirty-six years later, her fried chicken . . . the beautiful brown of it, the lightness of its crispness, the way the skin was never loose and globby, she had somehow married it to the chewy but just-succulent meat . . . and fresh butter beans, okra, sweet corn, sliced deep-red vine-ripe tomatoes, fresh crowder peas, fried squash, young, tender pole beans, the way she fixed them all, labor intensively and, yes, in the case of the pole beans, pork intensively, but with what a light touch . . . would still be my favorite meal if I could get it.

Of course I guess devoting so much time and energy to cooking chicken so well doesn't pay off when your son wants to argue with you. But I didn't, really, I wanted to *commune*. . . .

My mother's *intentions* were good, even outside the kitchen. I don't have any doubt that my mother loved me, and loved my daddy and my sister and our series of psychologically overstimulated but affectionate dogs.

I was taught that God is love. That, in my experience, is a little like saying God is whiskey. I like whiskey (I don't want to say I love it), but I don't want to depend on it. I'd feel better if God were those butter beans. Once I had a recording of a chorus of NASCAR drivers singing "Just a Bowl of Butter Beans," to the tune of "Just a Closer Walk with Thee," and somehow I lost it. If any reader, by any chance, has that record . . . I have lost a lot of things I wish I still had.

Those butter beans were not what you may be envisioning, big mono-chrome fleshy things like you get frozen in the North. No. Those butter beans were in part translucent, their color was pale green with hints of yellow, they were so delicate their skins hardly stayed on them, and yet they had substance to the tooth as well as the tongue, their lightly butter-bubbled nectar kept them moist in the bowl, and there was always a plenty of them at our table when the season was right. I would eat five servings. If I could write as well as my mother could cook butter beans . . .

Unconditional love it is now, that everyone goes on about, as if, okay, we've all agreed, that's par for a committed relationship. "Because of this unconditional love I have for my father," wrote the young woman who believed she was Bill Cosby's daughter, in her letter to Cosby's network demanding $40 million in hush money, "I do not wish to harm him."

"Unconditional love." It's partly redundant, isn't it, and partly senti-mental, and partly, quote, "just an expression." Like any other two words.

I was going on like that at the dinner table with friends the other night when I realized I was ranting. "Lord, Lord," I thought, "all of us would cut our arms off if necessary for at least our children, if they had murdered a busful of nuns, and here I am drinking and apparently coming out against love."

"You mean, people throw the phrase about too much," one of my friends said, trying to get me off the hook. It would have been sensible just to agree with that. To express the sentiment of the group as follows: the idea that, having come up with a phrase for something that we'd all love to get at, we have then *got* at it, is contrary to the spirit of whatever we're trying to get at.

But, no. I went on ranting. I love my children, I love my sister, I love my friends, but *unconditional* sounds too much like—I almost said "surrender"—too much like heaven. I will not agree, in an argument here on earth, with anything that sounds like heaven. Our children *wouldn't* murder that many nuns, and we *wouldn't* cut off our arms. Because cut-ting off our arms wouldn't help. Only hiring a lawyer willing to distort the truth would help. And we would hire such a lawyer to the extent of our for-tunes, but . . .

But here's something that just strikes me: my mother, who loved me with every fiber of her being, would sometimes look at me as if I *had* mur-dered a busful of nuns. And I *hadn't*. I might have stayed out too late, or something.

Once, when I was home from college, I had a conversation with my mother that somehow turned to the question of, if it came right down to it, which would come first, a principle or a person. And my mother said that to her, a principle would come first.

"It *would*?" I said.

She said yes.

Maybe I had been coming on college-snotty, but—well, to some extent I probably was, but if your son is coming on college-snotty, what is the unconditionally loving way to deal with him? Surely not to come on Methodist-orthodox.

For one thing, my mother didn't know what a principle *was*. We got to arguing about the House Un-American Activities Committee once, after I had gone off to college and learned that there was such a committee, and I just sort of mildly observed that it had persecuted people. I may also have said that I thought the great thing about America, you know, boilerplate liberalism, was that people had a right here to be Communists or whatever. And she got furious and said, "I would get down on my knees and kiss the soil of this country."

That's not a principle. Principles are abstract. Is there no mother out there, whom I could retroactively adopt, who would just say, "Well, if you want to be a Communist, son, then you'll have to take your meals out on the steps"? Is that so much to ask? From my mother, who introduced me early to the irony and incongruity of things? Exaggerate my position with humor. Play with me. Remember what I said earlier, that she would tell my friends that children had to eat outside . . . ?

But, hey, I'm the humorist. Why couldn't I humor her?

Nothing on earth exists except in some *condition*, in the sense of, to quote Random House's unabridged, the "particular mode of being of a person or thing; existing state; situation with respect to circumstances." You couldn't have unconditional love in a test tube, much less in a family. You could have it in your own mind, but then that's a circumstance, isn't it?

There are always *living* conditions, and there are always *loving* conditions. I'm not saying there is necessarily some kind of quid pro quo. I'm saying . . .

Does anything sound fishier than an "unconditional guarantee"? We'll replace this product with no charge *if* you don't misuse it.

What's an unconditional surrender? We'll give up *if* you stop shooting at us.

And in contemporary relationships doesn't it often come down to "I'm unconditionally loving you, how come you're not unconditionally loving me?"

"Uh, I am."

"No you're not. If you were, you wouldn't *argue* with me like this."

I shouldn't argue with men, even. I take it too personally, get carried away. I don't just want to win on points or to promote a course of action, I want to make them *just hear what I'm saying*.

When I was younger and trying too vehemently to make a point and a woman would demand that I be more respectful of her feelings, I would respond emotionally myself. Unable to put into words what her prim insistence reminded me of, I would wince and grimace and roll around and shout, in frustration. Now, I realize that being more respectful of a woman's feelings is what you have to do. Like being respectful of a police-man's gun. (Okay, badge.) She's probably being respectful of the loudness of my voice—though that's not what I *want* from her. The currency of per-sonal exchange is never pure.

But here's what was in the back of my mind when I was responding emotionally. It was: "Respect *your feelings*! How do you think *I* feel, when I come to you full of energy and contradictions and a desperate need for somebody to bounce my intimate thinking off of, and you want me to Be Sweet?"

CHAPTER 18 / **Sauce for the Genders**

Evil comes to us men of imagination wearing as its mask all the
virtues. I have known, certainly, more men destroyed by the
desire to have wife and child and to keep them in comfort than I
have seen destroyed by harlots and drink.   —W. B. YEATS

Once when Susan was a teenager, Mother mortified her in front of her
friends by declaring, out of the blue, "Susan should have been the boy,
and her brother should have been the girl."

Well. To be sure, Susan majored in math (but I was *good* at math), she
has a much better sense of direction than I do (but I can read a map), and
she manages money better than I do (but as much food as I have put in my
children's mouths, I'm sure they'll be happy to let me crouch under their
respective dining room tables—assuming my son Kirven ever becomes
bourgeois enough to have one—and battle the dogs for scraps when I'm
not funny anymore and no one will pay me to write). And according to
Mother, I had such curly hair as a tot that people thought I was a girl and
Daddy insisted that she take me for my first haircut. (She would recount
that anecdote in the same wistful tone in which she would tell people that
I quit taking piano because it took too much time away from baseball.
Preston Sturges's mother made him wear little Grecian gowns and hang
out with Isadora Duncan. Mine harped mistily on my normality.)

And, okay, in the early seventies, when I was divorced and the sixties
kicked in for me and I pretty much gave up barbers in favor of whacking
some off around the edges myself occasionally or getting a woman to do it
under the influence of marijuana and Häagen-Dazs (Ah, those days! I don't
even do ice cream anymore!), a gas station attendant in, as it happened,
Fruita, Colorado, approached my car from the rear and said, "What'll it be,
ma'am?" When he saw my face, however, he began to stammer—either
out of fear that I'd react violently or because I was the homeliest woman
he had ever seen (which, in that town, was unlikely).

But I have to admit that I have often felt, at some level, insufficiently gender specific. I don't like to shop for clothes or cry or watch the Romance Channel, but I do lack the simple male common sense to avoid *disputing* sore points with women. All my life I have been in a struggle—a *tangle*—with female consciousness. If a woman says something fond (if nonobjective and perhaps a bit proprietary) about how I smell to her, and then asks how she smells to me, I might think for a long time, trying to come up with something of commensurate perceptual interest. Something that clarifies how differently we perceive, yet brings us closer, somehow, to common ground. And the moment passes.

Or I may *plunge into it*. In what seems to me an altogether open and positive way. "Like soap—I don't know what kind, just soap—around the neck, and clean sweat—maybe *perfectly* clean sweat doesn't smell, exactly, but, you know, salty, and between your legs sort of like . . . have you ever eaten in one of those old fish camps on the Gulf where they fry, like, panfish, crappie or bream, in probably the same lard or oil that they fry, like, drum or alligator tail—what's the matter?"

A real man would just say, "Pretty," and give her jewelry. But I keep making a doomed attempt to be romantic on terms that I can *live* with. I want to find a way with women—a woman—that doesn't lead to an emotional wonderland where she's looking at me with a wild plea in her eyes that says, "This would be so cozy if you'd just . . ." Just *what*? I'm trapped, lost, and have no idea what I'm doing wrong.

I can't just say *"Vive la différence!"* I can't get over how differently men and women perceive. I'm *bothered* by it. I want either to avoid discussing it altogether or to really *get into it* with them. I want to *bridge the gap*. I want women to be *built* different from me, and have different tones of voice, and, Jesus, I'd rather see a pretty woman smile . . . But I wish we didn't *bond* so differently.

I swear, I have said things to women which, if any woman had ever said anything half so understanding to me, it would have lasted me for months. Years. But condensed, Roger-and-out sentiments soak into women like sprinkles of rain into parched soil. And I sulk. Brood. It's not manly to brood. Roosters don't brood. (But who wants to be a rooster? Have you ever had chickens? Roosters are *absurd*. They strut around, swell up, look for trouble. Hens look at them and just shake their heads.) It isn't even *my* idea of manly; it certainly isn't a woman's.

It may be that my most thoroughgoing male traits are negative. For instance, I don't know the color of anyone's eyes. I just don't. I don't notice. I wouldn't know the color of mine (hazel) if people hadn't told me. I am, in fact—I found this out in the army—a bit color-blind as to distinctions between some browns and greens. One of the reasons I was deemed unsuitable (I hate to say unfit) for a combat branch: I wasn't good at seeing through camouflage. In training we went through an exercise to determine that. Others noticed slight discrepancies with the background, and fired. The camouflaged person finally had to stand up and wave his arms in exasperation before I picked him up. And I was peering. Hard.

Why was I even *in* the army? Bizarrely enough, I went through college ROTC. In the late fifties, early sixties, pre-Vietnam buildup, you figured you were going to have to go into the service one way or another. And I may have been motivated in part by the fact that my father avoided military duty during World War II (he was the sole support of me and my mother and her mean, storytelling aunt Pearl) and you've got to do something your daddy didn't do. But then one night when I was dancing, badly, in a party scene in the movie *Philadelphia*—

I was playing a partygoer costumed (not very convincingly, I like to think) as Truman Capote. It's a party thrown by the Tom Hanks character, a lawyer who has AIDS. The character played by Denzel Washington comes into this costume party, and evinces discomfort, because he finds he has arrived at this predominately gay party. I am among those chatting with the Hanks character as the Washington character comes up to him. You have to look very closely to see me—not because I was *hiding* . . .

The point is, I was there, along with a lot of other friends of the amiable director, Jonathan Demme. During the breaks, I was talking with gay men who were also extras in this scene. Tom Stoddard, a straight-looking (pardon the expression) gay activist lawyer frequently quoted in the *New York Times* (movie makeup covered his sarcoma scars—he died a year or so later), was expressing good-humored chagrin over myths about gay men. For instance, that they were forever turning up in emergency clinics with shot glasses stuck in their rectums. "So, in other words, gay men are people who put shot glasses up their ass."

"Shot glasses?" sniffed a man dressed as, I believe, Marie Antoinette. Then he smiled as if in reminiscence. *"Tumblers."*

Well, said Stoddard, in *Everything You Wanted to Know About Sex* it was solemnly recounted that when you're in a men's-room stall you can tell a gay man has entered the room when somebody puts his foot under your door.

"I read that too," said the man dressed as Marie Antoinette. "And I've been waiting for it to happen," he added wistfully, "ever since."

Another extra was Quentin Crisp. He said his last movie role had been that of Queen Elizabeth I. "But not with black teeth," he said. "We are told that Elizabeth I had *such* black teeth that the king of Spain remarked upon them. From which, we may conclude that the Spanish royalty didn't have black teeth."

"Would you have been willing to play her with black teeth?" I asked.

"I'd have *killed* to play Elizabeth with black teeth."

I asked him why he lived in New York instead of London. The weather? "Yes, that, and, then, the people. In England, no one is your friend. So you must *make* friends. Which is so tiring. And then you are stuck with them. Which is so tiring. In America, everyone is your friend. And then they move along."

I was enjoying the company. I was thinking how much cooler I was than Denzel Washington's uptight-straight lawyer character. Then we were all told to choose partners for a slow-dance scene. And it hit me—*I was afraid to appear in a movie dancing with a man.*

Quentin Crisp was not about to dance with anyone, thank God. Marie was taken by Stoddard. I looked around, guardedly, and seized first upon an extremely attractive young woman who then informed me stiffly that she was playing Denzel Washington's date. Fortunately I was able to latch onto Black-eyed Susan, a thickset but clearly female veteran of the Theatre of the Ridiculous, who had perhaps noticed the panic in my eyes before they lit on her, because when I asked her what she'd been up to lately, she said, "You wouldn't know about any of it."

As we danced, stiffly, I went through this chain of associations: gay myths, Stoddard's campaign in defense of gays in the military . . .

And I flashed back to 1955, when we moved to Dallas for six months and I had to go into an eighth grade full of strangers in the middle of the school year, and one of the boys took me aside and said I was wearing a green shirt on Thursday.

"Uh . . . huh?" I said.

"That means you're queer," he said.

I had to go through the rest of the day in that shirt. And the next day I learned that red on Friday meant the same thing. And the last thing we did that Friday was to attend an assembly in which a recruiting film for ROTC was shown. Views of summer training. Surely no one could be suspected of being gay who had subjected himself to anything so grimly male.

And I remember thinking, a), that it looked like something I would hate, and b), that I was going to sign up for it when the time came. And I did.

I believe to my soul that my military commitment sprang from wearing construably homosexual clothes two days in a row in the eighth grade.

So maybe the reason I argue with women, so unproductively, is that when they look at me as though I ought to be able to empathize with them, I feel that I'm being drawn into androgyny.

Or maybe it's because my mother taught me to drive. In a straight-stick Studebaker. Driving filled my mother with a dread so pungent as to be almost musky.

Brave of her to teach me. But then it seemed to be brave of her to do anything. I taught my kids how to drive, and I know what it's like even when you can see straight and don't necessarily feel that the world is trying to collide with you. You sit there with your right foot jammed against the floorboard hoping somehow you can in that way exert some influence over a car hurtling out of your control.

For my mother, it must have been a little like a one-armed person who's convinced that she's drowning all the time she's teaching a kid how to swim. She, in fact, couldn't swim a lick herself. But once she leapt right off a dock to save an old lady who had fallen in and thought she was drowning. Fortunately, she found herself sitting next to the old lady in about two feet of water.

As a motorist, because she had one eye, she had depth-perception problems; she could never be sure exactly how far away things were; and she felt the world was not her home; so she steered as clear from things as she could. I knew you didn't have to be as leery of anything as my mother was of everything, so I tended to see how leery you really had to be. I ran into a lot of things when I was learning to drive.

"Oh Lord, son, there's a policeman!" I can remember her crying out as I came within thirty yards of hitting one. I can still hear her saying it. There was something almost sexy about it. My father was so responsible, he never courted trouble, at least not after courting my mother. I can't help thinking it would have been good for him to court some. He was all sound business practices and good faith—trouble was an imposition on his integrity. When people challenged his bona fides he took it to heart—to the extent, eventually, of a fatal heart attack.

Papa boo-boo bye-bye.

My mother's leeriness—no telling *what* might happen—excited her, I think. When I do something I know I shouldn't, something my father would never have done, something like going off down a stream in the Amazon rain forest in the middle of the night with a crazy Peruvian in a leaky canoe looking for crocodiles, or writing this book, I'm flirting with my mother's sense of disaster. Trying Oedipally to beat my father's time?

Well, I've never wanted to *marry* her, I know that. That would have meant feeling even more responsible for her. I flirt with her sense of disaster in order to acknowledge it—it keeps me from being frivolous—but also to evade it. I got off into the imaginary realm of reading and writing as a child (with her encouragement, inducement even) to escape the sense of dread that my mother evoked, and before I can get cranked up to write funny now I have to get into a state approaching that dread. I lurch around and agonize about what an irresponsible turd I am and what terrible work habits I have, until finally I can sink deeply enough into the sefflo to leap like a scalded dog into hilarity.

My mother's dread undoubtedly came from being an abandoned and mistreated child. I am not afraid of being alone. I like it. I have you. (Not you personally.) I am afraid of being made to feel unloving—like someone who *has abandoned* a child. My mother made me feel not like an orphan, but like an orphaner.

Methodism does not speak to that. "Sometimes I feel like a mother-orphaning child"? Jesus rolls his eyes.

Nor does business-community-service-boosterism—how could I compete with Big Roy in that department, and where is the room for absurdity?

Nor does psychology—what kind of complex can that be, where you kill your mother's parents? Anybody with any sense would know better than to have a complex like that. Who'd *want* it? It's silly. I've got it. The only way to dispel it is to come up with something equally ludicrous, but controlled, semidark but upbeat.

So, humor. It doesn't address a woman's deepest emotional needs, but—have you heard this one? God has raised Adam and Eve above the other animals by providing them with opposable thumbs and large brains and so on, and then he starts assigning each of them different gender-specific traits so that they will seek each other out and multiply, and he says, "Well, I've got two gifts left for you, each of you gets one. The first is the ability to pee standing up."

"Neat!" cries Adam. "I want that one. Me, me! I can range all over the Garden peeing anywhere I want to, and . . . Oh, hey, Eve, I don't mean to be pushy, but—"

"No, no, you go right ahead, be aggressive, have it your way, I'll take what's left."

"Okay. Thanks. Oh boy, I'm going to go right now and . . ."

And he runs over behind the Tree of Knowledge and commences to relieve himself mightily against it.

"So," says Eve, shaking her head. "What is the other gift?"

"Multiple orgasms," says God.

Maybe it was God who planted a seed of comedy in my mother's sense of disaster. She would never venture downstairs dressed in just her slip, because "the preacher might walk in." What was he going to do, batter down the door with the vice squad in tow? She adjured Susan not to drink at a dance because "you'll throw up on your pretty party dress."

Susan called me up from Houston the other day and said, "There are a thousand grackles in my backyard." When I E-mailed her that my computer screen was flickering slightly, she E-mailed back:

> It sounds like your monitor is dying. Years ago I had one whose dying conniptions included shrinking to this teeny weeny font size and then occasionally bouncing back to normal size. It was maddening. It finally went belly up, all letters collapsing into a single row in the middle of the screen. It was as if someone had folded a piece of paper and all the letters fell down into the crease in the middle.
> Love, Susan.

My mother taught me how to read, too, and she loved to read, but she was afraid of reading the wrong thing somehow. When my tenth-grade teacher, Ann Lewis, who got me started writing for publication, gave me a special personal list of outside reading—Thoreau, Ring Lardner, Thomas

Hardy, O. Henry, Clarence Day, Max Beerbohm, Ernie Pyle—my mother saw Galsworthy on it and said, as if the abyss were opening up, "This is awfully sophisticated, Bucky." Galsworthy.

I thought to myself, Well, gee.

But, hey, it's great to read dangerously. My father read for information, and confirmation. I read every newspaper I can get my hands on, hoping that it will include a passage like this one from the Mount Vernon, Ohio, *News* about a Mrs. Hazel Rousseau, who says that after her brother Vance's death from cancer, a song just came to her:

> "Maybe it is a message from beyond the grave?" she questioned.
>
> The portion of the song she refers to follows: "I visioned Jesus ascending into Heaven; glorified, glorified; and when Vance spoke these words to me, 'The answer to cancer, sulfonic cobaltite, petrified wood,' I knew that God was in His heaven and all was well."
>
> Although sulfonic cobaltite is not defined as petrified wood, nor is it defined in the dictionary, Mrs. Rousseau claims it makes no difference because of the mode in which the words came to her.
>
> "If music was not such an exacting art and that words just have to fit perfectly with the melody, what is revealed in the lyrics would not be a miracle," she explained, "and maybe the answer to cancer is sulfonic cobaltite."

My father was a rock-solid driver, in a car and in the community. He said a few words here and there and people rode with him. My mother kept trying to get him to take things to heart. I believe he *did* take them to heart, but there they ran aground, spun their wheels, dug deeper and deeper into tissue too soft to afford traction. He didn't know how to bring things back up out of his heart in a form that my mother would recognize. He just rolled—by no means painlessly, but so apparently stoically as to pain and enrage her further—with her punches.

When I'm arguing with a woman, I'm trying to get her to see how *differently*, from her, I take things to heart.

Or maybe I'm just scared of getting married again. So I get involved with *interesting* women. . . .

Hey, everybody is interesting.

• • •

People say I move and sound like my father. I am his son. So why didn't I learn to hunker down and—painfully—shrug off the fury? One reason is, I don't want to have a heart attack! But there's another reason.

If Oedipus Rex had been Oedipus Jr., he would have had a much knottier problem.

If I try to create Abraham Lincoln without having him born in 1809 and having him be the president during the Civil War, he would not turn out to be Abraham Lincoln.

—ARNOLD CAPLAN OF THE CENTER FOR BIOETHICS,

DISCUSSING THE FEASIBILITY OF CLONING A HUMAN BEING

You could at least get my name right.

—JOSEPH COTTON (JR.) TO ALIDA VALLI, WHEN SHE

REJECTS HIM BECAUSE SHE STILL LOVES THAT

SCOUNDREL ORSON WELLES, IN *THE THIRD MAN*

A postcard from a friend:
"I just heard an author say on public radio that there are more juniors in mental institutions than there are juniors walking around free outside. When are you checking in?"

That makes the third friend, so far, who has passed on to me, with relish, some variant or other of an assertion recently published in *The Language of Names*, by Justin Kaplan and Anne Bernays, as follows:

"A 1971 study found there were three times as many 'juniors' in psychiatric treatment as in the general population."

Let me say that I have no desire to contribute to the stigmatizing of people in psychiatric treatment. Psychiatric treatment is a good thing. Undoubtedly more people should be in it than are. Maybe I should be in it, and maybe because of my name. To be "in psychiatric treatment" is surely not necessarily to be institutionalized, but as far as that goes, my paternal grandparents met while working as guards in a mental institution, as I have mentioned, and my maternal grandfather (a junior) died in one. Although I have yet to find a fellow junior who shows any interest in discussing this with me—an unhealthy sign, right there—juniors do tend to have certain identity issues.

Furthermore, Kaplan and Bernays are good writers. I enjoyed their book. I think I speak for juniors—if that is possible—when I say that we don't want to pick a fight, in the name of juniorhood, with anyone. Juniors may have the most unraised collective consciousness of any class of people in America.

But like the fellow said, just because we're crazy doesn't mean we're dumb.

What is meant, in the Kaplan-Bernays assertion, by "general population"? The U.S. population as a whole? When you sign up for psychiatric treatment, you don't get subtracted from the population, do you? Then how can we account for there being fewer people identified as juniors in the general population than in psychiatric treatment? Either a lot of people not in psychiatric treatment are concealing their juniorhood, or a lot of people in psychiatric treatment are only imagining themselves to be juniors. Hysterical juniors? People who think they are Napoleon Jr.?

This seems unlikely, at least on the scale suggested by Kaplan and Bernays. The only estimate of the number of juniors in America I can come up with is based on another bit of data reported in *The Language of Names*: that in 1945 juniors constituted about 3 percent of the general population. If that remains true today, for a U.S. population of roughly 260 million, then there are 7.8 million juniors in the country and 23.4 million in psychiatric treatment.

It may seem more likely that by "general population" what is meant is everyone in the United States who is not in psychiatric treatment. I believe I have heard penologists in movies use the expression "general population" to mean everyone (including themselves) who is not in prison. But that would still mean that of 7.8 million American juniors, three fourths, or 5.85 million, are in psychiatric treatment. Even that figure is so high as to suggest that juniors constitute the overwhelming majority of psychiatric patients. If that is the case, then we had better consider legislation (Germany has it, in fact) prohibiting the naming of sons after their fathers.

What either Kaplan and Bernays or the study they cite must have meant to say, after all, is that the percentage of juniors among Americans in psychiatric treatment is three times as high as the percentage of juniors among Americans in general.

That is striking enough. Striking enough, in fact, to entitle us juniors to some sort of federal relief. But we won't demand it, because . . .

Okay, okay. It is about now that a woman I was arguing with would lose interest and start repeating herself and I would start yelling. So let's forget about the psychiatric angle. Let's look at public life.

The nineties is a pretty uncertain decade, isn't it? It's the era of the junior. Pick up a new magazine, and John Kennedy Jr. is the founder of it. Pick up another magazine, and Robert Kennedy Jr. is billed on the cover as "The Kennedy Who Matters." You turn on the TV and Jesse Jackson Jr. has been elected to Congress. It's as if America today were a sequel.

Al Gore Jr., who once sat on Richard Nixon's lap as the latter presided over the Senate, is now Vice-President himself. (According to Erich Segal, author of *Love Story*, the aspect of the preppie Oliver Barrett character that was inspired by Gore, whom Segal knew at Harvard, "was that he was always under pressure to follow in his father's footsteps.") Young George Bush is not, strictly speaking, a junior, because he did not inherit his father's entire plethora of middle names, but he's a junior in effect, and he's governor of Texas. George Allen Jr., son of the former National Football League coach, is governor of Virginia. Malcolm Forbes Jr. (who tried to bring back Reaganomics, and whose wealthy father once said, "I never knew a rich man's son who was worth a damn"), my college friend Andrew Lamar Alexander Jr. and Morry Taylor Jr. tried to get the 1996 Republican presidential nomination. Jimmy "Junior" Hoffa Jr. is trying to become president of the Teamsters, though he never worked as a Teamster. Frank Rizzo Jr. has been elected to the Philadelphia City Council. John Gotti Jr. is acting boss of the Gambino crime family while his father is away. Ross Perot (who has his own Jr. story, as we shall see) said that his party wouldn't put up a candidate for president—if the Republicans or Democrats "come up with George Washington II." The mayor of Chicago is Richard M. Daley, a far less imposing figure than his father, Da Mare, Richard J. Daley. Around town he is referred to as Little Richie or R2D2.

Cal Ripken Jr. (like A. C. Green Jr. in basketball) has set baseball's all-time record for consecutive games played. Ken "Junior" Griffey Jr. is the game's best all-around player. Other prominent baseball juniors are Sandy Alomar Jr., Larry "Chipper" Jones Jr., José Cruz Jr., John Smoltz Jr., Dennis Neagle Jr., Charles Johnson Jr., Bobby Bonilla Jr., Pete Rose Jr. and—still in the minors as I write this—Bobby Bonds Jr. and Tony Armas Jr. Often called the best active fighter pound for pound is Roy Jones Jr.—who, like Bobby Czyz Jr., Howard Davis Jr. and Tony Ayala Jr., has had a stormy relationship with his manager-father. "Big Roy didn't want Little Roy to be a champ," according to one observer, "because then he wouldn't have his son under his thumb anymore. As a champ, he'd belong to the world. And Big Roy couldn't live with that."

Big Roy Blount could, I'd say. I remember being home from graduate school for the 1963–64 holidays, trying to give my parents some sense of my ambitions. Getting a Harvard M.A. in English was putting me off scholarship. It was too much like accounting. I went into the next room and came back with *The Most of A. J. Liebling*, which I'd requested for Christmas. I held up that volume, and pointed to the Cartier-Bresson jacket photo of the awkwardly slumped author, looking very unhealthy, holding an empty but undoubtedly alcoholic glass. "I want to be like this fat Jewish man here," I said.

My mother thought I was being perverse, but my father took it okay. In fact, when I was twelve or so and counting on being a three-sport immortal he brought me a copy of *Bury My Heart in an Old Pressbox*, by Fred Russell. Maybe I'd like to be a sportswriter, my father suggested. I scoffed. Five years later I won the Grantland Rice sportswriting scholarship to Vanderbilt, a full ride in those days, and Fred Russell was on the selection committee.

My father had my interests at heart, I never doubted that. But there was a moat around him full of alligators. I know now that he hadn't put them there to keep me away, they were already there. He didn't know how to get over them himself, so how could he tell me how to? Best to set an example of keeping the drawbridge up.

Harry Connick Jr. is the new Sinatra. (Another knife in the heart of Frank Sinatra Jr.) Before Robert Downey Jr.'s heroin addiction became the best-known thing about him, a leading critic called him "the most skillful young actor today" (in the previous generation, it was Robert DeNiro Jr., and before that Marlon Brando Jr.). Fob James Jr., governor of Alabama and son of a former governor, has brought back an old form of prisoner employment for your viewing pleasure as you drive Alabama's highways: Chain Gang II.

Political turmoil of the present and recent past is thick with juniors:

Newt Gingrich (born Newton McPherson Jr., changed to Gingrich when his mother remarried and Newt Sr. agreed to the name change in return for not having to pay child support), Al Sharpton Jr. (who became a preacher at age four and insisted on heading his papers "Reverend Alfred Sharpton" after his father had an affair with his stepdaughter and moved out, leaving the family in poverty), Jesse Helms Jr. (whose father, "Big Jesse," was a police and fire chief, but who was influenced more by an eccentric right-wing radio commentator named Alvin Wingfield Jr., who opposed parking meters as unconstitutional and killed himself in despair over the growth of Communism), Vincent W. Foster Jr., John Hinckley Jr., Representative Ernest Jim Istook Jr., Johnnie Cochran Jr. (the plates of his Rolls say "JC JR"), Mayor Marion S. Barry Jr. (never knew his father, was born without a middle name, took Shepilov as his middle name after Dmitri T. Shepilov, editor of *Pravda* in the Khrushchev years), Benjamin F. Chavis Jr., Ed Rollins Jr., Ralph Reed Jr., San Francisco mayor Willie Brown Jr., Edmund "Jerry" Brown Jr., Representative Thomas J. Bliley Jr. (whose predecessor as head of the powerful Energy and Commerce Committee was Representative John Dingell Jr.), Senator Joseph Biden Jr., Whitewater investigator Robert Fiske Jr., Vernon Jordan Jr. and Harold Ickes Jr. Bill Clinton himself, of course, was born William J. Blythe III.

And by whom are the communications and entertainment industries dominated?

S. I. Newhouse Jr., emperor of publishing; John F. Welch Jr., CEO of General Electric, which owns NBC; Edgar Bronfman Jr., CEO of Seagram's, which owns 80 percent of MCA and is the largest stockholder in Time Warner; Roone Arledge Jr., head of ABC News; Arthur Sulzberger Jr. and R. W. Apple Jr., publisher and Washington bureau chief of the *New York Times*; Frank A. Bennack Jr., CEO of the Hearst Corporation; big-money man Herbert Allen Jr.; movie *macher* Alan Ladd Jr.; magazine founders William F. Buckley Jr., Bob Guccione Jr. and R. Emmett Tyrrell Jr.; pollster George Gallup Jr.; and talk-show host John Donald Imus Jr. Rush Limbaugh is a III.

How about William Gates, master of the cyberuniverse? Gates has lots of Jr. juju. When his father, born William III, went into the army he changed his name to William Jr. because he was afraid sergeants would pick on a III. So Microsoft's Gates is the son of a Jr. and the grandson of a Jr. He could call himself William Gates Jr. Jr. Jr. if he wanted to. Instead he goes by plain William Gates, which makes it appear that he is his father's father.

William Herff Applewhite, who induced all thirty-eight members of his cult to commit suicide along with him so that they could be taken up into outer space, was a Jr. (His father was a Presbyterian minister. The boy was called Herff. When he became a cult leader he had himself castrated and took the name Bo for a while and then the name Do.) The Reverend James Jones, mass-suicide leader in Guyana, was a Jr. too.

So what am I saying? The juniorfication of America is an ominous development? It's true that the first two punching bags lined up for Mike Tyson after he came out of prison were Buster Mathis Jr. and Peter McNeely Jr. It's true that Ed Wood Jr. was the worst movie director of all time and that Ernie Bushmiller Jr. (creator of *Nancy*) was the dumbest or at least the most minimalist cartoonist. Several serial killers (John Wayne Gacy Jr., Elmer Wayne Henley Jr., Lewis S. Lent Jr., Bill "The Riverside Prostitute Killer" Suff Jr.), assassins (John Hinckley Jr.) and mountebanks (Lyndon Larouche Jr.) have been juniors; also yuppie murderer Robert Chambers, subway gunman Bernhard Goetz, teenage killer-for-fun Willie Bosket (whose blithe confession led to tougher laws against youthful offenders in New York, and whose double-murderer dad Willie Bosket Sr. had become, by correspondence in Leavenworth, the first prisoner ever to make Phi Beta Kappa), My Lai massacre leader Lieutenant William Calley Jr., Fernando Waldo "The Great Imposter" Demara, Jr. (who took on any number of false identities, including that of a Trappist monk and a surgeon in the Royal Canadian Navy, performing several surgeries without training), Oakland Hell's Angels president Ralph "Sonny" Barger Jr., Soviet spy-ring leader John Walker Jr., legendary mountain-man killer-fugitive Claude Dallas Jr., Ronald DeFeo Jr. (who inspired the book and movie *The Amityville Horror* by murdering his parents and four siblings), and Charles Brooks Jr., the first person executed by lethal injection in the United States.

John Salvi grew up being called Little John and then Young John. He showed signs of severe psychological problems, but as his father, known as Big John, put it, "Kids do all kinds of strange things. I thought it was me: he doesn't like me, he hates me, what the hell did I do to make him hate me?" Young John shot and killed the receptionists of two abortion clinics, wounded five other people and sprayed the lobby of a third clinic with twenty rounds of ammunition.

I thought it was me.

Roy A. Brown Jr. was chief designer of the Edsel. Richard Bissell Jr. was chief architect of the Bay of Pigs fiasco. Charles F. Keating Jr. was the "poster boy" of the savings and loan scandal. Roy Michael Huffington Jr.

(of whom Representative Barney Frank said, "Even when he's around, he isn't") was elected to Congress but blew millions of inherited dollars trying to advance farther in politics at the prodding of his wife. Whittaker Chambers was named for his bisexual father Jay Chambers, but through high school went by the middle name that his mother insisted upon: Vivian. Except that his classmates called him Girlie, Stinky and Mr. Chamber Pot. He took his mother's maiden name, Whittaker, as his first when he went to college, and used any number of pseudonyms as a Communist spy. Earvin "Magic" Johnson, who put a straight male face on HIV, is a junior.

And although a number of highly successful American juniors come to mind (Adam Clayton Powell Jr., Arthur Schlesinger Jr., John McEnroe Jr., Angel Cordero Jr., Mormon founding father Joseph Smith Jr., Levi pants patriarch Walter A. Haas Jr., chewing gun pioneer William Wrigley Jr., Tip O'Neill Jr., Howard Baker Jr., Lowell Weicker Jr., Horatio Alger Jr. and the English-usage maven William Strunk Jr.), I can think of only two downright major American juniors who were *known* as juniors: Martin Luther King Jr.* and Oliver Wendell Holmes Jr.† Maybe the late Supreme Court Justice William J. Brennan Jr. qualifies as a third.

Here, however, is what people don't realize: All sorts of major and minor American (and occasional non-American) icons, from George Herman (Babe) Ruth Jr. to Andy Warhola (changed to Warhol) Jr., were born juniors:

Muhammad Ali (Cassius Marcellus Clay Jr.), Willie Mays, Billy Graham, Crazy Horse and Sitting Bull (at least they were given their fathers' names), Vladimir Nabokov (in the Russian form, Vladimir Vladimirovich), Ernesto "Che" Guevara (essentially, allowing for Latin metronymics),

---

*At birth he was named Michael Luther King Jr., after his father, but his grandfather, James Albert King, on his deathbed, asked Michael Sr. to change his name to Martin and "change little Mike's name too." From then on until at least as late as graduate school, the future great civil rights leader was generally called Marty. You have to wonder whether James Albert had some kind of deathbed vision. Would MLK Jr. have had the same resonance as Michael Luther King Jr.? In Christian tradition Michael is the angel with the sword.

†Perhaps the greatest figure in American jurisprudence, he was six three and lean whereas his father, one of the most famous writers of his day, was a foot shorter and round, but Jr. had to go to great lengths—the two of them never really got along—to stay out of Sr.'s shadow. Friends called him Wendy. In an uncharacteristically ungenerous opinion he wrote, "Three generations of imbeciles are enough."

Clint Eastwood, Charlie Parker, Thelonious Monk (born Thellous Junior Monk—his son Thelonious Sphere Monk Jr. is a jazz drummer), Jelly Roll Morton (Ferdinand La Menthe Jr.), Marvin Gaye, Willard Scott, Christine Jorgensen (born George Jr.), Oliver Hardy (of Laurel and Hardy), Robert Lowell, Walt Whitman, Edmund Wilson, Henry James, John Dos Passos, Gore Vidal (Eugene L. Vidal Jr.), Tom Wolfe, Thomas Pynchon, Yul Brynner (Taidje Kahn Jr.), John Denver (Henry John Deutschendorf Jr.), Mickey Rooney (Joe Yule Jr.), Jimmy Cagney, Van Cliburn, Bill Cosby,* Bing Crosby, Dr. John (a.k.a. "The Night Tripper," born Malcolm John Rebennack Jr.), Robert Redford, Rock Hudson (Roy Scherer Jr.), Richard Burton (Richard Walter Jenkins Jr.), John Cage, Florenz Ziegfeld, Tyrone Power, Burt Reynolds, Rip Torn (Elmore Rual Torn Jr.), Joe DiMaggio (Giuseppe Paolo DeMaggio Jr.), Y. A. Tittle, Joe Montana, Dan Marino, Kareem Abdul-Jabbar (Ferdinand Lewis Alcindor Jr.), Sugar Ray Robinson (Walker Smith Jr.), Minnesota Fats (Rudolf Water Wanderone Jr.), Walt Frazier, Willis Reed, George Mikan, Julius Erving (a II, but his mother called him "June," for Junior), Bill Veeck (Bill Sr. moved from one Chicago newspaper to another and changed his byline to Bill Bailey, inspiring the song "Won't You Come Home, Bill Bailey?"), Earl Weaver, the great golfer Bobby Jones, one-armed outfielder Pete Gray, George Wallace, Tom Joad, J. R. Ewing, Hamlet, Li'l Abner, Charles Lindbergh, four of the first six astronauts in outer space, Quincy Jones and James Brown.

Gloria Vanderbilt's mother was named Gloria Vanderbilt. Lola Montez, Erma Bombeck and Mark Twain's wife, Olivia, were named for their mothers. The Zodiac Killer lived with his mother and his sister, both of whom were named Gladys Reyes. As a young woman Willa Cather sometimes signed herself "William Cather Jr." But mostly this is a male thing.

Henry James, according to his biographer Leon Edel, signed himself "Henry James Jr." at first,† but "after a while, the 'Junior' got to be less and less. He hated being a junior, he hated number two. Papa was number one. There are a lot of juniors like that, who try to get around it some way,

---

*". . . a father figure for a black America that has become increasingly fatherless. . . . Since Cosby's father was absent for much of his childhood, he may be filling a void in his own life as well as the culture's: he has to be both the father his own father never was and a public paragon of kind strength and stability. He's doing double duty in the Dad department—no wonder he gets testy." (James Wolcott, in *The New Yorker*.)
†Incidentally, Ernest Hemingway signed things that he wrote in high school "Ring Lardner Jr."

with numbers for instance: Vanderbilt I, Vanderbilt II, Vanderbilt III, etc."
(This part about the Roman numerals is not quite right—a II is generally
not a junior because he was named not for his father but for his grandfather.) "What's interesting is the way that the 'Junior' in James's signature becomes, finally, just a little curve, a tiny curve with a dot over it. And
in a matter of days after his father dies, he writes a letter to his publisher
and draws a hand pointing to his signature—it's 'Henry James,' without
the junior—saying, 'this is the way I sign my name now.' "*

Raymond Carver, who was born Raymond Clevie Carver Jr., wrote, "I
hated the 'Junior' part. When I was little my dad called me Frog, which
was okay. But later, like everybody else in the family, he began calling me
Junior. He went on calling me this until I was thirteen or fourteen and
announced that I wouldn't answer to that name any longer. So he began
calling me Doc."

Donald Barthelme Jr.'s best book is *The Dead Father*.

Joseph Francis "Buster" Keaton was the sixth-generation Keaton
firstborn to be named Joseph. His actor father, Joseph Hallie Keaton,
called Joe, gave Buster the middle name Frank after Buster's maternal
grandfather, whose favor Joe was trying to curry. When it didn't work,
Joe changed it to Francis. Buster got his name as a toddler when he tum-
bled down a flight of stairs unhurt and a fellow thespian said, "He's a regular buster," and Joe said, "I'm going to call him by it." At five, Buster
joined the family vaudeville act. Billed as "The Child Who Can't Be Damaged," Buster was dressed as a replica of his father and thrown around so
extraordinarily—sometimes as far as thirty feet—that Sara Bernhardt
threatened to report Joe for child abuse. The joke of the act—Buster
became the headliner before he was six—was the father going to extreme
lengths to make the son obey. Buster was not allowed to cry, onstage
or off.

Many years later, it was discovered that he had been working since
childhood with two cracked vertebrae. When he turned twenty-one,
Buster broke up the act, leaving Joe drunk in San Francisco, but the son
later got Joe movie work and could never bear to hear any criticism of his
father, always insisted he owed him everything, and to be sure Joe fostered
the stage personality—skittery walk, deadpan expression—that Buster

*A later biographer suggests that James "may have performed his first acts of love"
with Oliver Wendell Holmes Jr., who "shrugged off the encounter."

carried on into the movies. Two of his best were *Steamboat Bill, Jr.* and *Sherlock, Jr.*, in the latter of which Joe played his father.

Charles Spencer "Charlie," "The Little Clown" Chaplin's father, who abandoned the family, was simply Charles Chaplin, and a drunk (and maybe not Chaplin's actual father).

More Hollywood juniors: Stacey Keach, Louis Gosset Jr., Harriet Frank Jr., Robert Montgomery, Tim Holt (his father, Charles John Holt Jr., known as Jack, was a top silent-era horse-opera hero. Tim, in his first movie, played Jack's character as a boy. Tim appeared, unstarringly, in a remarkable range of film classics—*The Magnificent Ambersons, The Treasure of the Sierra Madre, Stagecoach, My Darling Clementine, Stella Dallas* and *Back Street*—but mostly he made cowboy flicks like his daddy), Harriet Frank Jr., Rip Taylor (Charles Elmer Jr.), Bob Steele (Robert North Bradbury Jr.), Jason Robards Jr., William Broyles Jr., William Collier Jr. (friend of Buster Keaton's, helped him set up many of his stunts), Sam Goldwyn Jr., Lon Chaney Jr., William Holden (William Franklin Beedle Jr.), Noah Beery Jr., George Stevens Jr., Carl Laemmle Jr., Lorenzo Semple Jr., Jack Haley Jr. Douglas Fairbanks Sr. once said he had "no more paternal feelings than a tiger in the jungle for his cub," but he and Douglas Jr. became close friends when Jr. grew up.

Roone Arledge Jr.* and Chet Forte Jr. invented TV football as we know it today. Alexander Cartwright Jr. was the true inventor (though people persist in giving Abner Doubleday credit) of baseball. Earl Hamner Jr. created *The Waltons*.

There's an element of anointment in being named for your father. It can't be just coincidental that the first black American to go into space, the first black air force general, the first black admiral, the first black four-star general, the first black U.S. solicitor general, the first black president of a major university, the first black conductor of a major American symphony, the first black journalist to win a Pulitzer Prize, and the first male, native, African-American staff writer for *The New Yorker* (Henry Louis "Skip" Gates Jr.) have all been juniors. The first black man to play major league baseball—and the last, until Jackie Robinson—was

---

*I see by the paper that Roone Jr.'s daughter not only followed her father into TV production, she married a man named (Robert) Loonie Jr. Will there be a Roone Loonie, soon? And later a Roone Loonie Jr.? Anyway—I guess this goes without saying—if you want a sweet, strong woman, find one who likes her daddy.

(briefly, in 1884) Moses Fleetwood (Fleet) Walker, named for his father, a freed slave.

Thirteen American presidents—31.7 percent of the total—have been, whether they used the Jr. or not, their fathers' namesakes: Madison, Adams (not counting John Quincy), Jackson, Tyler, Buchanan, Hayes, McKinley, Theodore Roosevelt, Coolidge, Eisenhower, Ford (a double Jr.—born Leslie Lynch King Jr., adopted and renamed Gerald R. Ford Jr.), Carter and Clinton.* You don't get elected president if you keep your Jr. Al Gore didn't use his as a vice-presidential candidate, even. When Lloyd Millard Bentsen was chosen as Michael Dukakis's running mate, the *New York Times* reported that his father, Lloyd M. Bentsen Sr., was still living and known as Big Lloyd at the age of ninety-four, and that "Lloyd Millard Bentsen Jr. now uses neither his middle initial nor the 'Jr.' "

Deep down inside, I didn't want to be president. Of that, more later.

John Kennedy was a surrogate junior—when his brother Joe Jr. died, he became the family's standard-bearer.† Compare Ross Perot: his parents' first son, Gabriel Ross Perot Jr., died in infancy, and lived on in sainted memory. The man we know now as Ross Perot was born Henry Ray Perot, but at the age of twelve he changed it to Henry Ross. Compare, further, Governor Pete Wilson of California, who tried to be a Republican presidential contender: his older brother, James Boone Wilson Jr., was hit by a

---

*Four others have had their paternal grandfathers' names, one his paternal great-grandfather's. Five were named for maternal grandfathers—Bush was called "Little Pop" or "Poppy" because granddad's nickname was "Pop." Millard Fillmore was named for his mother, Phoebe Millard Fillmore. James Abram Garfield was named for his brother James, who died in infancy, and his father, Abram. Eleven presidents sired juniors. Of these, six died young—William Henry Harrison Jr. of alcoholism, Calvin Coolidge Jr. of a blister on his toe from playing tennis without socks. Chester A. Arthur Jr. became a playboy. John Tyler Jr. wound up in a minor Internal Revenue post. Ulysses S. "Buck" Grant Jr. and his father went bankrupt together. FDR Jr. had a fairly distinguished career in government. Theodore Roosevelt Jr. (named that although Teddy was a Jr. too) earned a Congressional Medal of Honor during the D-Day invasion at Normandy. John Adams II, son of John Quincy and grandson of John, was expelled from Harvard for taking part in a student riot, scuffled with a journalist in the Capitol rotunda and died at thirty-one.

†Ever wonder what kept the Smothers Brothers, Tommy and Dick, together as an act so long? They were both surrogate Jrs. Their father, Thomas Smothers Jr., was an army major captured at Corregidor and killed by American bombs. Tommy Smothers was III, and his father had wanted to name Dick Tommy IV.

truck as a child and became quarrelsome and inattentive, so Pete became the favorite son and was groomed for bigger things.*

America, to steal a line from George Carlin, began as Europe Junior, and the custom of naming people Jr. has always been far more more popular in this country than anywhere else. It originated in England after the Normans came from France and took over. Historical evidence is sketchy, but here's how I figure it: first you had a Jean, who on the formerly Anglo-Saxon side of the channel became John. John named his son after himself, and when the second John became a taxpayer, he was listed on the rolls as John Johnson. Then what if John Johnson wanted to name his son John? Designate him John Johnsonson? Instead, *junior*, Latin for "younger," was tacked on, and if Jr. wanted a namesake he could call him John Johnson III. Lewis Carroll was born Charles Lutwidge Dodgson Jr., and Voltaire was François-Marie Arouet "le jeune," but you won't find many British or French juniors today. In Hispanic countries, a son carries his mother's surname along with his father's, so Jr. isn't needed. In Germany it's actually illegal to name anyone Junior or to add Jr. to his name. Being a junior is as American as apple pie or violence.

Berry Gordy Jr., founder of Motown, worked closely with his father, whom he remembers fondly as "my greatest hero." You should know, though, that Berry Jr.'s father is known to history not as Berry but as Pop. Maybe he was able to live with that because he was a junior himself: "The first Berry Gordy," as Berry Jr. calls his grandfather in his autobiography, was born in slavery and was struck down by lightning before his son Berry had children.

Juniorhood is like Southernness in that there is no antidefamation potential at all. But at least Southerners can make common cause at a certain level of defensiveness. The only junior who ever invoked his juniorhood in an identity-politics sort of way, so far as I know, was Frank Mancuso Jr., producer of a movie that portrayed the late, straight Thomas Dewey as a crook. When Dewey's son expressed outrage, the ungratifying feel-your-pain response of Mancuso Jr. (son of MGM's chairman) was, "I'm a junior, and I'm sensitive to people trying to hurt the family patriarch."

*General H. Norman Schwarzkopf, commander of allied forces in the Persian Gulf, might almost be seen as a surrogate for the Lindbergh baby—he is the son of Colonel H. Norman Schwarzkopf, who headed the investigation that probably framed Bruno Richard Hauptmann for the kidnapping and murder of Charles Lindbergh's infant son, referred to as Charles Jr. although the father, the flier, himself was a Jr.

There is just one cause that might bring juniors together (after their fathers have died): No More Juniors. Clint Eastwood grew up being called Little Clint or Sonny and he didn't like it. "Every boy," he says, "should have his own name."

I agree.

"Males named 'junior,' " according to Dr. Murline Gatewood, a psychologist quoted in a Cleveland newspaper I happened to pick up, "have more trouble in adapting to traditional masculine developmental roles. It's hard to be 'Billy,' when there is always a 'Bill' around."

Good point. The problem with Dr. Murline Gatewood, she won't leave it at that. She goes on: "Particularly around adolescence, when there's opened mail—the love letter for Billy and it's read by William; and when the telephone calls come for Billy and William answers."

Well, I can't picture my father reading anybody's love letter. It was, to be sure, irritating to answer the phone after my voice changed and hear somebody say, "Roy?", and then, after answering, "Uh-huh," to be asked, "Big Roy or Little Roy?", especially since I topped out at six feet and a half inch and he was an inch or so taller, but, hey, I could live with it. It's Dr. Gatewood who won't let it go.

"And part of it is the given that we don't ever grow up in the eyes of our parents—'How do I feel at twenty-four, being 'Butch' instead of 'John'? The diminutive of any name implies littleness. And many of the names we give males when they have the same names as their father are like 'Chip,' as in Chip Off the Old Block."

Men, Dr. Gatewood says, have a "horrible problem" just being men. "There is no female equivalent to the question, 'Am I a man?' If I were to make a generality, it would be that the question most asked by young men I see in therapy is, 'Am I a man?' "

Well, in effect, maybe. But I'm sitting here trying to imagine having a conversation with anybody in which anybody would actually say, "Am I a man?" I hate to say this, but even if Dr. Gatewood's name weren't Murline, I would be able to tell she was a woman. Just as you can tell a writer is English by how unlikely her American characters' dialogue sounds.

"It's a scary thing to be a man—and add to that the burden of being some man's junior—Oh, God," Dr. Gatewood says.

Here's the problem: Juniors have to resist an inclination to become second bananas. Some of us overcompensate by becoming icons. Others of us just go with it. Elisha Cook Jr. was the quintessential gunzel, Slim

Pickens (Louis Bert Lindley Jr.) a heck of a sidekick, Claude Jarman Jr. flourished as a juvenile in *The Yearling, Intruder in the Dust* and *Rio Grande* (as John Wayne's son, whose mother, Maureen O'Hara, arrives in South Texas to buy him out of the cavalry, but he hangs in there and proves himself), then faded when he hit shaving age. Johnny Carson's bandleader and foil, Carl "Doc" Severinsen, was called "Little Doc" as a boy because his father was town dentist of Arlington, Oregon. Sammy Davis Jr. hung with Frank. Junior Gilliam, of the Dodgers, was the quintessential number-two hitter—not only is the second man in the order supposed to get on base so the big boys can drive him in, he's supposed to take pitches so the leadoff hitter can steal.

Orson Welles, the grandiose "boy wonder," was not his father's name-sake. His older brother was the junior of the family. The older brother never amounted to anything. In fact, he went insane (and while in an asylum wrote an unproducible play about John Brown and John Brown Jr.). Welles learned early on about the vulnerability of a junior. Probably the reason so many juniors have been larger than life is that they had to be, to keep from being smaller. It's not easy for Junior or Senior.

Kurt Vonnegut dedicated a recent book, "In memory of Kurt Vonnegut (Sr.)," of whom he wrote: "He died eventually, and in an act of Freudian cannibalism, I dropped the 'Jr.' from my name. (Thus in lists of my works do I appear to be both my father and my son, Kurt Vonnegut and Kurt Vonnegut Jr.)." While Kurt Sr. was alive, he called Kurt Jr. "K." That sounds like a girl's name, and it's what the profoundly stumped protagonist is called in Kafka's *The Trial*. Other Juniors get called Junior (which is what some of the dumbest characters on TV are called), or if they're lucky, as in the case of Willie Mays (who, however, has never quite seemed to grow up, has he?), Buck.

Ollie North was called Larry, growing up, to distinguish him from his father and grandfather, both of whom were named Oliver. But being a sort of crypto-junior may be more confusing than being an outright one. David Ernest Duke, the noted Louisiana racist, was so named because his father, David Hedger Duke, didn't want his son to have the "stigma" of being a junior. David Hedger never had much time for David Ernest, who drifted as a youth into the Ku Klux Klan, where he found father figures.

You know what? I never found any father figure, other than my father. I was too loyal to him. I still am! My father was a good man! When he died, one of his fellow pillars of greater Atlanta wrote to my mother, "Roy has been responsible to a large degree for the real progress of this metropolitan area and the stability of personal relationships in it."

James Brown, too tortured a soul to settle into his distinction as the father of contemporary African-American music, has described his naming as follows: "They were going to name me Joe Brown Jr. Then, for no particular reason, they added James. Because they didn't understand the flow, they had it James Joe Junior Brown. Eventually it got straightened out to James Joe Brown Jr., but the Brown should have been Gardner because that's what my daddy's last name was originally." For years he lived with an aunt and her grandson, who was called Junior. "Since I was called Junior too, he became Big Junior and I became Little Junior." Clarence Day Jr. wrote *Life with Father*. Theodore Seuss Geisel, son of Theodore R. Geisel, took the name Dr. Seuss to write *Hop on Pop*. Alfred C. Kinsey, the sex researcher, was the son of Alfred Seguine Kinsey, a strict evangelical Methodist who forbade dancing, tobacco, alcohol and pop music in his household and wouldn't let his children date as teenagers. Alfred C. has recently been revealed to have been a sadomasochistic homosexual who drew his wife, staff members and others into extensive sexual experimentation.

Marlon Brando was called Bud as a boy. He and dapper, womanizing Marlon Sr. never got over their resistance to each other: the world was too small for one Marlon Brando, let alone two. When Senior would introduce himself, people would say, "You're not Marlon Brando!" Once the father accidentally opened a letter addressed to the son. Marlon Jr. flew into a rage and demanded that his father change his name. Senior suggested that Junior change *his*. "His one regret," said an obituary of Senior, "was that he gave his name to his famous actor son."

I started using my Jr. in my byline thirty years ago when I was writing a column in the *Atlanta Journal* and my mother informed me that my father was hurt because I wasn't using it. Furthermore, she said, people had withdrawn their money from Decatur Federal Savings and Loan, of which he was president, because of liberal things I wrote. I moved to New York and the national media, but I kept the Jr. I still use it, twenty-four years after he died. Pauline Kael once advised me to drop it, it gave a lightweight impression; but I wouldn't.

Dean Martin was born Dino Paul Crocetti. When he died in '95, friends said he'd really stopped living in 1987 when his son, Dean Paul (Dino) Martin crashed his Air National Guard fighter plane and died.

Jim Thompson Jr., the noir novelist, caricatured his sheriff-embezzler father viciously. According to a biography of Jr., "Thompson Sr. recurs in various increasingly wild guises in his son's work, memorably as the insidiously grinning, just-folks sadist Sheriff Lou Ford in *The Killer Inside Me*," and as "the monstrous Sheriff Nick Corey in *Pop. 1280*."

I would never do that. It would be fun, but it wouldn't be right. My father was kind. Long-suffering. I banged up the family car several times and he never game me a hard time about it. On top of the refrigerator in my apartment I have a picture of my parents and Susan and me sitting on a couch together in 1958. (Ennis found it, framed it along with other family pictures, and gave it to me one Christmas.) My father is looking at me and smiling heartily, with what looks like pride. So is Susan. Inferrably, I have just said something funny. I'm looking straight ahead with narrowed eyes and a kind of shit-eating grin. My mother has her eyes shut, so her glass one won't reflect the flash, and her smile is pained and inward.

On the bookshelf next to where I write is a picture of my father at what would appear to be a business banquet, in probably the early fifties—so he's probably thirty-nine or forty. He is standing dapperly and merrily next to a really pretty accordion player, whose big, lovely smile he seems to have surprised her into. Astonishingly, to me, he even appears to be singing. My mother is nowhere to be seen. But don't get the wrong idea. Daddy is giving the accordionist an appreciative look—but wholesomely appreciative. Once at a convention—my mother's story—he got into an elevator and found himself alone with the bosomy, flirtatious wife of another savings and loan man. He was so unsettled he got off at the next floor. Remember Burt Lance, Jimmy Carter's ebullient Christian budget manager? My mother met him at a convention once and didn't approve of him. "He looked at me like he knew what I looked like in my slip," she said. Daddy wasn't like that. And I can't say I wish he had run off with that accordion player, because I was ten or eleven at the time and I would have been devastated.

(You think Dennis Rodman has an awfully plain name for such a flamboyant person? Well, his father was Philander(!) Rodman Jr., who as of September 1996 was living in the Philippines with his two wives and fifteen of his twenty-seven children. He hadn't seen Dennis in thirty years.)

Evan S. Connell Jr.'s father expected him to be a doctor. Embittered, Evan Jr. caricatured Sr. devastatingly as the dead, unfeeling—ironically unlinking—Mr. Bridge.

My father wasn't unfeeling. And my evidence isn't only all the times my mother told me I had hurt his feelings.

A woman I've never met, Fran Moreland Johns, read something I'd written a while back and wrote me a letter about my father. She and her husband, and then just she herself after their divorce, were in real estate in Decatur, "so we were periodically buying a house, or a little duplex for the kids' eventual education. What we would do was drop into Decatur Federal, poke our noses into your dad's office and ask if he had a minute to talk about this good thing we found. Which of course we couldn't buy without a lot of help from his funding sources. So he'd say, 'Well, let's go take a look, then,' and we'd pile into the car and drive him wherever. Once there he would eyeball the property and its environs, and if it looked pretty good we'd close in a week or so. Sooner, if necessary. Since he already knew the metropolitan area, the communities, the economy, the market, the reasonable financial potential of the property and the probability of our (or other clients') paying back the loan, it makes perfectly good sense that his success record in this gentlemanly way of doing business was infinitely better than the subsequent records of all those dolts with their calculators and seven-copy forms.

"I don't think your dad was ever a Good Old Boy S&L person, either. I know of loans he helped procure for people whose race, creed or economic circumstances might've argued strongly against them, but when he believed in the people and the property, he had a way of eliminating the detail problems. He reminded me of my own pedagogue father and I thought he was wonderful.

"So did the Junior League and other doers of good around town. You may not have known about the manila envelope. When we needed money for the Decatur High band trip or some great community project, everybody would moan about going out to solicit all those folks who had to be photographed for the newspapers as they handed over the check. But you would just amble into Mr. Blount's office, tell him about it, and wait while he pulled out the manila envelope and handed over a couple of bills."

"Be a good man." He said it with feeling. And at a certain level, I get it. I just don't know how to go about it. That's the only explicit advice or instruction I remember him giving me, ever.

"Part of the sad irony" of our family, my sister wrote me after reading the first draft of this book, "is that while you characterize your relationship with Daddy as distant, I recall how often you withdrew to your room, leaving me downstairs with Mother and Daddy, who would be wishing you would spend time with us. This was high school and beyond, so by then I suppose the damage was done."

Marvin Gaye, born Marvin Pentz Gay Jr., was shot to death by Marvin Gay Sr., a transvestite who whipped all his children mercilessly, after making them get naked. The most defiant child—eventually he seemed to be inviting the whippings—was Marvin Jr. His mother said her husband had always been jealous.

My father was widely, publicly acknowledged to be a good man. When he died the *Atlanta Constitution* editorialized, "Mr. Blount was a soft-spoken and friendly man, but he maintained a firm strength in his beliefs and his integrity was unquestioned. Humanity could use more of his kind." When integrating the Decatur schools was no longer avoidable, my father took on the responsibility of being chairman of the board of education, because it was hard for people to say that anything Roy Blount was behind was immoral or tyrannical, even if the federal government was behind it as well. Susan says, "I remember Daddy saying that it was coming, it was the right thing to do and the best way was to take charge rather than waiting for somebody to force it done in a certain way." By then I was off up north, married and fecklessly seeking mutuality.

It's amazing to me that Daddy and I never talked about the most important issue of my youth and his prime of life, the integration question. When, as a student newspaper columnist, I came out in favor of— pardon my radicalism—admitting black undergraduates to Vanderbilt University, I heard through my mother that he was proud. The year before, when I was a sophomore, she said, "Your father says your writing is getting more professional every day."

My parents may have thought I was too callow-liberal to appreciate their moderate (his paternalistic, as I saw it, as I *would* see it) approach to things. No doubt I was. But I could see where they were coming from. I remember half overhearing them chuckling over a demand placed before the board of education, when he was not chairman but just a member of it, by a delegation from the black community: "What we want to know is: Is you is or is you ain't going to integrate the schools?" That sounds like white folks quoting black folks condescendingly, and that's what it was, in part, but it was also Southern folks savoring how well some other Southern folks had hit the nail on the head.

I have a letter from my mother that accompanied, sometime in 1972, a newspaper clipping about one of the wrangles involved in pushing through the Metropolitan Atlanta Rapid Transit Authority system, my father being chairman of the authority. "Thought you might be interested in this write-up. Your father looks this tired too. He has been the liaison between the blacks and whites. Fighting for them on this [trying to keep the price of a fare down to fifteen cents] to the annoyance of some whites. He has been very fond of Jesse Hill, a black man on MARTA.* I heard him tell Bill Hicks that Jesse was as white as Bill except for skin. Now they (white group) keep filing suits—MARTA can't do anything until these are settled because they can't collect the tax until then. So Jesse and blacks have turned—saying he's double-crossed them. I wish he'd get out of it. He feels since he pushed it this far he is obliged to see it out of this muddle. I'd spit on them and go home but guess that shows I'm not the person he is."

How come he couldn't share any of that with me directly? Was it the president in him, or the tattletale in me? It's not as though I was still working for the Atlanta paper. I was writing sports up in New York. I wouldn't have revealed anything he didn't want me to anyway.

Oh, wait. I know. I kept on writing columns (twenty-five bucks a pop) for the *Atlanta Journal* after I went up to New York to work for *Sports Illustrated*. I wrote a column defending Atlanta's alternative newspaper, the *Great Speckled Bird*, whose offices had been firebombed. When I was still in Atlanta I went to *Great Speckled Bird* picnics, and felt like I ought to be part of that crowd of hippies and radical labor organizers and old lefties, but I was married and had a baby. Also, I was still pretty stiff at the time, if you want to know the truth.

The least I could do was come out against their being firebombed. But somehow it all got involved in DeKalb County politics. Decatur is the county seat of DeKalb, which is one of the counties of the greater Atlanta area. There was the establishment, good-government faction, of which my

---

*Jesse Hill Jr. was an important figure in Atlanta history, along with Ivan Allen Jr., John Portman Jr., Sam Massell Jr., Maynard Jackson Jr., Andrew Jackson Young Jr., Joe Martin Jr., Lewis Grizzard Jr. and many other Jrs. It makes me wonder whether I should have stayed. If I'd followed Daddy into the savings and loan business, though, I'd've been in it when it went bad in the eighties. One of the worst things my mother ever said to me was, "I don't see why you can't come back down here and write a column like Lewis Grizzard." Bad enough that people in New York often confused me with the now late Grizzard, the worst famous humorist of our time.

father was a pillar, and there was Brince Manning's faction. Manning was a rough-and-tumble politico who presented himself as antiestablishment. Neither of these factions was anywhere near the *Bird* on any conceivable spectrum, but somehow the Manning faction was accusing my father's faction of tolerating this filthy Commie rag. And here I was, Roy Jr., playing into their hands.

My father didn't explain any of this, he just sent me a page from the *Bird* with a note saying, "Now you see why this shouldn't be supported."

The page he sent contained a picture of Jesus holding a machine gun and saying, "Up against the wall, motherfucker."

Today, of course, it would not shock me much to hear of a mainstream rock band called Jesus Motherfucker. But at the time that was pretty startling.

But, hey, that's what you a send to a son who is a newspaper columnist? "Now you see . . . ?"

I didn't answer his letter. I wrote another column attacking anybody who was against the *Bird* for any reason.

If you're going to send your grown son a bullying letter, the least you can do is put some personal flavor into it.

I can see my father being a funnier *talker* than he generally let on at home, because he did show flashes of that. But I have never seen a word he *wrote* that would have been out of place in an interoffice memo.

My first wife, Ellen's, Texas grandfather, J. D. "Dunny" Kirven (for whom my son John Kirven was named), was a reserved person and a businessman—he made a bundle building levees along the Mississippi—but he wrote us funny little letters. Here's one to Ellen and me:

"Congratulations on the arrival of Miss [Ennis] Blount. We, here, are so happy the lady has arrived and is alright. You know Gammy has said all along that when you had children she wondered if it would be a possum, since she has such intelligent parents.

"All we need now is for Jolie to bring us about 4 cute pups, she must be pregnant as she has wet on the floor twice today, which is out of the ordinary."

And here's one to Ennis herself, six years later:

"Your pictures and your letter with Mommy's necktie gift to me came this morning, and we sure do like those pictures. That old boy Kirven looks like a fattning pig doesn't he? Tell Mommy we can hardly wait for you darlings to come to Texas to see us.

"Lots of love to you all from Gammy, Grandmother, Robin, Rusty [the next three are dogs], Jolie, Mollie, Frauline, the cats, and old Dunny."

Of course Dunny was retired by then and had the time to be whimsical.

Maybe my father sensed that he had to hold back so that I could achieve my destiny. (I actually think this about my children sometimes—should I disappoint them in some way that would be good for them? But it's too confusing.) Humorists tend to have highly vocal mothers and receding fathers. My father was prominent in many respects, but the most nearly interesting piece of writing that has come down to me from him is a diary he kept while touring Russia on a People-to-People exchange in the mid-sixties. The entire diary is 174 words long. The closest thing to an observation in it is "These people don't even realize what we have back home."

Salvador Dali's father was named Salvador Dali, and so was the father's first child, who died in infancy less than a year before the artist Dali was born. Dali was haunted throughout life by being looked at by his father as if he were someone else, by growing up with a picture of his dead name-sake brother on the wall over his bed and by being taken to see his brother's grave, with "Salvador Dali" on the headstone.

Lewis B. Puller Jr., son of the eminent World War II hero General Chesty Puller, tried to follow his father's footsteps in Vietnam, lost his legs doing it, wrote a memoir entitled *Fortunate Son* and killed himself.

Billy Tipton Jr., adoptive son of a well-known jazz musician, found his father on the floor after a heart attack and called paramedics, who discovered what no one, including twenty-five-year-old Billy Jr., had known: that Billy Sr. was a woman.

Morton Downey Jr., the vitriolic talk-show host of a few years ago, hated his crooner father Morton Sr., darling of radio's golden age, who would come home every three weeks and beat him with a long shoehorn carved out of an elephant trunk given him by Paul Whiteman.

My father never hit me. My mother spanked or switched me occasionally when I was little and contrary, but I can't picture my father hitting anybody. Though, come to think about it, there was a Sunday afternoon when we were all out for a Sunday drive after church. A car pulled alongside us, and apparently the driver said something drunkenly rude to my mother—I didn't hear it, I was probably sitting there wishing the hell I was somewhere else, somewhere interesting. My father chased the car down and made the man apologize. Cool.

Before Daddy worked for Edsel, he worked for Packard. I quote from a 1950 Packard Motor Car Company employee psychological profile, which Susan found among my father's papers:

> Mental alertness score ranks higher than 99% of persons of all ages and educational levels.
>
> Above-average word-usage ability.
>
> Tends to be cooperative, poised and confident. Possesses the ability to make decisions based on facts.
>
> Some readiness [?] and unevenness of response, sometimes accompanied by annoyance and faultfinding toward others. Temperament may be erratic and peevish at times.
>
> Some evasiveness or unwillingness to face reality, "passing the buck" and projecting blame on others.
>
> Strong attitudes, usually unfavorable, towards others. Intolerance and prejudice, often disguised as "high" standards and ideals.
>
> Few unsolved problems and absence of worry about them if they do exist. Usually stable, cooperative and well-adjusted to his work.

He was placed at the ninety-ninth percentile on intelligence, ninety-eighth on stability, fifth on tolerance.

And there was this: "Normal ways of thinking. Feelings are not intense."

Yet he no less than my mother could ooze intense, imperious disapproval. It wasn't as scary as my mother's, but it was scary enough. One Saturday afternoon when I was seventeen, I spent the afternoon hanging out with the girl next door, who was fifteen. I guess her parents weren't home. But we weren't dating or anything, and I was too nice to even think of making out with somebody who wasn't my girlfriend. She was my friend's girlfriend. We were just hanging out. When I came home my father glared at me as if I'd been doing something filthy. "What if your mother knew?" he said, and then he looked away.

Jeez, Dad.

Now I wish I *had* been making out. I wish I were making out right now. Making out in high school—with my girlfriend, Patti, a cocaptain of the majorettes—was great, troubled as I was about the unspeakable un-niceness of it.

One day during my freshman year in college my mother called to say that she wanted me to come home. My father was in the hospital with kidney trouble. Eventually he had to have one removed. And here's something terrible I had done:

I had sent him, in the hospital, a sick-comical get-well card that had a buzzard perched on the foot of a hospital bed. Did I not realize how sick he was? Was I trying to fend off realizing how sick he was? It was a stupid card to send, anyway. He was in danger of dying.

But did my mother call and say, "Son, I need you to be with me, your father is very sick, please come home and help"?

No. She called and said that Patti's mother had called her and told her that Patti and I had, when last we were in town together, made out very heavily in her living room.

I put myself in either mother's shoes. If I'd been Patti's mother, I would have run me off. If I'd been my mother, I would have said to Patti's, Well, why didn't you just run him off? Of course that is the most inoperative of clauses: If I'd been (anybody else).

What my mother did was tell me to come home, not because she wanted my support because my father was so sick, but because she needed to give me a talking-to about how I had embarrassed the family by making out.

I might have been *cured* of being a humorist if my mother had treated me like a real person from whom an appropriately feeling response could be expected. But no.

She was afraid I'd get somebody pregnant and my future would be ruined. A reasonable concern, but. . . . Listen, I know the sixties, for which I was born too soon, were extreme in their own way, but I'll tell you what, they beat the fifties, for which I was born just soon enough, all hollow. Once after a dance my mother found lipstick on my collar in the laundry hamper, showed it to me and said, with a furious, semi-oblique look on her face, "You're playing with dynamite!" Believe it or not, I had sense enough, even without any shred of birth-control information, to avoid teenage paternity. I was too intent on getting out of Decatur. It was too nice a place, I couldn't stand it. My parents made sure of that—so their approach to sex education worked, to my advantage though not to theirs.

I was going to be a humorist. On the national level. But the primary reason I would never have knocked anybody up was that I knew it would have killed my parents.

I didn't want to hurt them. I did, though. I left them, flat.

Theodore John Kaczynski, the Unabomber, developed his love of nature on camping trips with his father, Theodore R., who taught him such survival skills as how to kill and eat a porcupine. But the father was called Ted Sr., or Turk. The son was called Young Ted or Teddy. Ted Sr. committed suicide. Teddy stayed away from the funeral.

Daddy would never have killed himself. Well, people said he did, from overwork, from giving too much to his church, his community, his work. Although people tended to see me as presidential in high school and college (I was nice, and affable, and made good grades), my father's example has helped to keep me from doing anything civic. Now that my children are grown, I don't even live anywhere specific. Nobody ever tries to appoint me to a committee.

But I certainly didn't stay away from his funeral. I was a pallbearer. I cried. At a certain level I was relieved: I was freer—though God knows there was still my mother—I was more nearly free to write.

John J. Royster confessed to four brutal attacks on women (one fatal) in New York City. When he was twelve, his father, John P. Royster, who had little contact with him after early boyhood, murdered a woman who had spurned him. The son, also spurned by a woman, seemed to be taking it out on his victims. From prison the father said the son was "a chip off the old block." Papers (except the scrupulous *Times*) referred to the son as John Jr. A former girlfriend: "He said he had the same power that his father had, and that it was passed down to males in his family from generation to generation. He said they could all read minds and see the future."

Eric Star Smith Sr., on a fishing trip, decided his sons were possessed and beheaded fourteen-year-old Eric Star Smith Jr. on a roadside while the younger child watched and motorists drove past. Truckers reported seeing the father on the side of the road, hacking at the head. When the police came, Eric Sr. raced away in his van, throwing his son's head out the window about a mile down the highway.

In 1973 John C. Bradley Jr. killed his parents and was declared insane.

His mother was found in the driveway with a stab wound in her back; his father was found sitting in front of the TV, the back of his head smashed by a sledgehammer.

Ray J. Macaro Jr. was hospitalized afer allegedly murdering his father and two aunts, then, in a feud over the deed to the house, setting the family home on fire.

Thomas Sullivan Jr., fourteen, Jefferson Township, New Jersey, after having visions of Satan ordering him to kill his family, stabbed his mother to death and set the living room couch afire, apparently in an effort to burn down the house and kill his father and ten-year-old brother.

Hulon Mitchell Jr., of Enid, Oklahoma, became a sect leader in Florida, calling himself Yahweh ben Yahweh or God the Son of God, not to say God Jr. He was found guilty of conspiracy in the murders of "white devils" and of firebombing an entire block of Delray Beach.

Founding a sect is the last thing I would do. I'm more of a guest-observer type, bordering on sidekick—I'll appear on my friend Garrison Keillor's radio show, I'll do a turn on my friend Al Franken's TV special, I'll write movie dialogue for my friend Bill Murray (which he will improve upon). But I won't create anything but a one-man show. I did one off-Broadway, *Roy Blount's Happy Hour and a Half* (no room for a Jr. in a title like that), just stood up there talking for ninety minutes. Then I'll move on.

It's hard for me even to bring together a book! I have all these random notes:

Dan Mayfield says it kills a tree to shoot milk into it. Loggers slip around and cut a plug in an environmentally protected tree trunk and inject milk, because when it dies they can cut it. Called milking trees.

Song Title: "A Gentleman Doesn't Boil His Handkerchief for Soup."

Personal ad: "I have in the not far-distant past suffered the loss of my dog. I will keep your dog gratis, no fee, for any time in my apartment."

"You won a match the first time you ever played?"
"Yep."
"What was the score?"
"It was 0–6, 0–6, 115–113, 6–0, 6–0. That was back before tie-breakers. I started catching on to the game, that third set."

The word *text* derives from "Texas." We first find it used in an anonymous antideconstructionist cowboy poem entitled "I Feel Like I Been
Read Hard and Put Up Wet."

They don't gather into anything. Here is the type of distinction I have
as a writer: I believe I am the only American writer—indeed, the only
writer internationally—who has both gotten drunk with Ernie "Fats"
Holmes and cracked up John Ashbery.

Ernie "Fats" Holmes was a 260-pound defensive tackle for the Pittsburgh Steelers. I spent the 1973 season hanging out with the Steelers, and
wrote my first book, *About Three Bricks Shy of a Load,** about that experience. After it came out, I sat down next to Fats in the locker room,
expecting a friendly talk, and he said in a suppressed furious growl,
"What'd you put that shit in your book for?"

I thought to myself, Uh-oh. I remembered a time in training camp
when he had come up to a table where I was drinking depth charges (a
shot glass of whiskey dropped into a glass of beer) with some other players. He fixed a mild-mannered rookie defensive back with a sulfurous glare
and demanded, "Where's my brother?"

Nobody at the table—least of all the rookie—had any idea what he
meant. The rookie's shot glass clunked softly on the bottom of his beer glass.

"What'd you do with my brother?" Fats insisted. The rookie said, "I'll
go find him," in a strangled voice, slipped away and never returned. By
that I mean he gave up football.

"What shit?" I asked Fats as lightly as possible.

"Said I had the mind of a six-year-old child."

What I had done, in the book, had been to quote Holmes as saying,
over a number of martinis, "Ever since the incident"—the time when he
broke down under the pressure of personal problems and started shooting
from his car at trucks and eventually ran off into some woods wearing flip-
flops and inflicted a bullet wound in the leg of a policeman pursuing him
from overhead by helicopter—"I'm praying. With the mind of a child and
the brains of a sixty-year-old warrior."

*If I were doing a dissertation on my work, it would surely not escape me (although it
did until recently) that the titles of my books—*Not Exactly What I Had in Mind; One
Fell Soup, or I'm Just a Bug on the Windshield of Life; Now, Where Were We?; What
Men Don't Tell Women; Camels Are Easy, Comedy's Hard*—have tended to imply
incompleteness, noncommunication, gaps.

I tried to assure Fats that he'd said it, and that I'd been struck by how poetic a statement it was. To tell the truth, I was less terrified physically than disappointed as an appreciator of eloquence. It was as if I had quoted Wordsworth as saying, "I wandered lonely as a cloud," and he had chewed me out for accusing him of not having any friends.

He was not to be mollified. "Get away," he said, and I did.

"Don't mess with Fats," people warned me. "He's running on a forty-watt bulb." But I hated to let it go. I believed that he was, essentially, a nice person. I was standing in the aisle of the team plane when I saw him walking toward me. The aircraft seemed to shift slightly from side to side as his left foot, then his right foot, advanced.

"Fats . . . ," I said. He moved me aside with the backs of two fingers of his left hand.

Then, the afternoon before the 1974 Super Bowl, I dropped by a hotel room where the defensive line—the Steel Curtain, they were called—were drinking quantities of Mateus and dancing the bump with wives and dates. The first person I walked head-on into was Fats.

"Hello, Archenemy," he said.

I said the soppiest thing I have ever said to anybody, maybe. To any male person, anyway. (If only I'd been willing to say more soppy things to female persons over the years . . . but they seemed so obvious.) "I'm not your enemy," I said. "I'm a good man. And so are you." We exchanged a soul grip and were friendly again after that.

So—it occurs to me just now—what my father told me when I said I was going to get divorced came in handy after all.

John Ashbery, on the other hand, is a distinguished poet, whose work is so highly refined in a thing-in-itself sort of way that I've given up on trying to give you a representative whiff by way of quotation. Suffice it to say that his poetry to my verse is as Hyperion to a tater. It was he who called Elizabeth Bishop "a writer's writer's writer." Which makes him . . . even more literary. He was in the audience recently when, in a fund-raising talk for the Academy of American Poets, I proposed a radical reconfiguration of the entire canon of poetry in English.

No, not to add my own verse to it, though I do believe . . .

I realize that this is a touchy issue, one that pits advocates of multi-culturality against defenders of everything that the Visigoths tried so hard to tear down. Perhaps I should feel reluctant, as a white male, to commit myself on this issue until I am dead.

But I've got to be honest with you. I believe that, yes, there should be a canon—a body of required reading that must appear on syllabi so that college students, having read or at least purchased these texts, can feel fully and truly justified in confining their cultural pursuits henceforward to watching cheesy television—but that there should be such a canon only if I am in it. Now. While I can enjoy it.

Not so much for the honor as for the long-term book sales. Since Dante never pops up on the best-seller lists, I assume that *The Divine Comedy* never moves as briskly in a given week as *All I Really Need to Know I Learned in Kindergarten* did for so long. But surely canonization—even though so many students buy books secondhand—would amount to a steady annuity. Like, if you're in formal-wear rental and someone is buried in one of your tuxes.

I don't mean to suggest that I should be the only author canonized. I would also welcome the following:

- Some friends and acquaintances of mine. Otherwise a certain chill would develop in my relations with writer friends and acquaintances, which would be a shame. Though I would understand their feelings.
- Not all of my friends and acquaintances, though. That would take some of the charm out of it for me. I do not specify which friends and acquaintances should be immortalized and which not, because I would rather not be put in that position.
- *Silas Marner.* I feel this work should be included for the same reason that I feel the military draft should be reinstated: it stared me in the face during my puberty, why should young people today get off easy?
- A booklet, which I could get together myself for the forthcoming school year, entitled "Deconstruction as Dyslexia." The fly in anointment is that once you become canon fodder, academic critics will be taking notice of you—which is to say they will be demonstrating, to their satisfaction, that you, the author, do not, in any rigorous sense, exist.

I do exist. If I don't say it, who will?

In my remarks to the Academy of American Poets, however, I proposed not to add to the canon, but to boil it down. There are certain short poems that are sublime because they don't make any sense. For instance, Dr. Johnson's:

> *If a man who turnips cries,*
> *Cry not when his father dies,*
> *It's a sure sign he would rather*
> *Have a turnip than a father.*

But there is another short poem that is sublime because it makes all the sense in the world. Conveniently, it is often the first or second poem in anthologies of English literature. It's anonymous, dates back to the early sixteenth century. That poem is:

> *O Western wind, when wilt thou blow,*
> *The small rain down can rain?*
> *Christ! That my love were in my arms*
> *And I in my bed again.*

All the sense in the world. There has been something of a falling off in the English poetic tradition ever since. What I proposed was that the canon be boiled down to all those poems that can be rounded off in the same way. For instance:

Keats:

> *When I have fears that I may cease to be*
>   *Before my pen has glean'd my teeming brain—*
> *Christ! that my love were in my arms,*
>   *And I in my bed again.*

Matthew Arnold:

> *And we are here as on a darkling plain—*
>   *Christ! that my love were in my arms*
>   *And I in my bed again.*

Browning:

> *And did you once see Shelley plain,*
> *And did he stop and speak to you*
> *And did you speak to him again?*
> *Christ! that my love were in my arms,*
> *And I in my bed again.*

Donne:

> *When my grave is broke up again*
> *Some second guest to entertain,*
> *Christ! that my love were in my arms,*
> *And I in my bed again.*

James Thomson:

> *When Britain first, at Heaven's command,*
> *Arose from out the azure main.*
> *This was the charter of the land,*
> *And guardian angels sung this strain:*
> > *Christ! that our loves were in our arms*
> > *And we in our beds again.*

James Whitcomb Riley:

> *'Long about December, poppin' corn with Liza Jane,*
> *I found myself a-thinkin', oncet er mebbe twicet,*
> > *"Christ!*
> *That my love were in my arms and I in my bed again."*

Afterward, Ned Chase (who happens to be Chevy Chase's father) came up to me and said, "You cracked John Ashbery up."

So didn't that make me, just for a moment at least, a writer's writer's writer's writer? Natural-born storyteller, is it? Pah!

The trouble is (well, one trouble is), the audience that knows who both Ernie "Fats" Holmes and John Ashbery are probably numbers into the low tens. If you think I'm scattered, how about y'all?

Whereas my father's savings and loan was sort of a sect, in a nice sense. Savings and loans have a bad name now, but in the sixties and early seventies, when my father was in the business, it was about as populist as capitalism can get. I bristle when people tell me in a certain condescending-from-the-left tone that they've been surprised to learn that my father was a banker. My daddy wasn't no banker! He didn't own Decatur Federal Savings and Loan . . . well, I'll tell you more about it when I get a little older. Bear in mind that in the arc of this narrative, I've only recently been born.

Maybe the key to the junior thing is *Shane*. If there is a cultural achievement that even other nations' culturati will concede to America, it is the Western movie, and *Shane* is the most famous Western. Some call it the essential one. What is *Shane* about? The historical conflict between cattlemen and sodbusters over whether the frontier will stay range or be turned into plots? The necessity of standing up, together, against oppression? The inevitable victory of good guys, who resort only reluctantly to violence, over sadistic bullies? (So what happened in Vietnam?) No. Those are cherished American themes, all right, but in *Shane* they're boilerplate.

Brandon De Wilde is the young son of a sodbuster. Alan Ladd is Shane, the gunfighter who wants to retire but straps on his iron again to do the requisite kick-ass thing for the farmers. What we remember is the boy crying, "Come back, Shane," at the end, as Shane disappears from his life.

The screenplay is by A. B. Guthrie Jr. (His autobiography does not mention the Jr. factor, except to reveal that people have always called him Buddy or Bud.) Ladd, the star, and George Stevens, the director and producer, were seniors—fathers of juniors* who would go on to film careers of their own but were just coming into manhood at the time *Shane* was made. Van Heflin, who plays the sodbuster father, was born Emmett Evan Heflin Jr.

The screenplay adapts the novel of the same name by Jack Schaefer, which—although I found it in the children's section of a bookstore—is both subtler and more substantial than the movie. The fight scenes are

---

*Alan Ladd Jr., known as "Laddie," was expunged from his father's bios and cropped out of family photographs when his father left his mother to marry another woman. When the second wife became pregnant, Louella Parsons reported that if the baby was a boy, it would be named Alan Jr.

nastier and better. (We might call the movie a junior that outshone its superior source.) In the novel, the father is Joe Starrett and the boy—as Joe introduces him to Shane—is "Robert MacPherson Starrett. Too much name for a boy. I make it Bob." In the movie, the boy is called Joey or Little Joe.

Most of the movie's characters come straight from the book, but a key one is different. In the book, Frank Torrey is just one of the other sodbusters. In the movie, "Stonewall" Torrey is the smallest man but the biggest talker, an Alabaman who swears "Nobody's going to buffalo me." In the book, Ernie Wright is the farmer whom Wilson, the cattlemen's hired bad-guy gun, provokes into gunplay (by suggesting that his mother was an Indian), thereby lighting the fuse for the final showdown between Wilson and Shane.

In the movie, it's Torrey. "They tell me they call you Stonewall," says Wilson—played memorably by Jack Palance. "I guess they name all of that Southern trash after old Stonewall."

Torrey realizes that he's in over his head with Wilson, but he's not backing down. He responds, in a pinched voice, "Who'd they name you after, or don't you know?"

"I'm saying Stonewall himself was trash," Wilson says.

Torrey can't stand it any longer, he goes for his gun, Wilson outdraws him and shoots him down in the mud.

In the movie, so much is about who you're named after. And Torrey is played by that quintessential movie little guy, Elisha Cook Jr.

You know who remade Shane, as Pale Rider? Clint Eastwood Jr.

But forget the name factor as such. America is "an immature culture," groused an Englishman I knew after he found himself unable to communicate with his New York cabdriver (who was probably from Biafra) in English.

America is always developing. America is adolescent. Therefore we romanticize fathers. Expect them to be more than they are. It goes without saying that those of us who are mothers and daughters do. That is so everywhere. But in America, so do men: fathers as well as sons expect fathers to be more dashing.

Hey, there are no flies on Joe Starrett Sr.—a strong, brave, ambitious, hard-working, caring family man and cultivator of the soil. And yet Joe Sr. himself acknowledges quick-drawing Shane in his fringed buckskins to be a better man. And Little Joe calls for Shane to come back, he needs Shane. Shane is the embodiment of being big without having to grow up.

• • •

Richard E. Byrd Jr., namesame of Admiral Richard Byrd, famed polar explorer, was discovered dead in a Baltimore warehouse in 1988, age sixty-eight. He lived his whole life in his father's shadow, obsessed with building a museum to his father's memory. My father deserves a better monument than this book, so far. But I'm not finished yet.

I'm going on and on about this junior thing. But if there's nothing to it—why do I, a junior, feel compelled to make so much of it?

Do you fault that bottom line? Is it any less convincing than Shakespeare's?

If this be error and upon me proved,
I never writ, nor no man ever loved.

And consider this:

My father called Susan "Petunia." She remembers that fondly. Try as I might, I can't remember him calling me anything.

I can remember my mother calling me "Bucky" and "Bubba" and "Son," but I can't remember her ever calling me by my name. And try as I might, when I think of my father, amiable, pillar-of-the-community Roy Sr., big old authoritative gray head, general overall reassuring presence—he was organized, he founded things; to this day in Decatur, Georgia, where I grew up, most of the tall buildings have plaques with his name as head of the building committee. . . .

Well, I guess I can remember him calling me "Son," maybe. But I can't quite hear him saying it.

And here's another junior angle: my maternal grandfather, the progenitor of the family curse (if you hold the man responsible in this sort of thing), whom I never knew at all, was George Henry Floyd Jr.

But of that more later.

It is certainly possible to be a well-adjusted junior. I know no one more widely celebrated for his infectious niceness than Ken Griffey Jr., who is called Junior the way Ruth was called Babe, and is generally regarded as the best player in baseball. When Junior was seven he took 277 aspirins because of tension between himself and Ken Senior, and thought about killing himself "with my father's gun or something." But in time they became the first father and son in big-league history to play on the same team. To be a teammate of your father, and better than he is, and it's okay all around! Can there be an American son or father who would not feel that he had died and gone to heaven? Junior (as he is called by his teammates) was briefly the highest-paid player in the game. Asked by Murray Chass of the *New York Times* "if the concept of being No. 1 enters his thinking," Bonds replied, "No, why should it?"

Chass: "Ego?"

Junior: "Don't have one."*

He added that it never bothered him to go unrecognized. "I can go into a Dairy Queen, walk in, walk out, nothing's said. . . . Because I'm Ken Griffey, you're supposed to let me eat here, get this for me? I don't need that.

"If you're busy, you're busy. I'm not going to ask you to alter your business because of me. . . . That's just the way I was brought up, I guess. My dad has never done that—'Hi, I'm Ken Griffey, I want to eat here.' "

I was brought up the same way, and I am the same way. Not that I am likely to be recognized in a Dairy Queen, but if I were, the only reason I would enjoy it would be that it would bolster my self-loathing. In a Dairy Queen it's my job to notice things, not to be noticed. I never had the sense that my father tried to be a big man.

I don't know that I even needed him to notice me, in any very personal way. I knew he had his eye on me, and I mine on him (rather differently, of course, but not all that differently), from a distance. God knows he never told me he loved me, but it never occurred to me that fathers were supposed to. Mothers did, and as you got older it made you uncomfortable. Up to a certain age, I guess my father and I kissed each other, because I can remember my mother saying to me as he and I hugged awkwardly, "You better not stop kissing each other." I don't think we ever kissed after that. It astonished me to see my friend Edwin kidding around with his father, the two of them poking at each other playfully. It also astonished me, when I'd visit home in my twenties, to see Susan, who had become a

---

*Joseph Cornell, the reclusive, very eccentric assemblage artist, was the sixth male in his line—his father, who died when young Joe was thirteen, being the fifth—to be christened Joseph I. Cornell. He never learned, according to his biographer (who didn't either), what the *I* stood for. He lived his whole life with his mother, who continued after the father's death to go by the name Mrs. Joseph Cornell. If you are a junior, your mother is, of course, Mrs. (insert your name here) Sr.

teenager (she and I had played together some, making ourselves a house out of packing crates, for instance, but as children we were never close enough to the same age to fight or share our concerns),* fondly, cheerfully, prolongedly brushing my father's (thick, wavy, distinguished-silver) hair. He steered her into computer work—for Decatur Federal, to begin with—and she has done very well in that field.

My father's father, Noah Charles Blount, was a carpenter and small-time contractor, a smart man (one of the few things I remember my father telling me about him was that he could calculate the square footage of a complicated roof in his head), who could find no work during the Depression except for nailing up the windows of houses whose mortgages had been foreclosed upon. My father loved carpentry all his life, and wanted to be an architect, but my grandfather advised him against it because of the Depression. My father was never really happy in his work—executive for Libby Foods, Packard Motor Car Company, Ford Motor Company (the Edsel)—until he got into savings and loan, lending people money to build homes.

Once, when I was nine or ten, I stayed with my paternal grandparents in Jacksonville for a week. Louallie and Noah (which she pronounced "Noey"). I didn't have any grandparents on my orphan mother's side, and Noah and Louallie Blount weren't what you'd call forthcoming. The only things I much enjoyed doing at their house were climbing their chinaberry tree and digging in the sandy dirt for doodlebugs. Louallie didn't want me playing with the kids in their neighborhood because she regarded them as trash. To be sure, the younger ones ran around in dirty underpants or even no clothes at all, and I wasn't much of a mixer anyway. Once I made myself a caveman costume out of Spanish moss, and learned that chiggers live in Spanish moss. Just on the other side of a canebrake next to my grandparents' house was a colored neighborhood. It was clear that I

---

*Now we share news and feelings about our breakups (Susan is single too), our kids (although we have never since childhood lived in the same town, we always spend Christmas together with Ennis and Kirven, who grew up playing frequently with Susan's two stepchildren, Audrey and Stuart, and Audrey is still one of Ennis's, and, for that matter, Kirven's, best friends), dogs (Mumu got *very* close to dogs—"You get so attached to them," she would say, "and then they die"—and so do Susan and I, and Kirven) and the abiding mystery of our mother. The other day Susan told me she'd had a nightmare that Mumu was mad at her, she couldn't figure out *what for*. The only person who ever expressed real raw hatred toward me, I told her, reminded me of someone as he was doing it, and I realized it was Mumu. She knew exactly what I meant. "Venomous," she said.

shouldn't go there. A black woman would come and do their washing out-doors in a big kettle with a fire under it. I watched from the chinaberry tree as a black boy rolled a hoop down the sandy street with a stick. One afternoon my grandfather set out to get a wasp's nest off the roof, which sounded like fun, but when I started to go with him, he looked at me like he wished I wouldn't. "Noah, remember about Roy," Louallie said. I've often wondered what she meant exactly—I guess she was reminding him that he wished he'd done more with my father when he was a boy. He let me tag along, but it was by no means a shared moment.

I admired my grandfather. Partly because of his hands—the most busted-up fingers I've ever seen on a person, and I've studied old catchers', fighters', bluesmen's hands. His fingernails looked like cracked bits of oys-ter shell. He made things with his hands—a walking stick with a brass doorknob for a handle, a paring knife whose handle and blade and rivets he'd fashioned out of bits of scrap. He didn't show me how to make any-thing, though, and he cared even less than my father did about the things I was interested in: sports, books, radio comedians.

Partly because he was so *resolutely* unforthcoming—and yet he was, I think, the only person I ever heard my mother admit was sweet to her. He called a bicycle a "wheel" and pronounced *put* like *putt*. My mother once said, "Poppa, why do you pronounce *put* that way?", and he stood her down, politely: *"P, u, t: put."* To rhyme with *but*. My mother was pleased somehow by that bit of personal spelling, often mentioned it—with maybe a touch of condescension, but mostly affection—when Poppa's name came up. I can get similarly adamant about pronunciations, for instance (*pace* my third-grade teacher and highly educated people who have disagreed with me since), that distinct, audible, evident-to-the-tongue *h* sound before the *w* sound in *what*.

Maybe I made Noah feel undereducated. A while ago I ran into some-body who said his sister used to baby-sit for me. "She says you had a smart mouth," he said. I was startled.

Maybe my grandfather, the carpenter, sensed what I am always afraid people are going to sense about me—that I don't live sufficiently in the physical world, that I am somehow cheating, taking the verbal way, the humorous way, out. Doomed to make a living being silly.

Maybe he regarded me as an idle fantasizer, which I guess is what I was. I can remember striking poses in his yard with a football, a basketball and a baseball in my arms, imagining that I was a three-sport immortal.

CHAPTER 20

Ball

I can't explain it in simple terms, but . . . that's the reason I
didn't quit, because a little man inside me never went away. I
knew I could do it because I used to go in the outfield and throw
the ball three hundred feet. That's the reason I didn't quit,
because a little man inside me never went away.

—STEVE CARLTON, PITCHER (NOW RETIRED)

I might have lived a more purposeful life if I had played some position
other than outfield in my first years of organized baseball, in 1952 and
'53, when I was ten and eleven.

Great demands were not made on Little League outfielders in my
time. The best players were pitchers, shortstops and, to some extent,
catchers and first basemen. Our park lacked fences, and we outfielders
were expected mainly to keep the long ball from going to ridiculous
lengths. Nothing throws off the tempo of a game more than a winded and
perhaps even tearful outfielder still scrambling, long after the bases have
cleared, to retrieve the horsehide from a crowd of slightly smaller children
under a jungle gym, as he half hears distant cries from the game he had
been involved in:

"Use another ball. Let's go on without him."

So basically you kept the ball in front of you, or you regarded it as
gone.

I took part in the second Little League game ever played in Decatur,
Georgia, and I caught one fly ball in two years in the outfield. For a while I
filled my time in the field by chattering to the pitcher: "Come, baby, come,
boy, you the baby, you the boy, humbabyhumboy." My chatter reached its
apogee when Tom Hay was pitching. I would shout:

HeyTomHayheybabyTomTom, hey,
Hay. Humbaby

182

TombabyTomHaybabybabyhumTomTomHay
humTomTom You the baby, you the one.
Fir't by'im baby, heyTomHay, hey, baby,
heyTomTomTomTomHayBabyheybabyboy.
Hey, TomTomHay, hey,

until our coach called me in from left and told me in a nice way that he felt my chatter was one of the main reasons Tom had hit so many batsmen that inning. After that I was less active on defense, and began to muse.

People assume that what is wrong with every male American is that his father played catch with him feelingly and then left him to figure out everything else himself. But my father did not invest much emotion in baseball either. I don't recall ever playing catch or following a pennant race with him.

I played catch with both of my kids, and taught Kirven to hit. I don't know what the record is for Earliest Age, Making Contact, but Kirven was fifteen months old. I was pitching. Then, okay, he and I both were probably pressing, overthinking there for a while, and I believe he went zero for the whole age of two. Sophomore jinx they call it. At three he began to find his stroke, spraying the ball around, and we started using a real baseball, and I remember the afternoon in Waxahachie, Texas, visiting his maternal grandmother, Christmas of '71—jeez, he hit a *shot*, right back at me, I just got my glove up in time. His mother and I were in the process of breaking up.

Now he's better than I ever was, looks like Darryl Strawberry out there in softball, so that's that until I'm eighty and his son has to play catch with me, chase down my weird little loopy tosses, and I'll fill my grandson in on life outside baseball. Paternal-line advice (aside from "Get in front of the ball") often skips a generation. When you're a son, you resist believing what your father tells you he knows. And until he's a grandfather he's not sure he knows it. My grandfather showed me some things, like how to draw a star and a box and a rabbit, and a face in one continuous line, that I adopted absolutely. I still draw a star and a box and a rabbit the way he taught me, and my children admire, but do not imitate, the way I draw a face in one continuous line. Most of the things I picked up from my father were by osmosis, filtered through Oedipal reservations.

My father was a business executive and a Depression survivor who didn't have much time for sports when he was a boy because he worked several part-time jobs to help support his younger siblings. When I was a boy his recreations were catching fish to fry and doing needful carpentry in the home. In one of my strongest visual recollections of him, he is awash in sweat, gritty with dust and almost violently absorbed in ripping out plaster and lath to expand the kitchen, and my mother is nagging him to take me down to the local swimming pool to teach me to swim. He is reluctant to tear himself away from his handiwork, but he does, and I have a vague memory of thrashing toward him over gradually increasing distances (very gradually increasing, and he seems distracted) of chlorinated water. His father—a carpenter and small contractor who, as I have mentioned, talked him out of his true calling, designing and building houses, because of the Depression—had taught him to swim by throwing him out of a rowboat.

Perhaps because of this heritage, I resist lessons: prefer to learn how to do things by plunging in and doing them less and less clearly wrong. My father was passably familiar with sports, and he must have played some ball, because I remember running around at a very early age with his old, cracked, hardly-any-webbing glove. And I remember dancing around the house in anticipation of his taking me to see the Atlanta Crackers (Southern Association, Double-A) in old Ponce de Leon Park.

I had read somewhere that in America, the land of the free, I had the right to throw a pop bottle at the umpire, and I was disappointed when my father told me I couldn't. However, I liked the bleachers, which is probably where I first heard raffish talk: rank, beery guys betting on every pitch and yelling at the umpires. (If these guys weren't throwing things, I had to admit that my father must be right.) Also yelling at the players. Not only at the visitors, who might have been the Memphis Chicks or the Birmingham Barons or the Chattanooga Lookouts or the New Orleans Pelicans or the Little Rock Travelers (also called the Pebs, short for Pebbles), but also at Crackers who popped up or booted plays. These guys in the bleachers seemed to feel more on top of things than the players. I didn't quite approve of this presumption, but it was striking; when I got into sportswriting, the press box was like that.

My father, while affable with persons of all classes, was above such contentiousness. He saved it for business. When someone under him at Decatur Federal said, "We're getting our share of the market," he said, "I don't want just ours, I want part of somebody else's." Otherwise he was above the fray. Didn't unload much emotion—even on our dogs. Mother would say, "I always dread getting a new puppy, because I get so involved with the dern things and then when they get old and die, it's so hard." The dogs always "worshiped" Daddy, as my mother would observe, even though he never gave them much affection, at least by our family's standards. He knew them, though. One of the last things he said before his sudden fatal heart attack was that he thought he heard Chipper—a mixed (like all our dogs) black-and-white terrier, who had been dead for some years at that point—barking. Once Chipper was looking off into the distance as if she were turning something important over in her mind. "Chipper," I said, "you've got a *tail* hanging out of your mouth." I relieved her of it. It appeared to be all that was left of an extremely desiccated mouse. Chipper looked embarrassed. "Chipper is humiliated and sick," Daddy said. A send-up—a joke between Daddy and himself, or maybe even between Daddy and Chipper—of the way the rest of us projected emotions onto our pets. We took a great deal of comic pleasure in the way Chipper would hang out the car window and bark viciously at cows we drove past. One day, all of a sudden, Daddy stopped the car and let her leap out the window and go after a herd. Chipper ran, barking at the top of her voice, until she came up beside an actual cow, whereupon, realizing the animal's size, she turned without missing a beat and ran back to the car, still barking. "Are you satisfied now?" he asked her. Perspective. I suspect the bleacherites were of Chipper's disposition. After the game you could run down onto the field and ask for autographs; I remember doing this once and being flatly ignored by Dixie Walker, the manager. The Crackers had several old Dodgers who were playing out the string after their big-league careers: Whitlow Wyatt, Hugh Casey, Kirby Higbe. Crackers who went on to the majors included future Hall-of-Famer Eddie Mathews (who hit a ball all the way over the magnolia tree on the bank in deepest center field), Art Fowler, Leo Cristante, Chuck Tanner and Dick Donovan, a power-hitting pitcher who once struck a 117-mile home run: it cleared the right field billboards and landed in a freight train going to Chattanooga.

In my first year covering baseball I saw Eddie Mathews in a coffee shop. I started to go over and tell him that I had been a big fan of his since he was eighteen and I was eight, but then he ordered coffee in a voice that sounded like a backhoe scooping riprap. Here, clearly, was a man whose hangovers dwarfed mine.

But when I was a boy I planned to bridge the gap between me and the players by growing up to become one. Through two years of indifferent

Little League outfielding I waited to develop, and when I was twelve I became an all-star third baseman, like Eddie Mathews. My father never discussed my baseball career plans with me except once when he suggested I might want to become a sportswriter. I chuckled inwardly. The first person I distinctly remember playing catch with is myself. This may be how my personality started to get scattered, because neither of us was me. I was in the side yard bouncing a tennis ball off the side of the house, being a pitcher throwing at the corners of a bush that defined the strike zone up against our house's stone foundation, and then I was the fielder scooping up the ground ball, and then I was the first baseman digging out the throw. Or I would deliver a fastball that was a little too sweet in the bush there, so I'd move in and throw the ball up against the wooden part of the house at such an angle that it drove me back, back, all the way to the drainage ditch, where I would make an incredible leaping catch.

I did play with other children. We played games in my side yard, with all the bases but no right field (that's where the woods were), no left field (that's where the house was, but there was a good deal of left-center beyond it) and no catcher (therefore no stealing). Third base was a big square can in which my father carried out clinkers from the furnace until we converted from coal to natural gas, and in which I would sometimes keep a captured box turtle for several days (with lettuce). Clinkers were nasty, spiked chunks of noncombustible coal-impurity residue. Traces of clinker cropped up in the yard, so we didn't slide much.

We also played flies and grounders: one player threw the ball up and hit it until one of the others caught three flies and six grounders and got to take a turn batting. Or roll-a-bat: one player threw up the ball and hit it and then laid the bat down in front of the plate, and the fielders tried to throw the ball so as to hit the bat and take it over.

But I was the only one who read baseball history. My father brought me, from one of his business trips, a book called *Big-Time Baseball*, in which I learned about the greatest players of all time, and the great moments, and the screwballs—I can remember a picture of Rube Waddell from that book more clearly than I can remember the faces of the boys I played with. I don't think any of my friends had done enough baseball scholarship to know about the Hall of Fame, which I planned to be a member of, and I don't think any of them played baseball solitaire the way I did. One day I was absorbed in throwing the ball up and hitting it to certain spots so as to create an imaginary game, when I heard someone say, "Is that as far as you can hit it?"

I looked up and it was Mr. Elliott, our neighbor from across the street, the semipro softball pitcher. His daughter, Jerry Lynn, was a friend of mine, and sometimes we would go to his games, in which he struck nearly everybody out. He threw a rise ball that I can still see; it would seem to upshift in midair like Michael Jordan.

That day Mr. Elliott came over, I'll bet he was wanting to show a boy some stuff. His son, Neil, was still just a little kid. But I didn't have sense enough to be responsive; my horizons were too unreal. I muttered something and Sambo Elliott went back home. Years later I attended a ceremony honoring him as one of the first members of the Softball Hall of Fame.

I would also make up box scores featuring my name and several imagined or borrowed ones. I remember once when my friend Francis Rowe happened to see one of those box scores, with Blount batting third and Rowe fourth. I think Blount was four for five that day (the hardest thing was keeping Blount's batting average within the bounds of credibility) and Rowe got only a couple of hits. Francis gave me a funny look, whether because of the disparity in hits or because of finding himself statistically fictionalized. "You hit more home runs than I do," I said lamely. By that time I was far gone into what I might call—if that movie weren't so soppy—the field of dreams.

I spent a lot of time looking for balls I had hit, in my reverie, into the woods beyond center field. Poking around under old leaves, looking for an old ball that was tan and scuffed or even covered with friction tape instead of horsehide; sometimes turning up a moldy brick-hard relic lost many rains before. A mildewed ball is an awful thing, but there's something to be said for the feel of a soft, scuffed one, and even one of those black taped-up jobs had a certain distinctive tactility, until the tape began to unwind and get dirty on the sticky side so that you had to keep interrupting play to cut off a bit of the tape, and the ball got smaller and smaller. The game itself is complex enough without the ball becoming a problem.

One day at school, during recess (in the, I don't know, second grade?), we were playing football, and somebody mentioned baseball, and I said, "I hate baseball," and then it dawned on me that I didn't. Not much of an anecdote, but it seems significant that I remember very few snatches of conversation from grade school and that is one of them. Another, curiously parallel, fragment has floated up, and I'm sure that I do remember that one, because I'd rather not.

I'm standing in the same spot where I remember saying I didn't like baseball. I'm telling Jody, the prettiest girl in my class (I think this may actually be first grade), that I hate Maylene (we will call her), and to my surprise Jody is not siding with me but coming on the great liberal—demanding to know why I hate Maylene. It hits me that I hate Maylene because she is dumb, rednecky and bad-looking; and what kind of person does that make me? Still, today, I remember a resentful look on poor old Maylene's boney-nosed face (maybe she was listening to my conversation with Jody) that makes me wince. So maybe I have transformed the memory of saying I hated Maylene, and then realizing I shouldn't, into a memory of saying I hated baseball and then realizing I loved it. I was an American boy. Maybe I had a mean streak (to be fair, Maylene was not sweet-tempered), but I had love in my heart for baseball.

Here's a moment I remember from my earliest playing days, second grade, I guess. I'm just learning the game. My position is what we called "hindcatcher." (In his autobiography, Jimmy Carter says that when he was growing up in Georgia they used that term to refer to a boy who stood behind the catcher in case of passed balls, but it was our term for catcher.) With a big run on base I allow a pitch to get away from me—a long, long way away from me—and I'm forever trying to get a handle on it, and the guy comes all the way around to score, and my teammates yell at me. My friend David Leveritt (who later died piloting an air force jet) runs up to me and says, "I know what you were doing. You were trying to pull that trick in the story." We had read a story in class about an unpopular boy who won his fellows over to him by letting a ball get past him, luring the runner off base and then throwing him out.

"Yeah," I say. Lying like a dog.

I hustled. I ran things out and slid hard and got my uniform dirty and held the ball down in front of the base so the runner had to slide into it and I stayed down on the ball to dig those short hops out. I liked to have a layer of clay dust and the odd blade of grass stuck to me by sweat.

I thought too much. They tell you to "stay within yourself" in sports, just do what you're capable of, but that was too depressing a prospect for me. Once, before a game, Johnny Tingle, our second baseman, and I were reflecting on not having turned a double play all season, and I took the position that a triple play ought to be pretty easy to pull off. You'd just have to have two slow runners on base and nobody out and a sharp ground ball hit over third. . . .

Which is exactly what occurred in the first inning. A sign. To me. From the baseball gods. As I moved to my right toward the perfectly playable ball, I saw the whole thing in my mind: I'd snag that big hop I saw coming and plant my foot on third and whirl and throw to good old Tingle (he later married LaMerle Thompson, who thus became LaMerle Tingle, which undoubtedly was a factor in her being singled out by a *New York Times* reporter, in the sixties, for a spirited quote about the effect on her of Elvis in concert), and with a light of recognition in his eyes he'd take my chest-high throw and pivot, and over to first—a triple play! I'm on my way, now. What a story this will make, when I'm interviewed at the height of my fame: in Little League, I started a triple play! A predestined triple play!

I completely missed the big hop.

At least I was integrated enough to grasp the historic opportunity to root for Jackie Robinson. I don't recall being offended as a boy by the fact that the Crackers' home right-field seats were called, with unconscious, grinding irony, "the nigger bleachers," but Robinson was my first favorite big-league player. (My favorite Crackers aside from Eddie Mathews were Ebba St. Claire, Junior Wooten, Bob Montag and Ralph "Country" Brown.)

My scrapbook preserves a Fawcett *Jackie Robinson* comic book from 1950. "There was just one way to answer the taunts and Jackie found it by singling to right!" Old photographs of my family, even of my dogs, are mysterious to me, but every panel in that Jackie Robinson comic book jumps out at me like a lifelong friend. Lots of great stuff about epic struggles between the Dodgers and the Cardinals. The anonymous artist had a great way of capturing a hitter swinging and connecting in one more-lasting-than-video image, with comments popping in from all sides.

"WHAM!" "ATTA BOY, STAN!" "MUSIAL AND SLAUGHTER! YEOW!"

In 1951, though, I switched over to the Giants and Willie Mays. You could hardly help it, if you had no geographical affiliation. The miracle Giants came from thirteen and a half games behind in August to tie the Dodgers at the end of the regular season. I ran home from school to watch the final innings of the final play-off game, got there just in time to see Bobby Thomson win it with a three-run homer, and I was dancing around gleefully and couldn't understand why Georgia Stockton, who came to our house once a week to iron and clean, couldn't share my enthusiasm. She did have an affiliation, with the Dodgers. Twenty-some years later I thought of Georgia when Dick Allen told me he grew up in Wampum, Pennsylvania, rooting for the Dodgers: black people everywhere were Dodgers fans then, he said, because of Jackie Robinson.

I never met Robinson, but Mays was the first baseball player I wrote about when I went to work for *Sports Illustrated*. In April of '69, Mays was batting leadoff for the first time in his career. In Atlanta I heard Sonny Jackson of the Braves say to him, "You just want to get more fastballs." So I asked Mays if he got more fastballs as a leadoff man.

"No, no, don't you write that," he said. "I'm not getting nothing to hit, never give me anything to hit. You go and write that, and it's not true. I don't even *want* fastballs. You guys write all our secrets, and don't leave us anything to work with."

There I was in a big-league locker room. *Interfering* with Willie Mays.

When I was thirteen we moved to Dallas for half a year, and my father's colorful friend W. O. Bankston, the Packard dealer, took me and my friend Eddie Guepe to the home of Dizzy Dean. Ol' Diz was himself all over, tried to give me a ball autographed by the Gashouse Gang but his wife wouldn't let him. He said his brother Paul's son might make a pitcher; ever since the boy was a baby he and Paul had pulled on his fingers a lot, because long fingers were vital in pitching.

Bankston also took me around to the Dallas police station. In the same halls where Jack Ruby later shot Lee Harvey Oswald, I heard a lawyer tell Bankston, "I had my witness all set to say what I wanted him to and then the son of a bitch got up there and told the truth," and I was shocked. But also pleased. This, more than Sunday school, had the ring of truth. My father was too upstanding to introduce me to people like that.

It came as more of a shock, in young adulthood, to be perceived by Willie Mays as a threat. Not only was I not ever going to play major-league ball (maybe because nobody pulled on my fingers—but then, Paul's boy never made it either), but I seemed to be getting in Willie Mays's way. I felt—well, hell, I felt rejected, wouldn't you? Spend your boyhood wanting to be Willie Mays, and then when you meet him he doesn't even want to hear you praise him? I was told that he was mad at *Sports Illustrated* because the magazine had run a story about his being in decline, and had also said in its series on the black athlete that black ballplayers didn't respect him anymore because he wasn't militant. So he felt rejected himself, I guess. Say Hey, Willie Mays!

I'll say this, though. Old and tired as he was then, he got himself up to an appropriately mythical level both times I was following him around. The second time—in 1970, when he was thirty-nine—was to write a cover story about his advance toward three thousand hits. In six games he was ten for twenty-three. Once he ranged past his right fielder to make a running catch. He cut off a drive to deep left-center barehanded. He went from first to second on a fly ball in the ninth inning of a game after playing fourteen innings (and hitting a ninth-inning homer) the night before. He stole one game with a burst of eleventh-inning speed. "He was running on three and two, and it was a wild pitch, and he turned second and I mean, he ran to third like a sprinter and he slid hard," said a young Giant named Frank Johnson. "A lot of guys wouldn't have done that—especially somebody thirty-nine. And the way he runs, his feet flying . . . we were in the dugout behind third, he was bearing down on us and we jumped up and said, 'Did you see that?' He does things that just thrill me to death."

I felt like Mays was playing for me. I wrote: "When Mays is poised in the outfield or at bat he still seems more eager, or anxious, than anybody else. He has the air of that kid in the pickup game who has more ability and fire than the others and wishes intensely that they would come on and play right and raise the whole game commensurate with his own gifts and appetites. Mays does not say so, but it is hard not to suspect that he feels that way toward it all—the fans, the park, the press. And these days he must finally be saying, 'Come on, play right' to himself, too. When he does, and when he responds as he has over the last two weeks, Frank Johnson is not the only one who is thrilled to death."

If you took out the words *ability* and *gifts*, the first two sentences could be about me as a kid. Once, when Mays was fielding questions from fifth-grade students, he was asked, "When did you first know you were good?"

He answered, "Every time the ball went up in the air, I felt I could catch it."

I felt that way when I was a kid, when a new word came up.

But Mays made me doubt for a long time that I would ever be good at talking to ballplayers. I kept at it doggedly, warily, until finally in 1973 I established a hanging-out relationship with an interviewee: Dick Allen, a great player who had trouble adapting to off-the-field life. People kept wanting him to go to meetings. He was guarded with the press, but Walter Iooss Jr., the great *Sports Illustrated* photographer with whom I had some great times on the road, had gotten to be friends with him. The three of us smoked dope together, and after that Allen lost all reticence with me.

Allen was with the White Sox then. He had just broken his leg. We were in his apartment in Chicago. A remarkable place: the refrigerator needed defrosting so badly that not only wouldn't the freezing compartment close all the way, the refrigerator *door* wouldn't. His phone rang almost constantly, and he never answered it—except, he said, sometimes when he was by himself and felt like talking to someone, then he'd pick it up. "Woman in there got me worn out," he said, indicating the bedroom. "You, uh . . . ?"

"No, uh, thanks," I said. An extremely good-looking woman came out a few minutes later, looking hastily dressed and a bit miffed, but not as miffed as you might think; he told her good-bye.

"Well," I said, "I've got to get a plane back to New York."

"I'll give you a ride," he said.

"No, you've got a cast on your leg. I'll get a cab."

But he insisted. Got out a briefcase, into which he tossed an Afro pick and a bottle of Yago sangria, and the next thing I knew we were driving not to the airport but all the way to his farm in Allentown, Pennsylvania, from which I could take a bus into New York. We drank that sangria and smoked hash and took turns driving all night long. Once we asked at a tollbooth what state we were in, and when the collector said Ohio we figured we were going in the right direction. At daybreak we were well into eastern Pennsylvania, and Allen was admiring the land.

"I like to ride along these roads and see the farms," Allen said. "I like to get out on the ground. The open country does something for me. When I was a kid, the ball diamond was just across the road."

Allen was a bad conditioner, and he put too much pressure on himself going to such lengths not to play ball, in the go-along-to-get-along sense; so he didn't have a Willie Mays career, won't make it to the Hall of Fame.

Reggie Jackson made it. Once in Cleveland, when I was doing a story about him, and the hotel he was staying in was full, he said, "I'll get you a room. I'll tell them you are my parents."

Since I was but one person, white, and only five years older than Jackson, I didn't see how I could manage that impersonation. In fact, the next morning there was a knock on the door, and I answered it, and a kid was standing there with an autograph book, and he looked at me and said, "Man, you ain't no Reggie's daddy."

I interviewed Reggie's daddy once. He was a single parent. "I didn't say the name 'Mom' until I was thirteen or fourteen," Reggie told me. I talked to his father, Martinez Jackson, in his tailor shop in Philadelphia. We had a drink in a little room in the back of the shop. "I spend the night back here some nights," he said. He showed me a heavy pistol and said there was a rifle too. "People come in here, I fill their black ass full of holes. One night—it was when the shop was in another place, with a skylight—a guy came down through the skylight and I jumped up with the rifle on him and said, 'I got you!'

" 'Oh, I came into the wrong place,' he said.

" 'You sure did,' I said. "He made it out the front door. The police got him out there. He was bleeding. I shot him in the behind, in the arm, in the shoulder. Had some coats hanging by the door; I filled them full of holes. I was shooting. You should have heard that shine sing out!"

When Barbara Walters interviewed Reggie on one of her specials, she gave him a word-association test. "Black," she said. "White," he said. "Mother," she said. "Father," he said. "Love," she said. "Daddy," he said.

"Did I ever think Reggie would do anything major?" his father said. "Never entertained that thought. I always impressed the boys to observe along the line of obedience and aggressiveness."

Maury Wills told me that he got interested in baseball, around the same time I did, when he heard about Jackie Robinson breaking the color line for the Dodgers in Brooklyn, New York. Until that moment, growing up in Washington, D.C., he'd never heard of the Dodgers, Brooklyn, New York or baseball. But he decided he wanted to be a baseball player himself.

After he had become one—captain of the Dodgers, in fact—a reporter came to get Wills's reaction to something Robinson had said: that the trouble with the post-Robinson Dodgers was, they had no leaders. Wills's reaction was, "What the fuck does Jackie Robinson know?" When that got back to Robinson, he wrote Wills a letter chiding him for letting a reporter provoke him into saying such a thing. Not long thereafter, Robinson died. One of Wills's great baseball regrets is that he never answered his inspiration's letter.

But, hey, Robinson let a reporter provoke him into saying the first thing, didn't he?

My main baseball regrets both have to do with my father: one, that I never said to him something I've been wanting to say since I was fifteen and my Babe Ruth League team had a father-son game. My father was clumsy at third base but he hit a clean line single, to left, off our best pitcher, Doodle Crane. Doodle used to lie down next to the bench with his girlfriend between innings and rub her bare legs, but that's another story. What I want to say is, CRACK!

ATTA BOY, DADDY! YOU THE BABY, YOU THE BOY!

And two, that I probably wouldn't share with my father, even now if he were still alive, my theory of why I started loving baseball so much:

The sweat and dirt of baseball evoke for me my father working on the house. And the reason I have felt so good when I hit a line drive—or even just saw and heard a line drive hit—is because, hey: good wood. (My father loved wood.) And something hard but responsive hit square, the way my father drove a nail, or made a home loan. The way I wish I could write. A four-hundred-page beeline to the inevitable climax. "When you take over a pitch and line it somewhere," Reggie Jackson told me once, "it's like you've thought of something and put it with beautiful clarity. Everyone is helpless and in awe. Included in your ability are your philosophies, your theories. You tap that mental reservoir and it goes."

I'm a wanderer. My mother taught me to drive. I lose my way in words, to the detriment of what male writers are supposed to have: narrative drive.

Narrative drive is like your father's agenda on a family trip: making the best possible time over distance. Whereas your mother wants to stop and poke around in antiques stores. I like to do both. But if I have to sacrifice one for the other—if it's a choice between averaging over sixty miles an hour and stopping off at a place that something tells me I just can't bear to pass by . . .

Why didn't my father and I relax with each other, joke and kid around? I do with Kirven. (As for Ennis, you can ask anybody: if you can't kid around—and also get down to brass tacks—with Ennis right off the bat, you must be dead.) Of course Kirven and I like the same movies and ballplayers and country singers. We even notice the same great names. Kirven said the other night that he was going to start calling himself Deuce, and I knew immediately where he'd gotten it: from the liner notes on a CD I'd passed on to him, a sideman named Deuce Spriggins. You know that scene in *Blue Velvet* when Kyle McLachlan is being held by scurvy guys while Dennis Hopper smears lipstick on him? Kirven once gave Ennis, for her birthday, a tape of that movie into which—right at the most unbearably tense point of that scene—he had spliced in about three seconds of himself dancing the twist on the top of a car. The greatest bit of comic relief I have ever seen in a movie. When Kirven was watching the Godard film *Contempt*, he noticed—as I would have noticed, if I'd been with him—that the subtitle for something Brigitte said to Jack Palance in reference to his sportscar was punctuated as follows: "Get back in your Alfa, Romeo." Daddy was too busy working to pick up on a comma like that.

At Ennis's wedding, my uncles Charles and Fred started telling me about my father, their big brother. "He was a great man," Fred said, and he wasn't talking about my father's prominence in the greater Atlanta community.

"It was the Depression," Charles said, "and there wasn't much construction work. In fact, the way Papa made a living was that he took out a thousand-dollar loan from a bank to build a house for a man, and then when he finished it the man decided he didn't want it. Papa was stuck, so we moved into the house, and to keep the bank from foreclosing on the loan, Papa worked for the bank—when the bank took over a mortgage on a house and the people in that house had to move out, Papa would put up a sign in front and board up the doors and windows. That's the kind of carpentry that kept us living in that house in Jacksonville. And because of that loan, Papa never borrowed anything again. He said, 'If you really want something, save up for it, and by the time you save enough money for it, you probably won't want it anymore.' Other than what he did for the bank, there wasn't much construction work. Maybe Papa would get a half a day's work here and a half a day's work there. And your dad, who was in high school—he was eight years older than me, and I'm eight years older than Fred—had a paper route, and he worked in a grocery store, and two nights a week he would take over from the man who supervised the children's home. He'd watch the orphans so the man could have some time off. And all the money he made, he brought home and put on the kitchen table. If I needed a pair of shoes, I'd use that money to buy it. Otherwise I was going to school in a pair of Papa's old shoes, worn out and the bottoms flapping. Your daddy was a great man."

Did my mother remind my father of those orphans he watched? Did his savings and loan success spring from that menial bank job Papa had to resort to? Set those questions aside for a moment: my grandfather couldn't support his family; my father had to take on a good deal of the burden. He was, in effect, already a daddy in high school. That confusion of roles can't make for closeness between father and son.

In savings and loan, my father had a mentor, Julius McCurdy, whom he succeeded as president of Decatur Federal. McCurdy was also connected with the law firm of McCurdy, Candler and Harris: three of the oldest families in Decatur. Years after my father died, a Decatur newspaperman informed me that the people who made the real money were the partners in the law firm, which collected a fee every time Decatur Federal made a loan.

We were arrivistes in Decatur. We'd moved there from Ohio while my father was with Libby Foods. Then he'd worked for Packard Motor Company, which transferred us to Dallas in 1955. The whole family hated Dallas, so my father quit and we moved back to Decatur. He sold real estate for a while, and then he got a good job with . . . Edsel.

He was working himself to death for that automobile—and the Methodist Church, of course—when Decatur Federal came to him. Those old families groomed my father to be the unimpeachable up-front man, who got a nice salary but no piece of the action.

My father proceeded to transcend his mentor. Decatur Federal built the biggest building in Decatur as its new home. My father was named chairman of the board of education, in which capacity he handed me my diploma when I graduated (I made the graduation speech, got a couple of pretty good laughs) and thereafter oversaw the integration of the Decatur school system. He also headed up committees that built a new YMCA and a new Decatur First Methodist sanctuary (the steeple exceeded by two feet that of Decatur First Baptist's, which had been the tallest in town). My father became such a dynamic force in the community that he was named president of the Atlanta Chamber of Commerce, and then of the National Savings and Loan League.

"The problem of this place is too much leadership," an overpressed Decatur Federal janitor said, to my father's great pleasure but not necessarily Julius McCurdy's. One April afternoon in 1974, McCurdy, who was chairman of the board, accused my father of thinking too much of his own aggrandizement.

Did this stir deep Oedipal mud? Was he being made to feel guilty again about doing—overdoing—what he thought his father figure needed from him? Daddy came home highly agitated, went outside to work off some steam by cleaning out the gutters, stopped to check out the azaleas, told Mother it was funny, but he thought he heard Chipper barking. Chipper had been dead for a couple of years. Daddy felt dyspeptic, came back inside and sat down in his BarcaLounger, had a heart attack and died, at sixty. Didn't smoke or drink or stay out late, and lived twenty-one fewer years than Harold Robbins.

One of my mother's favorite stories from my infancy was of the time my father consented to take the middle of the night feeding. She heard me bellowing and got up and found my father asleep with the bottle in one hand and me in the other arm, the bottle just out of my reach. So he never fed me, apparently, anymore.

My mother also used to say that when I was a toddler I would follow my father around with a hammer in my hand, saying, "Hammer-nail, Daddy, hammer-nail!" I can remember driving nails with relish. But I never went so far as to build anything, and in time I drifted away from nails toward my mother's world: words.

Laird Cregar to Veronica Lake: "I want to know all about you."
Veronica to Laird: "That's a big word, *all*."   —THIS GUN FOR HIRE

I don't know what the first word I ever read was. I do remember that the first word I ever made out in handwriting was *all*. I was looking at something my mother had written, a mystery to me because I knew only block letters, and then I thought, "Oh. That would be *all*."

I got a piece of paper and a pencil and wrote out *all* myself. And stared at it. Here I am now, staring at it on the screen of my computer.

My mother never published anything, but she had a flair for language. I can hear her now, saying, "I bet you a cookie," "keeps my coattails popping," "on the hop all the time," "bless Pete," "bless my soul if he didn't up and . . . ," "bless gracious," "bless goodness," "my goodness alive," "just as barefooted as he can be," "you don't eat enough to physic a jaybird," "that's no more so . . . than pea-turkey," "poor as Job's turkey," "Well, I guess we better start moseying on." She had more different expressions for gaits than anybody I have ever known: hightailing it, lightfooting it, hotfooting it, highballing it, going at a dogtrot, coattails in the breeze, with coattails flapping, lallygagging, traipsing, sashaying, moseying, ploughing along, parading along, prissing along, frisking along, flouncing along, shooting along, barreling along, galloping along, poking along, dragging along, trucking along, breezing along down the avenue, waltzing right in, shaking a leg, going *zrooop*, going lickety-split, going at a dogtrot, going like a house afire, going like a crazy man, highlining, flying low, burning up the road, making a beeline, going dancing by, slewfooting. Many of these were judgmental. She didn't approve of breezing along down the avenue; she didn't have time for it; but you could tell she liked the idea.

"Mother had a great sense of drama," says Susan. "Delivering lines, at poignant moments, that any playwright would have been proud of. But not the kind of lines that you wanted to be on the receiving end of."

" 'I see,' said the blind man to his deaf daughter." That's something she'd say when you tried to explain something to her. "You talk like a man up a tree," she might also say.

"Don't fuss at me, Bucky." Ooo. That's something she would say when I tried to explain, Lord help me, why I disagreed with her about something. That one always got my goat, because it left my goat at such a loss: now the issue was not whatever I was trying to talk to her about, but the unkindness of my fussing at her. That was never the issue when she was fussing at me.

Neither of my parents told long stories. My father would send me a postcard occasionally: "All fine here. Write us." My mother would write me a chatty couple of pages from which a stunning passage would leap out. A year after my father died in his BarcaLounger of his sudden heart attack as she held him and begged him not to, she wrote:

"Atlanta is a blaze of glory just now. The dogwood and azaleas are competing for beauty. The spring brings back such a rush of memories, however. Somehow I see Roy's face in my hands in every azalea bush. I dont want to stop loving spring, but will be glad when it is over this year."

James Dickey once said that he realized he was a writer when, while writing letters to women, he started thinking, Hmm, this is pretty good, instead of, This'll get her. I'd say my mother had a foot in each of those camps.

Why do so many women say they can't tell a joke, that they blurt out the punch line too soon? Because to delay an orgasm is not a female thing? I can tell a joke—a long joke. But when your first act in life is to nearly kill your mother, how are you going to build your life story masterfully to a climax?

Memoirists tend to recall early childhood either as hell or as golden days, a time of innocent pleasure without compromise or misgivings. I remember it as a kind of holding pattern. I was holed up, waiting till I could get to where I didn't have to answer people's questions in ways that they could understand. I'm told I had three imaginary playmates: Bobby Jones, Mincemeat and P'tar Homer. Now I have the reader. Adults would ask me what I was doing. They asked me that only when I was doing something hard to explain. Like looking at dirt. Sometimes when I was a child, I would just look at dirt. Soil out in the yard, or dust under the couch. But

I didn't want to say, "Looking at dirt," because adults would think I was being crazy, or perverse, or, at best, cute.

You were supposed to look *for* dirt, in order to get rid of it or to avoid getting any of it on you. There were no grounds for looking at dirt. No established procedure, no rationale. Looking at dirt didn't make me feel like an American or a Methodist or a good boy or a beloved son or a member of a family highly regarded in the community. It only made me feel like myself. But I knew better than to tell anybody that. In college, years later, Vereen Bell, the English professor who, more years later, would be best man at my second wedding, lectured my aesthetics class on organic symbolism. He cited a learned critic's commentary on a short story (I forget which one) by James Joyce. There was a bicycle pump in the story. The critic held that this pump stood for the Holy Spirit. This was hooey, said Vereen, a bicycle pump was a bicycle pump—but it might evoke certain things. A good example of organic symbolism, he said, was the train that runs over Anna Karenina. We all know what a train is like. We can all imagine what it might be like to be run over by one. We can all consider that a dictate of society, say, may be like a train.

Literature wasn't a secret code, it was palpable. The substance of literature—of *education*—was the substance of everything else.

When I was a child, I didn't have that concept. I was given to believe that we had to proceed from religion, from guilts and abstract notions that adults had settled upon us. Something, however, kept me from signing off on things that stuck in my craw. My mother had taught me to sound out words. She also had a compulsion to banish dirt. I couldn't grasp the compulsion. I could grasp the dirt.

So when adults asked me what I was doing I would say, "Uhh," or "Playing," or "Nothing." And I would get up—the spell of dirt observation having been broken—and do something that at least looked like something comprehensible to adults. I was wary of being comprehensible to adults. Once I was drawing a naked man. I was a little kid, I didn't see anything wrong with it.

"What's that?" my mother said. "A man," I said with some satisfaction. She had always admired my drawings. She wouldn't say, "That is the best picture I ever saw—if you looked up the word *picture* in the dictionary, there ought to be a picture of that picture there." But she would usually say, "Oh, that's nice," with sufficient sincerity.

This time she said, "What's that?"

"That's his tinkle," I said, nothing loath.

And she got *mad* at me. It was a different time and culture back then, and all, but how can you get mad at a little kid for drawing a man with a tinkle?

"We don't draw that," she said darkly, and withdrew. Okay. I haven't drawn one since. If Caravaggio could do without drawing them, I certainly could. I don't want to come off reactionary, here—when I see Tom Wolfe talking about modern art on TV, I am distracted from the plausibility of his conservative critique by an urge to paint big black bold abstract (yet literal) brush strokes on his white suit. But I do think that a lot of artists today who are into *transgression* are not exploring the organic fruitfulness of dirt. They are jerking their parents' chains.

I know how the line goes: "He was one of our greatest photographers, and the five so-called offensive photographs were only a small part of the show, off to themselves where no one had to notice them, and his unemotional men with large objects in their orifices and his small children exposing their genitals are as austerely rendered as his flowers, really. . . ."

Uh-huh. So's your old man.

There's something to be said, I think, for being raised—as folk artists generally are—by people who don't care for the arts. Folk artists aren't hurling challenges, they are making pretty things out of the materials at hand. By the time they get discovered, they are either dead or too set in their ways to be patronized. Once I talked to Nellie Mae Rowe, an elderly Georgian whose "Pig on the Expressway" and other studies in felt-tip pen, as well as her used-chewing-gum sculptures, had found their way into New York museums. I asked her whether she was surprised when suddenly in her sixties people from around the world started showing up at her tumbledown door wanting to represent her and show her and buy her and interview her.

She looked at me as if I evidently hadn't given that question much thought.

"Yes," she said.

And did she wish she'd had a chance to study art in school and learn all the accepted ways of drawing figures and so on, so she could explode them? She looked at me as if I evidently hadn't ever given anything much thought.

"No," she said.

She didn't need an arts council, just a sense of the actuality of sacred things (she chuckled at the notion that anybody could get her to believe that men had walked on the moon, but when her dealer took her to her first museum she could not be lured away from a Renaissance oil of minor importance because it was the biggest picture of Jesus she'd ever seen) and stuff she could pick up anywhere.

My father didn't care for the arts. He hated it when the June Taylor dancers would break in on Jackie Gleason, and he didn't see any point in *Hamlet*. I know because I talked the family into attending a performance of *Hamlet* once, when I was home on vacation from college (did I mention that Hamlet was a junior?), and Daddy was forthrightly reluctant to go, and afterward he said he wished he hadn't.

Of course he was right about the June Taylor dancers. And T. S. Eliot had reservations about *Hamlet*. But T. S. Eliot liked *some* things about *Hamlet*. My father didn't. In fact, I don't think anybody on either side of my family liked the arts until my generation. They all liked church. So it did not seem outlandish to me when a prospective juror in an obscenity trial in Cincinnati a few years ago said he had never been to any kind of museum and could not relate to art or to people who did relate to it: "They're into that type of stuff. These people are in a different class. Evidently they get some type of satisfaction looking at it. I don't understand artwork. That stuff never interested me."

What is outlandish to me, quite frankly, is taking a picture of yourself with a whip up your ass, or suspending a crucifix in urine. It's a free country, people have every right to do these things and other people have every right to show them as art. I am curious, myself, as to what people who think of themselves as artists will think of next. What I don't understand is how people can be so ignorant of American democracy as to be shocked, *appalled,* when government funding of dunking Jesus in pee plays into Philistines' hands.

By Philistines I don't mean just the obvious ones like Senator Jesse Helms. When Lamar Alexander—with whom, in college, I campaigned against segregation—was running for the presidential nomination of (God help us) the Republican Party, I saw him address a Christian Coalition rally in Columbia, South Carolina. He was introduced by his friend William Bennett—who, when it comes to virtues, has produced a best-selling anthology. In rambling, draggy remarks Bennett conceded that "Lamar is not a man who'll light the house on fire." Bennett confessed furthermore that he himself had once been head of the National Endow-

ment for the Humanities. "Not the arts. Arts is the one with the dirty pictures. Humanities is the one with the dirty books." Before a liberal, arts-
and-letters-indulgent audience, that might have been witty. Before this
literal, arts-and-letters-phobic audience, it was what I would call, I don't
want to say vicious, let's say abjectly unvirtuous. You don't catch me telling secular New York audiences, "I used to be a Southern Methodist. Not
Baptist. That's knuckle-dragging Christian. Methodist is just fingertip-
dragging."

My man Lamar did not give these Christians the red meat they craved.
He said that he, "like every boy," used to carry a pocketknife to school, and
now there was a federal law against it. The reason boys didn't use their
pocketknives against each other in his day, he said, was not federal laws, it
was community pressures. Relatives, preachers, teachers, nosy neighbors
who kept boys in line. Lamar had the air of a boy who was trying to tell all
those monitors at once—and the hardened pols and the business interests
and the media elite—what he was planning to do on a date.

He said nothing that dishonored the library card that his mother told
him was all a boy needed to get started in life. He didn't rouse the Christians, either. They wanted dirt.

Once, when he was governor of Tennessee, Lamar told me, sadly, that
he had come to realize it was impossible to tell the truth every time somebody in the media asked a question. He had been reading about Huey
Long. Wistfully, he recounted an anecdote: one of Long's minions came to
him saying that reporters were bugging him to explain two contradictory
statements Long had made. "Tell 'em I lied," Long said.

Hey, misrepresentation is the backbone of democracy. When Bob Dole
got up before that same South Carolina Christian audience, he did not
shrink from dishing dirty art. First he paid a grotesque tribute to nonage-
narian Strom Thurmond, who was standing very, very still, as if stuffed,
behind the candidates on the podium—"People ask me, 'How do you stay
so young?' I just follow Strom around and eat what he throws away." Aside
from its making no sense, that remark was, to my taste, vaguely emetic.
Then Dole exclaimed, "And I know the difference, believe me, between
Mapplethorpe and Michelangelo."

The Christians whooped. They knew too. Just as clearly as they saw
the point of eating Strom Thurmond's chicken bones and peanut hulls.
But I'll tell you something. In the bad old days of integration resistance,
old Southern-pol sayings were often mendacious, even despicable, but

they also tended to have an inner logic and might well be insightful. They weren't just vague allusions, they were similes and metaphors. Old Marvin Griffin down in Georgia said, "Politics is like killing rats. It's all day and all night." Jim Folsom in Alabama said, his opponents might sling mud at him, but "one day outside church a boy slung mud on my white shirt. Mama told me 'Don't rub it off. Let it dry. It will fall off by itself.' " I'll bet Folsom or Griffin would have felt obliged—would have been happy—to say what the difference between Mapplethorpe and Michelangelo *was*. Whether he had ever seen a Mapplethorpe or a Michelangelo or not.

If Dole had said something like, "Michelangelo reached out agonizingly toward ecstacy. Mapplethorpe just shows people poking things into each other as if it doesn't hurt," I would have said right on. Or if he had said, "Michelangelo is *soft-core* homoerotic." But Dole (like Mapplethorpe, if you ask me, or at least like the people in Mapplethorpe's scandalous photos) was just pushing dirty buttons.

I remember when selling liquor was illegal in Mississippi. Efforts to repeal that prohibition were for many years overwhelmed by a powerful lobbying axis: the demon-rum-denouncing preachers and the bootleggers. There is a similar de facto alliance between people like Jesse Helms and various dirty-art-bashing men of God, on the one hand, and enthusiasts of subsidized nose-thumbing art, on the other. The former get to holler praise the Lord and pass the dirty pictures (and to throw around words like *filth*, surely a much dirtier word than *fuck*), and the latter get to be cause célèbres.

In officially dry Mississippi, the victim was he or she who wanted to order a drink or to shop at a package store like a civilized person. In the controversy over the funding policies of the National Endowment for the Arts, the victims are arts projects that need public funding because they are neither conventionally vulgar enough to attract the broad ticket-buying public nor unconventionally vulgar enough to make Helms lick his chops and *Newsweek* take pictures and so on.

Here's what I think about government money: it ought to be readily available to people who can't get by without it, but if you can avoid taking any, you ought to. I believe that if you take money, you are obliged, and I'd feel less comfortable being obliged to Jesse Helms than I would with a whip up my ass.

But listen here now: is there a kind of art that could use some funding, and yet is held in high esteem and displayed with pleasure by people all across the aesthetico-political spectrum?

Children's art. A delicate blossom, of course, too soon blown by authority-figure and even peer review ("That's not the way a cat's foot goes"). I hate to think of children's drawings coming within the purview of arts councils.

Now that I am an adult, I no longer look at dirt, per se. But I still do things that don't seem to have much point. For instance, I collect pairs of words that look as though they might rhyme but don't, like *baseline* and *Vaseline*.

People run into me on the street and ask me:

"What are you working on?" What I am working on at that moment is turning *poultry* and *sultry*, or *miseries* and *miniseries*, over and over on my tongue and, loosely speaking, in my mind. But I know better than to tell people that. So I say:

"Oh, well, a lot of little things, and trying to make some progress on this book, which is sort of a memoir, well, not a memoir exactly but . . ."

In other words, I'm still saying, "Uhh" or "Nothing" or "Playing," but in somewhat more respectable terms.

Once someone asked me what I would do if I could indulge myself with anything. My indulgence, when people ask me what I'm up to, would be . . . Not to tell the truth, which might damage my reputation. My indulgence would be to say any old thing that pops into my head:

"Well, I'm bringing out a new fragrance we feel is going to do very well for us—Senator Malcolm Wallop, of Wyoming, has agreed to wear it the next time he addresses the Knesset. And I believe I've got ahold of a really good story for an upcoming issue of the 'Cruise Control News': the Disney people are diversifying into the extermination field, and they've agreed to give me an exclusive as long as I don't comment directly on the irony involved. There's movie interest in my uncle Dipper's 'Bio of a Bayou Boyo,' which, as you probably know, I ghosted, and I'm angling for a permanent slot on the 'February 29th Show.' "

People also ask me, "Are you seeing anybody?"

My indulgence would be to say, "Yes, Latasha and Letitia, Siamese twins—but with Letitia it's platonic, she's the shy one. They share a common foot, which their parents didn't have the heart to deprive either one of them of. They live in Elmo, Texas, where I met them one night when I was playing alto sax with a retro-country quartet called Meat and Three. They were smiling at me from their table—Latasha, mostly—so during the break I sat down with them and didn't realize until we got up to go to their place that they only needed three shoes between them. To make a long story short, I wound up in Latasha's arms, while Letitia just sort of perched on the side of the bed. After a while, Letitia said in a little, soft voice, 'Could I try your saxophone?' She was good, too—I think we had all had enough retro-country for the night, so she played ' 'Round Midnight' and 'Keepin' Out of Mischief,' and 'Tangerine,' all night long while Latasha and I were rolling in each other's arms.

"Then the next time I came through Elmo, there they were again. I went straight to their table. Latasha nudged Letitia and said, 'See? See?' Letitia blushed.

" 'See what?' I asked.

" 'We started not to come,' Latasha said. 'Letitia didn't think you'd remember us.' "

"You'll grow up and forget me," Mother would tell me when I was a child, giving me a look of near flirtatious and yet impenetrably sealed-off longing. Then when I grew up, "You can't write about me. You don't know me." As late as the age of eleven, I got homesick at camp, brooded, missed my mother so much that I never learned to paddle a canoe. In high school, I was out of it; loyal to my mother's apprehensions. Then I started writing for the school paper, and dating, and hanging out at Tatum's drugstore—which was the cool drugstore, the one the bad boys habituated. I was still prudent, didn't want to do anything that would kill my mother. Then I won a full scholarship to Vanderbilt University in Nashville. I still got luscious pecan pound cakes from home; I reflected my striving, respectable upbringing well; I actually wrote a letter or two home every week. But I wasn't dependent on my parents anymore, and I never had a homesick moment. Except for a few perhaps delusory years in my late thirties, about which more later, I never felt at home again, but I never felt entirely out of place either. I was beginning to realize that the world, strange as it was, was more comprehensible than home. I got A's on term papers and exams, I spoke my mind in the school paper, and in the summers I wrote for newspapers in New York and New Orleans. Since then I have written my way to all the United States except the Dakotas and Alaska and all of the usual countries (except Spain), plus Iceland, Uganda, Kenya, Senegal, Venezuela, Peru: places where I could get as lost as I was in childhood but could find my way—by negotiating the river of language, which my mother first dipped my paddle into.

But I've never felt that I was quite getting at what I was meant to get at. Whatever we think we are telling our children, I am inclined to believe, we are setting them up to do what we wish we could. I've been all over the world, trying to find the key to the castle my mother and my heart are still locked up in.

CHAPTER 22 / **Reverse English**

In addition to summit meetings, ordinary Americans and Chinese can help. . . . Only through continued dialogue at many levels can we resolve differences and build a foundation for better understanding.   —JIMMY CARTER

The Ruptured Chinaman, by Wun Hung Lo.
                              —THE FIRST OFF-COLOR JOKE I EVER HEARD

Nixon went to China." That's what people say, meaning that if you're anti-Communist enough, you can traffic with Communists because nobody will accuse you of liking it. By that logic, my mother in her widowhood could have visited the most luxuriant island paradise, because nobody could accuse her of doing something because *she* wanted to. "There must be a leper colony in Bora Bora," people would have said.

She, of course, didn't visit island paradises. She took my children to Disney World. How can I criticize that?

We rarely ate out when I was a child, because (at least according to my mother), Daddy got enough of that old restaurant food on his business trips. Evidently he got enough of exotic places, too, because on our vacations we visited his family in Jacksonville. We could go to the beach in the afternoon without broadening our horizons.

And yet we were *strange* people. My mother regarded herself as "a freak of nature"! Wouldn't it have done her good to realize that freakishness abounds?

I wanted to go to China. The first thing I remember learning about geography was, if you dug straight down you would eventually come out in China, where everything was upside down. Talk about a switcheroo! I couldn't picture it. No point writing anyone in China for information, because if the Chinese were upside down they presumably always had been and wouldn't realize it. The only way to clarify China in my mind was to dig straight down. All I ever did was look down at the dirt and think about it.

That's what I was doing recently when it struck me that the China turnaround might undo the family curse. My friends the Swans were spending a year in Beijing. I flew there, with Kirven and our friend Lois Betts.

I was in my room in Beijing's Friendship Hotel, studying the TV schedule. "Gigh Anxiety" and "The Lords of Disciping" were the American movies on tap. The Chinese one was "Look These Elderly Men and Women." Earlier that day I had purchased, in a street market, a T-shirt (not crepe de chine, but it did have a sleazy feel) that said . . .

Okay, I know, you've been around, you've seen strange T-shirt English in, like, France. But the English on Chinese T-shirts is off on another level. This particular T-shirt had on it—beneath a hastily sketched hedge-hog, with (maybe) strawberries stuck to his spines, and a couple of smaller, less determinate animals, one of which might or might not be gnawing on a mango—the following English:

"We can to communicate. ALL OF THE WORLD IS COCORABBIT."

A knock at the door. A young Chinese man, looking determined to straighten out some irregularity. And this is what he said:

"Please sing."

I was unprepared. In my own country, I am never asked to sing. It is not uncommon, in my own country, for people to suggest by word or gesture that they wish I would stop singing. And here, halfway round the world. . . . Maybe everything in China *was* upside down.

After all, the tiny pellets of herbs-and-toad-venom that I had taken to stave off the flu (they worked) had come in a tiny vial (inside a tiny plush-lined box like a casket) that unscrewed backward. But . . .

"Sing, please," the man said.

Surely by "sing" he didn't mean "confess." In order to get a visa, I'd been required to write a letter promising not to interview anyone in China. Just that morning at breakfast I had asked a man—an Australian businessman, though, not Chinese—how he was, and before I knew it he had told me that the Chinese word *ma* meant so many things, depending on tone of voice, that the sentence *"Ma ma ma ma ma"* could mean "Do I scold my mother for smoking marijuana while riding a horse?" Perhaps he was an agent provocateur. The waitress had looked at me as if I were a subversive, but I thought that was just because I had asked for another napkin. The Chinese government has a way of locking up people it deems to be irregular.

The man at the door frowned. Chinese hotel employees tend to give the impression that working in an international hotel would be a pretty good gig if there were no guests.

"Sing this," he insisted.

He was holding out a piece of paper. I took it—a form, something to do with laundry. I had left some dirty clothes to be picked up earlier.

"Oh!" I said. *"Sign."*

"Sing," he said. I signed.

China is Westernizing. "One Country, Two Systems" is the official word. Market Leninism. People stream in from the provinces to visit Mao lying waxily in state, and portraits of him abound, but he is cheek by jowl with McDonald's, Kentucky Fried Chicken and a Hard Rock Cafe. Makeup and bras, until recently banned, are widely in evidence. And may I say that bright red lipstick harmonizes awfully well with Beijing women's white teeth and black hair. Under Maoism they had to keep their hair cut short, but now you see long, elegant, glistening pigtails bouncing, and a high incidence of full but perky lips.

Bright-red, inscrutable lips. Just-post-repression lips, lingering fifties lips. Lips that haven't yet come to the conclusion that the sexual revolution is bad for women, so sort of seventies lips; but, hey, Maoist lips, so also sort of sixties lips—and thirties lips, even, because remember, these women have just now started wearing bras. . . .

I used to see a woman, from Alabama, who pronounced the word *moist* like *Maoist*. As in, "Ooo, I'm all maoist."

Once, in the south of France (*National Geographic* sent me there), after my English ladyfriend Christabel and I had enjoyed a fine vinous lunch, she wandered outside the restaurant while I went upstairs to the rest room. Relieved, I walked out onto a little balcony overlooking the little street where Christabel was sitting reading a book. I shouted out to her, as vulgarly as possible, "Hey, mamselle!"

And you know what happened? A quite attractive and perfectly respectable Frenchwoman who happened to be passing by thought I was addressing her. She smiled and responded, *"Enchantée."*

All these years, I should have been just shouting to women, "Hey, mamselle!"?

But I was not about to try shouting anything like that to a Chinese woman. I had read—in the "Comrade Language" column in the *Beijing Scene*—about the pitfalls of trying to give the right impression in Mandarin:

"Bianfan means 'simple home-style meal.' It's fine to say: *'Qing ni dao wo jia chi yidian bianfan*—Please come to my home for a simple meal.' But a foreign businessman, trying to be overly polite, added the word 'little' when extending an invitation to his Chinese colleague and said: *'Qing ni dao wo jia chi yidian xiao bian-fan."* The problem is, *xiaobian* means 'urine.' So what the businessman said was: 'Please come to my home and have a little food and urine.' "

There are four tones in Mandarin, and common Beijing parlance is an accent unto itself. In a certain tone of voice *bi* means "pen," but a male student, being from South China instead of Beijing, pronounced *bi* so that he inadvertently said to a female student, "Something's wrong with my vagina, may I borrow yours?" Which is apparently an even worse pickup line in China than it would be in the United States.

In Beijing it's twelve hours later than daylight saving time in New York—when it's noon in New York, it's midnight in Beijing. Seems simple. But we left New York at 6:55 a.m. on a Tuesday by American Airlines to Toronto, from which Canadian Airlines took us via Vancouver to Beijing. When we got there it was thirty-three hours later, 3:45 a.m. on a Wednesday, New York time, but by Beijing time it was 3:45 p.m. To get to the mysterious East we had flown westward, gaining twelve hours, but then we crossed the international dateline and lost a whole day, so . . .

Here's how I worked it out in my notes on the plane: "Tonight is really this morning, only it's tomorrow morning—if it weren't this morning, it would be two days . . . Look at it this way: Tuesday morning is really Monday night, but they call it Tuesday night so it won't be Wednesday. This morning, then, is really last night but they call it tonight—otherwise, it would be tomorrow."

Fortunately, we were met at Beijing's big, modern, but somehow extremely Chinese airport by our friend Marianne Swan. She and her husband, Jon, were living in Beijing for a year. She taught us rough phonetic versions of important phrases, including *Nee yu bing ma*. This is what you say when you get run over by a cyclist. It means "Are you sick in the head?"

Beijing days are gray. The automobile population has exploded, there is no unleaded gas and in the spring the air is suffused with sand blown in from the Gobi Desert. Many of the buildings are concrete ugly-as-we-wanna-be blocks erected by the Soviets. In the fifties the government ordered all the city's grass and bushes dug up, because they harbored an overabundance of insects, which had resulted from the government's having previously ordered the extermination of all the city's birds. (Citizens walked around town banging on pots, to keep all the birds within earshot up in the air until they collapsed in exhaustion and could be gathered up for cooking.) We saw lots of newly planted saplings, though—with all their limbs cut off so the trunks will grow higher quicker. There's a good deal of rubble around, where boulevards are being widened. A given boulevard's name may change from, say, Dongzhmenwai Street to Dongzhmennei Street to Jiaodaokoudong Street to Guloudong Street in the space of five blocks.

Beijing is boxes within boxes: there's a third ring of multilane freeways, and within that there's a second ring, where there used to be a wall, and within that there's—well, actually there is no first ring, except for the perimeter of the heart of Beijing, what the Chinese for over five hundred years regarded as the very center of the center of the universe: the Forbidden City. The Forbidden City was where the emperor, the Son of Heaven, lived surrounded by thousands of concubines and eunuchs. Often a eunuch carried his testicles around in a pouch, not out of nostalgia but in the belief that you couldn't get into the afterlife if you weren't whole. The Forbidden City is a network of courtyards and palaces within walls within walls, surrounded by one big wall, which is surrounded by a moat. From nowhere within the Forbidden City can you see anything but the sky and the walls of the Forbidden City. If you had been caught sneaking in there as recently as two hundred years ago, you'd have been killed in some interesting way—perhaps had your throat cut and the flesh sliced from your bones as your life gurgled out, which also happens to be the first step in the preparation of Beijing duck.

Now the stone stairs of the Forbidden City are being worn away by tourists' feet, and you can get T-shirts that say things like "Treat with Disdain Powerful Gropu."

A nice sentiment, assuming that "Gropu" means groups. But not a revelation.

Beijing's principal circulatory system is a river of healthy looking, dead-earnest-looking bikers and pedestrians. We rented bikes and waded in.

At Bamboo Park, where people go to do various exercises in the mornings, we saw a man walking backward; a man standing in a rigid pose and emitting a long, impossible, drawn-out shout, "Ooooowaaaaaaaaaaaaah"; women doing tai chi with big lethal-looking swords; a cha-cha class; and a group of people doing some nifty hip-twitchy dance that resembled a cakewalk.

At various markets, most of them in the street, we bargained for antique jars, cast-iron household demons, strings of pearls and startling faces carved out of roots. A Belgian told Lois he frequently financed a flight to Beijing by buying sixty or eighty silk ties haggled down to under a dollar apiece and reselling them back home. Lois said carpets were a good buy. I picked up a T-shirt that said: "Smallest Cigarette Lighter in the World! One glance ghows theg bring you big saving on potent vitamins and organic mineraisi. But please oct now while these low prices are in effect. It's easu to orxer. KIOK POTENCIEB."

Too enigmatic. Even in America, Chinese menus have streaks of mysticism.

In the enormous Hong Qiao Market, Kirven and Lois and I saw—well, it was as if a net had been dragged across the bottom of the sea and everything it picked up had been moved, mostly live, to a many-aisled butcher shop. An enormous vat full of writhing eels. Long-necked turtles blinking intelligent-looking eyes—"What is a turtle like me doing on a counter?" Great mounds of sulking frogs. Displays of the least sightly inner organs (octopus pancreas, for instance) of creatures that even from the outside are not among nature's more edible-looking. A tray full of what I assumed to be little pod people, twitching—they may, or may not, have been locust chysalises. Poverty and a highly disproportionate ratio of people to arable land have taught the Chinese to dine on anything that crawls, hops, flies, swims or slithers. To make sure meat is fresh, they like their animals "killed lively." In the markets you can see people feeding live snakes head-first into meat grinders to make snake tartare, or taking live snakes and jamming their heads onto the upturned point of a nail and ripping the meat out of the skin that way. In some upscale bars you can have a live snake brought to your table, where your waiter will cut it open and squeeze out the bile or the blood for your cocktail-sipping pleasure. I never talked to anyone who had actually seen a monkey served live with the top of his skull cut open so you could eat his brain while imagining his thoughts. Several people told me that this practice was still extant, however. "The monkey does not know what is happening," I was assured by a Chinese man (whom I didn't interview exactly, I just sort of raised the monkey issue). "Boiling water is poured into his brain." In restaurants, I kept steeling myself to eat—just so I could say I had—dog. Statues of "lion-dogs," which is to say Pekingese, abound, but we saw only one actual dog—to keep one as a pet is a sign of wealth, like keeping a plump pig around purely for show. Dog was on several menus we saw, but I kept picturing a puppy being brought out. . . . Does anybody ever send the dog back? "This puppy isn't very roly-poly." Or "I distinctly ordered my puppy pink inside." I did point to "Stewed Snake, Tiger and Chicken" in one place, but the waiter (a Chinese friend of the Swans interpreted) said they were out of tiger. He also said tiger was cat.

Here were some of the items we saw on semi-English menus:

Traditional Snake Soup
Cool Colour Crab
Fried Sliced Soyed Pin's Intestines
Spiced Goose Web and Wine
Braised Sea Slug with Fish Maw and Fish Lip
Spiced Pig's Offals
Preserved Fried 2 Kinds of Foods
Fried Cicada with Scorpion
Stir-Fried Fragrant Cedar
Eight Jeweled Congee
Water Melon and Tomato Fresh Juice
3 Kinds of Eating of Turtle
Bear Gall Wine
Steamed Glutinous with Sugar

The Win with Beer Blood
Tonic Tincture of 3 Animal
Green Bean Drink

I didn't have any of these. Whenever I pointed to one, it was not available. In many restaurants, English-language menus—picked up from international hotels—are a sort of courtesy unrelated to the dishes actually served. We learned the Chinese for dumplings, and had some excellent ones with who knows what fillings, and we also had some tasty noodles and vegetables and chicken and pork—not much different from what you can get in a good, unpretentious Chinese place in the States. We had a hard time getting them to bring us rice along with our other courses—Beijingers generally eat rice toward the end of the meal. We were disappointed in Beijing duck, which we tried in one of the restaurants best known for that dish. Every part of the duck was brought in at one time or another, and every part was too bland and fatty for our tastes. I nibbled on the head; the beak was the best part.

No fortune cookies. And don't ask for a doggie bag.

None of this seemed to touch the family curse.

There are more than eleven million people in Beijing, and six million registered bikes. I nearly collided with most of them. We found nice old alleyways to tool down away from traffic, but to get to them we had to work our way along thoroughfares jammed with cars, buses, three-wheeled carts, pedestrians and bicycles, all jockeying for position. The trick was to keep a steady pace while thousands of wheels all around you were doing the same thing far more expertly. Many of the bikes had platforms built onto the back, and strapped to such a platform you might see a couple hundred pounds of celery and noodles, wooden night-soil buckets, a canvas tub full of water and live carp, a dozen twenty-foot-long two-by-eight planks, a couch with an elderly couple sitting on it.

Then too there were people selling hedgehogs on the sidewalks, vendors tossing out bad fruit, watermelon farmers camping out on the street while they sold the wares they'd brought to town and lots of people taking naps. Beijingers have a grand lack of self-consciousness about sleeping in public—also spitting. And when it comes to nose picking, my hat is off to the Beijing man in the street. I saw every finger used, expertly.

The mass of bikes, as turgid as a pack of marathoners at the start of a race, would swing way out into the line of vehicular traffic. A lovely young bright-lipsticked woman with her skirts tucked up around her handlebars would float through the pack like a swallow through a fog. Bike bells disputed with car horns and little chirruping bus tooters. We saw only one out-and-out dispute—somebody got off a bus, a biker dismounted and picked up a chunk of concrete, the bus rider grabbed the biker's bike and threw it at him. Otherwise the collective-slash-competitive jockeying instinct was refined to a high economy of movement, and since I tend to swoop latitudinarily on a bike when I'm looking around and feeling good, I often complicated the flow in ways that made me feel like I was hitting clinkers in the midst of an enormous choir. From time to time I heard an exasperated grunt from an elderly woman compelled to swerve uncoolly around me, but generally the locals no more called attention to themselves individually than waves do in the sea. Kirven and I made some neck-risking dashes across four-lane intersections, and pretty soon he was going just about as fast through the mélange as he did in the scarcely peopled outskirts of town. And yet the three of us stayed in touch, like small, hardy boats in radio contact.

Kirven is six foot five, Lois is black, and I couldn't resist buying and wearing hats (one of them a duck's head with a big bill that opened and closed) that now, looking at myself in our snapshots, I regret. But our odd threesome attracted hardly any incredulous looks. Kirven found a perpetual full-court basketball game at a college near the Friendship Hotel. Although he was dunking over players a good foot shorter than he was, he was always welcome. Nobody kept score, and when you accidentally passed the ball to someone on the other team he would hand it back to you.

We didn't do much nightlife. Amy Tan had advised me, "You can get taken up the yinyang. A Chinese expression. You're taken to a special place, where they offer you the special fish, and a special drink, and a special girl to sing for you. And the bill will be $2,500. And they will kill you if you don't pay."

We did check out the karaoke bar in the Friendship Hotel. Upscale Beijingers really get into karaoke, which they call MTV. One man was crooning along with a syrupy love ballad when his beeper went off. He went right on crooning without missing a beat. I had a special drink, all right: a "Folating Immortal Happiness," which I couldn't quite place the taste of until Lois had a sip and said, "Ginger ale and Robitussin." Kirven passed up the "Harvey Wall Banker" for a "Love Is Happiness," whose taste was so special that he had to rinse his mouth out with some of my Folating.

We got up on the Great Wall, of course. To keep itself the center of the universe, China built a wall around itself. Didn't work. Mongols and other barbarians kept coming in. A lesson to us all. Toward the top was a guy dressed as a Mongol, waving a wooden sword, who gets peeved if you don't want to pay him to pose with you for pictures.

We also flew to Xian to see the 2,200-year-old, formerly subterranean terra-cotta army. In 1974 some peasants were digging—not trying to dig through to America to see whether we were upside down, they just needed a well. They came upon some ancient pottery fragments, didn't want to get in trouble, so notified authorities. Subsequent excavation revealed something genuinely astonishing. Emperor Qin Shihuang, who held sway in China during the third century B.C., apparently had a highly developed interment instinct. He set back Chinese culture considerably by burying Confucian scholars alive. He also arranged to have a military escort in the afterlife. When he was laid to rest in his underground mausoleum, thousands of lifesize terra-cotta soldiers—each one with individual facial features and armor and weapons—were buried along with him. Also horses and chariots. No one had known for centuries that this army was there underground. Now the earth has been dug and brushed away from over 7,000 of the warriors and 100 chariots. The restored soldiers, standing heartily at attention in rank after rank, look like they're ready to kick ass this minute, though it looked to me as if one of them was whispering out of the corner of his mouth to another one, "I forget—what is it we're protecting?"

A metaphor for the curse? No, just for the defenses around it.

In the lobby of Xian's fine New Asia Era Hotel, Kirven and Lois saw a Russian tourist with his necktie sticking out of his fly. "It was zipped halfway up, and the end of his tie sort of flounced out like an ascot," said Kirven. "An old-style big tie, of course. And it must have been a style, in this guy's mind, because if it had been a mistake, the guy with him would've said, 'Your tie's sticking out.' "

"Maybe the other guy didn't want to give the guy with the tie the satisfaction of calmly answering, 'Yes, I know,' " I suggested.

"Yes," said Lois, "he looked like the kind of person who would say that."

We were less sure how to interpret Chinese signification.

What to make of this, on a package of condoms we saw for sale: "Dispensing male and female maladjustments." Or of the Chinese tendency to hyphenate the English word *the*:

PLEASE KEEP TH-
E HEALTHING OF
ENVIRONMENT.

Lois took the position that the Chinese were perfectly capable of writing straightforward English, but did it the way they do it to be charming. "They know exactly what they're doing," she said firmly.

I don't know. A lot of women have insisted to me that I knew exactly what I was doing.

Our last night in Beijing, Lois and Kirven and the Swans and a couple of other Americans and I walked around Tiananmen Square. During daily visiting hours we had seen Mao in state there—people bought flowers at the entrance to his mausoleum and placed them around his casket as they filed by, then attendants took the flowers up and brought them around to the entrance to be sold again. We had bought souvenir Mao pocketknives and Mao pens and Mao calendars.

Now we stood around under the enormous portrait of Mao at the Gate of Heavenly Peace. Historic Chinese places tend to have names like that— Pavilion of Shared Coolness, Studio of Quieting the Mind, Library of Embracing Simplicity, Hall of Nourishing Heavenly Nature, Garden of the Palace of a Peaceful Old Age, Gate of Supreme Harmony. In 1989, as many as 3,000 students and workers who had been demonstrating on the square were killed by government tanks and gunfire.

"We are actually hoping for bloodshed," a student leader told an American reporter the night before the massacre. "Only when the square is awash with blood will the Chinese people open their eyes."

The government disposed of the bodies secretly.

Just before we arrived in Beijing, local people were locked up for commemorating the bloodbath by tossing up shredded white paper on the square, to symbolize the release of doves.

"Treat with Disdain Powerful Gropu," is it?

Easy for a T-shirt to say.

There we were at the center of the universe, and the quiet was eerie.

People are afraid to commit street crime in Beijing. We strolled into the lobby of the luxurious Palace Hotel, where a Chinese string quartet was playing, earnestly, exquisitely, "I Dream of Jeannie with the Light Brown Hair."

It's a good thing I never got around to digging straight through the earth when I was a boy, because, in fact, the diametrically opposite spot on the globe from where I grew up is somewhere in the middle of the Indian Ocean. I would have drowned. But let's just say I had gotten around to it, and had taken care to remain right side up, myself, all the way through, and eventually—right after I came upon a, yep, upside-down terra-cotta soldier—my shovel had broken through the surface of China, and I had looked down between my feet and seen the sky. I would have felt oriented. As it happened, no such breakthrough.

It wasn't until we were on our way back home that I Came to a Realization. Our layover in Vancouver was long enough that Lois, Kirven and I were able to take a cab to the waterfront and sit on a bench and jet-laggedly enjoy a beautiful Western morning, feeling a nice breeze, sharing coolness, embracing simplicity, quieting the mind, and . . .

Then it hit me. My children and my friends enjoy hanging with each other! And I with my children's friends!

Not only that, but we three, Lois and Kirven and I, had not had a single argument. In an inscrutable place we had a harmonious ten days: coordinating offhandedly, keeping an eye out for one another, laughing at the same things, enjoying the same Swans, and each of us instinctively playing a different unshowily supportive, sufficiently independent role.

Lois is a mom, Kirven is a son, I am a dad. We love each other. A family. The words of the T-shirt: "We can to communicate."

Maybe families should be assembled platonically.

And they never will be.

Once you factor in somebody for each of us to sleep with—and in my case, someone to risk getting married to and breaking up with after having children who might turn away from me the way I turned away from my parents, which I don't think I could bear, which I don't know how my parents bore, which in fact probably sped my mother's death . . .

"ALL OF THE WORLD IS A COCORABBIT."

CHAPTER 23 / **A Road Not Taken**

I guess you children wouldn't have liked any of the friends
Daddy and I had when we were young.
—MY MOTHER TO SUSAN ONCE, SEMI-PITIFULLY

No, I guess we wouldn't've.   —SUSAN, IN REPLY

O f all my friends, Lois's husband, Roland, is most like my father. When I
got to be friends with him, he was more like me. A couple of years ago
I realized that he had become something very like the man my parents
would have liked me to be. And yet we are *still* friends.

"What's the point of having a corporate jet if we have to get up early?"
Lois asked Roland one morning. My sentiments exactly. Which is probably
one reason I am not a mogul, and Roland is. He can get up better. Which is
why, at his insistence, we met at the Bettses' Manhattan house at 7:20 a.m.
to fly to their Santa Fe house. I believe he had already run several miles.

I can *stay* up better than he can. Not that Roland can't have a good
time: the night after the birth of his first child, my goddaughter Mags, we
were up late buying drinks for several houses. And after we watched the
second Ali-Frazier fight—the Thrilla in Manila—on closed circuit, we
were out on the town till the wee hours exchanging near ecstatic shouts of
AH-LEE, AH-LEE with pimps and cops and ad salesmen (that was a great
communal occasion in the New York streets—everybody knew what everybody was hollering about).

But both those nights were back before Roland was a mogul. A couple
of years ago in the Bettses' house in the Berkshires (they have also built
one on the island of Tortola), family and friends went on talking uproari-
ously for a couple of hours as Roland slept peacefully on the floor in our
midst. He generally goes to bed early, gets up early, runs and then works.
He loves to work. That's another reason he's a mogul and I'm not. I'm not
saying I want to be a mogul, particularly, at least full-time. I'm not even

saying that I want to know moguls. It's not as though I hang out in mogul bars hoping to strike up acquaintances. But there's no getting around it: one of my closest friends is a mogul, in several fields.

Roland's company, Silver Screen Management, financed almost all the movies made by Disney from 1985 to 1990. He is the largest single stockholder of the Texas Rangers baseball team—which Roland's group is in the process of selling for some $200 million more than they paid for it. His company, Chelsea Piers Management, has developed a highly successful 1.7-million-square-foot sports and entertainment complex (TV and movie and fashion photography studios, a rock-climbing wall, two skating rinks, deep-sea-fishing access, a summer-games facility, a driving range with "ball plumbing" and computerized tees) in Manhattan on the old ocean-liner piers sticking out into the Hudson River between Sixteenth and Twenty-third streets, where the *Mauretania* and the *Lusitania* used to dock.

I should be in charge of an institution by now. Garrison developed "A Prairie Home Companion," my friend Ruff (the one who appears tangentially in the Bird Dog Hall of Fame) is chairman of all sorts of interesting things. Back in college, Ruff was president of the honor council and I was editor of the student newspaper; we were executive peers.

At what point did I turn, once and for all, from the path toward becoming a responsible executive like my father? When Lamar Alexander suggested I stick to writing—I succeeded him as editor of the paper—instead of succeeding him also as president of our fraternity, Sigma Chi.

I had been president of my seventh-grade class and of my senior class at Decatur High School, but never again. Lamar went on to be governor of Tennessee, president of the University of Tennessee and a contender for the Republican presidential nomination in 1996. He has never used his Jr., in fact, has always gone by his middle name instead of his and his father's first, Andrew. No Little Andy, he. You may recall that his campaign posters said, simply and insistently, "LAMAR!" When I saw that analysts were saying he might be the party's best threat against incumbent Clinton, I had second thoughts about removing my hat from the ring back there in college. Here I sit, I said to myself, composing limericks—

A pokerface man in Mobile,
When women ask "How do you feel?"
Will only say, "Well,

I ain't gonna tell.
Who says that is part of the deal?"

"Come up and see me," said Flower,
And then, when I entered her bower,
"The shower—I'm in it—
Just give me a minute. . . ."
I saw her and raised her an hour.

—and Lamar is running for president.

The Phil Gramm campaign distributed biographies of all the other Republican contenders that contained what, to Gramm people, must have seemed clever little subliminal digs. "By his senior year," the Gramm bio of Lamar noted, "Alexander became editor of the college newspaper and used his position to promote racial tolerance, a major source of conflict at the time."

A civilized person would put it that racial *in*tolerance was a major source of conflict at the time. It was 1962, and black students had been admitted to most of the South's state universities, over stiff white resistance, but the University of Mississippi was still holding firm—the bloody riots at Ole Miss over the admission of James Meredith were a year away—and the Vanderbilt University undergraduate body (like Duke's) was lily-white. Lamar was editor of *The Hustler*—yes, that was the name of our paper. Larry Flynt, editor of *Hustler*, which enjoys nothing more than to put diarrhea and naked women together, is a folk hero, and the editor of *The Hustler*, who attacked racism, is . . . not.

In the January 5, 1962, issue of *The Hustler*, Lamar dropped what at the time was a bombshell: "Presently a carefully worded statement offering admittance to Negroes who can not find an equal education at another Nashville university restricts colored students from all schools except divinity and law and a few graduate departments.

"This is a cowardly policy. At best it is avoiding the issue. How consistent is it to say that Vanderbilt is one of the nation's best universities but that Negroes may find equal educational opportunities at other Nashville schools?"

At least that was on the side of making white bread available to people of all colors. He and I kept pushing the issue in the paper, and in the student senate our fellow Sigma Chi John Sergent introduced a resolution to admit "qualified Negroes." The senate bumped the issue over to a campus referendum.

Sergent and I debated anti-integrationists in a raucous special assembly. Another Sigma Chi, Alan Gibson, threw the weight of the Student Christian Association behind . . .

We brothers were all white ourselves, of course. It was students of predominantly black Fisk College, on the other side of town, who went out and got hit on the head integrating lunch counters. (I went along on a sit-in led by John Lewis, who went on to become a hero of the movement and a congressman, but I didn't get arrested, I just wrote a column.) However, we got written up by the Associated Press, and once after I became editor I answered the *Hustler* phone and was delighted when a voice very much like that of the guy who cornholes Ned Beatty in *Deliverance* threatened to "git" us, and although the student referendum went two to one against receiving qualified Negroes into our bosom, Vanderbilt did, the year after I graduated, finally accept its first black undergraduates.

To tell the truth, although I am a staunch anti-Republican, I always thought it would be nice for Lamar to be president some day because he'd be *civilized* (Lamar is from East Tennessee, where Republicanism derives from hill folk's incompatibility with the Confederacy), and my college crusading might piggyback into history.

But Lamar was right. I am not presidential timber.

After spending a couple of days with him on the campaign trail, I said to myself, "Well, I may not have achieved my destiny, but at least I haven't been reduced to running for president."

I want to be one of the boys in the back of the bus. Let some denounceable politician or captain of industry have the *tsuris* and the vainglory of driving the damn thing. And let the other, nicer boys sit up near the driver and behave themselves. What is sweet, to me, is to sit in the back with the boys who guffaw and snigger and throw things at the backs of the heads of the ones up front. I don't want to beat anybody up, which the boys in the back sometimes do, but I want to *command* the bus, attitudinally. I have had to work my way with difficulty to the back of the bus, because I started out so *nice*, but I have made it.

Being a president helped kill my father, when he was five years older than I am now.

But maybe if I'd CEO'd the way Roland has . . .

I believe I mentioned all the Bettses' houses, and the corporate jet. I flew on the jet, with Roland and Lois, and I didn't pay my way. There are several other matters I will have to explain if I ever run for president, but let's don't go into those now. Let's just clear the air on this mogul-jet deal.

Roland wasn't a mogul when I met him, back in 1972. He was a reform-minded assistant principal in an inner-city high school in New Jersey. He had a beard. Actually, I met Lois first, at the mailboxes of the brownstone where I had a tiny apartment. I was hoping she was a new tenant. She informed me that she and some guy were now my landlords. In those days you could buy a brownstone on West 102nd Street, in a neighborhood whose population tilted heavily toward winos, for a lot less than it would cost to buy a small co-op apartment around there now. The Bettses lived on the ground floor and paid the mortgage with the rent from the apartments on the three upper floors. Roland went down into the basement and knocked out some walls (another reason I'm not a mogul: why have walls if you're going to knock them out?) and single-handedly added a floor to their living quarters.

We got to be good friends. Roland and I scalped tickets—purely for journalistic purposes—outside Yankee Stadium during the 1977 World Series. Roland and Lois were the only people with me when I got the news that my father had died, and seven years later that my mother had. Lois picked me up at the hospital after I had a sinus operation. Mags (now a student at Princeton after a year in Paris) took her first step in my house in the Berkshires, and I think I am also the godfather of her sister Jessie (now a student at Yale), though that title may belong to Jimmy Rogers, an old Yale buddy of Roland's who is the architect of the Chelsea Piers project. Tom Bernstein, Roland's partner in Silver Screen and Chelsea, is an early lawyering friend of his (I'll explain how Roland got into lawyering in a minute). The younger George Bush, operating partner of the Rangers, was Roland's roommate at Yale. "I won't do business with anybody unless I like them," Roland says, which is another reason I am not a mogul: I don't like anybody who does business.

Except Roland, who is grandfathered in. Here was his background when I met him: he had devoted his senior college year, in Aquarian 1967–68, to an independent study of Intermediate School 201 in central Harlem. When he found that he couldn't be deferred from the draft for law school, he became a teacher and a teacher-trainer in the wilds of way-uptown Manhattan. He worked with The Teachers Incorporated (one of whose organizers was Harris Wofford, later to be a Pennsylvania senator), which was determined to bring community control and a new wind of organic order to a school system that made *Blackboard Jungle* look like *Little Women*. Lois, who was teaching at P.S. 75, came to a Teachers Inc. meeting. Roland was cutting a broad sixties swath through the women teachers, but Lois would not be mowed. Feelings deepened in due time (he realized he loved her even when she was throwing up—not that that was a common occurrence), and commitment flowered.

The public school system, however, resisted improvement. "We realized we were white boys trying to do it," Roland says, "and we got tired." He was going to have to do something else to support his family. But first he wrote *Acting Out—Coping with Big City Schools*, which was published by Little, Brown in 1978 and remains one of the best books on the subject, and the funniest. It treated such matters as how a teacher can get away with farting in class without diminution of authority.

So you can see that this is the kind of mogul I might legitimately like. (Even after I was displaced by the Betts household's expansion into the entire New York brownstone—what used to be my apartment is now their living room.)

Acting Out also includes a sober, thoroughgoing analysis of every aspect of inner-city schools: domineering chief custodians, insensitive veteran teachers, variously resourceful substitute teachers (for instance, one woman who was expert at holding the attention of students, who referred to her reverently as "No Drawers"), struggling or irresponsible parents, conniving board members, and touchingly game kids, including Theotis Davis, who had three fingers on each hand and three toes on each foot and starred as the catcher on the baseball team Roland organized, and James Thompson, who said he had two ambitions in life: "to go to Harvard Law School and to knock off Chicken Delight."

While writing the book, and while Lois continued to teach, Roland went through Columbia Law School. He had in mind becoming a litigator, but a summer job at Paul, Weiss and Rifkind revealed the delights of entertainment law. After he got his degree, that firm hired him. He devised new ways of financing films—most notably, *Gandhi* and *The Killing Fields*—then started his own film-financing company, Silver Screen.

And made a series of deals with Disney. Frank Wells and Michael Eisner had just taken over the company, and they needed cash. Roland sold them on an arrangement whereby Silver Screen would raise money through public stock offerings to finance films with budgets of no more than $20 million each. In return Silver Screen got 50 percent of the profits and, by the way, the copyrights to the films. Five years and four stock offerings later, Disney decided they could make a better deal with Japanese investors (although Wells remained a close friend—Roland was invited on the helicopter skiing trip that took Wells's life last spring). By that time Silver Screen owned the rights to ninety or so films, including *The Little Mermaid*, *Beauty and the Beast*, *Pretty Woman* and *Ernest Goes on Vacation*. Between 1995 and the millennium, at ten-year intervals after each of the eighties offerings, Disney must buy back the rights or Silver Screen can sell them to the highest bidder. The value of all the films together, Roland told me at his house in Santa Fe (zestfully furnished six-bedroom faux-adobe with four-hundred-year-old doors imported from Pakistan and Afghanistan, a kidney-shaped pool, mountain views, lots of paintings and sculpture and a leased orchid plant) has been estimated at a figure that I am not at liberty to disclose, but let's just say a shitload.

And I mean a shitload. Until that figure came up, I had not quite realized what kind of ballpark my man was playing in. True, he *had* mentioned in recent years that he was looking into buying Epcot Center and a nuclear plant, but those deals didn't go through, and frankly (a nuclear plant?), I kind of blocked them out. I did think it was cool when Silver Screen bankrolled the salvaging off Cape Cod of the sunken pirate ship *Whydah*. (Roland still hasn't given up on his plan to raise the whole ship and turn it into a museum, but black activists in Boston and then Tampa managed to block that project in those cities on the grounds that the *Whydah* was a slave ship before the pirates seized it—although Roland made the case in community meetings that the slavery angle would be treated with proper seriousness and that the pirates ran the ship democratically, and although a photograph in the *Tampa Tribune* made it evident that Lois was herself glowingly African American.)

Most of the time, Roland doesn't even seem overworked. He throws himself into projects, gets them set up solidly, and then he plays a powerful game of tennis; golfs in the seventies; takes pleasure in his bulldog, Maxx (who once jumped between me and the fire in my fireplace when I threw a lot of paper into it and it flared out threateningly); devotes lots of time to his kids (and on occasion to mine) and to his and Lois's relatives;

serves on the executive committee of the Harlem School of the Arts; and roots merrily for the Rangers from the visiting owners' field-level box whenever they play in Yankee Stadium. (He once startled then Yankee Dave Winfield, after Winfield steamed into third, by loudly denouncing the chili served at a restaurant Winfield then owned near the Betts brownstone.) If I were a mogul I would be constantly frazzled. I am constantly frazzled now, and I am not connected to anywhere near a shitload of anything, except little scraps of paper that I have scribbled notes on that I can't read. I'm still doing the fart material.

> *Professor emeritus Carter*
> *Is quite without qualms as a farter.*
> *Goes* FPLT! *with some force,*
> *Betrays no remorse,*
> *Indeed looks vaguely the martyr.*

I forgot to mention that Roland owns the Sistine Chapel ceiling. Well, a full-scale reproduction of it. Remember the scene in *Six Degrees of Separation* in which Donald Sutherland and Stockard Channing are given a close up tour of the Sistine ceiling, and she slaps hands with the depiction of Jehovah? That scene was filmed in a studio at the Chelsea piers. When they were tearing down the set, Roland asked what they were going to do with the ceiling. Bust it up and throw it away, they said. Roland gave them $5,000 for it, and he has it stored, in panels, at the piers. You can talk about a rich man having to go through the eye of a needle all you want, but if I were a religious person, I would bet you that God (as for Michelangelo, who knows?), in spite of *Ernest Takes a Vacation*, would not be loath to slap hands with Roland.

As for me, well, I believe I do a certain thing as well as anybody. For instance, this couplet of film criticism, a review of *I Wake Up Screaming*, with Betty Grable, Victor Mature and Carole Landis, which I rented the video of, to my regret, because of the title:

> *Blondes who don't go far enough,*
> *Film that isn't noir enough.*

The rhyming syllables are three-sevenths of the poem. Aside from the *r, ee* and *uh* sounds in the rhymes, consider how the *ah, n, d, s, oh, t, f* and *ih* sounds interplay. The *f* sound spelled *gh* gliding across the central comma into the *f* sound spelled *f*. The mixture of absorbed French and unreconstructed Anglo-Saxon. The macro-balance and micro-imbalances.

The question is, is this something *worth* doing that well?

I'm not going to develop an institution at this late date.

And do you know why?

Because I'm stuck with lifting the family curse.

CHAPTER 24 / I Go Home Again

'Tis an ill cook that cannot lick his own fingers.

—*ROMEO AND JULIET*

What is so rare as one's own hometown, in my case Decatur, Georgia, where both of my parents are buried in that sweet potato–colored dirt. I went down there several summers ago planning to do a lot of research for this book, but the first thing I did was run into a guy I went to high school with, who proceeded to remind me of the time we put cherry bombs in the toilets in high school, which never happened, and then I walked to the cemetery. As I was looking for my parents' graves, I was thinking for some reason of the time when I was fourteen and not fitting in in high school and my mother told me, "Lilah McGee says you and Joe have the best posture of any boys she knows."

I remembered how angry that made me. How could my mother have possibly thought it would make me feel good to hear that Joe McGee and I, neither of whom were particularly popular at the time, had extraordinarily good posture! I didn't want to have good posture! And my mother was so hurt that it made me so angry. And how about the time, I was thinking, when I was eight or nine and my mother made me go along with her to visit a friend of hers, and I was fidgeting and sighing and sullenly trying to entertain myself while they spoke of antiques or something, and suddenly I noticed the two of them looking at me and my mother saying, "But he doesn't have much stamina!"

What? That bothered me for years, until finally I became a divorced sportswriter and started staying up till all hours drinking and chasing women and realized that if there was anything I had, it was stamina. There was nobody I couldn't stay up with. And I could arise, hungover, the next morning and remember key things defensive linemen had told me in the middle of the night, and write.

I'll bet I had stamina when I was a kid too. I was just bored! Why would anybody say such a thing about the son of her bosom to some old church lady when the son of her bosom was right there listening? No telling what she said when I *wasn't*.

As I was walking through the cemetery thinking these ill-humored thoughts about my poor dead mother, a car pulled up alongside me and stopped, and somebody said, "Roy?"

Do you know who it was? It was Joe McGee. I hadn't seen him in thirty-six years, or so, but I recognized him immediately.

And do you know who was with him in the car? His mother, Lilah.

Too eerie. Eerier than Tiananmen Square. I couldn't do research under those conditions.

What got me back home, as it happened, was that *Sports Illustrated* asked me to help cover the 1996 Atlanta Olympics. If the image that Olympics left in your mind was either the *Star Spangled Banner* playing or a bomb bursting, I can understand. I watched U.S. teams win a couple of events, and I came out of a restaurant right after the bloody Centennial Park explosion—felt tension in the air, smelled cordite, rushed to the scene, scurried from survivor to survivor (you could tell them by the TV cameras already surrounding them), trying to find out what song the band was playing when the bomb went off (none, apparently).

But I'll tell you what the Olympics left planted firmly in my mind: certain passages from the *Dogon-Peulh*, a seduction dance of Burkina Faso that, if writing could do it justice, might be said to go sort of like this:

She: HEY! *Watch my booty move, big boy, beyond your wildest dreams, kapocketaboonkboonkboonkboonkboonk kapocketapock-etaboonkapocketa boonkboonkboonkboonkboonk . . .*

He: *Yehhhh-heh-heh-heh boomalammaboomalamma, it is a right good-moving booty. Heh-heh. Baloomaloomaloom. Smelllls good, too.*

And it did. Even muskier than the Delta. Could there be any way that my little old Methodist family tied into that musk?

• • •

Burkina Faso, the West African country adopted by my hometown for the Olympics, used to be a French colony, later an independent republic called Upper Volta. Its capital city is Ouagadougou. Its people are the Burkinabe. None of its five Olympic athletes made it to a victory stand, but thanks to its thirty-five-member Olympic delegation—in particular its percussion and dance troupe, Bonogo—I finally came to feel at home in the place where I come from, where the Burkinabe were honored guests.

Before I explain, let me tell you a quick football story. Back in the sixties, a professional wide receiver and his quarterback were passing through the latter's hometown. They were expected for a family dinner at the quarterback's parents' house, the house where he had grown up. But these two famous athletes got high (the sixties, remember), so high that when they drove to the quarterback's neighborhood, he couldn't focus on how to find his house. Here was their solution: they drove to the quarterback's old high school, the quarterback got out of the car and the wide receiver drove slowly along behind as the quarterback walked home from school.

Maybe that story isn't morally edifying. (I was told that Burkina Faso means "land of morally integrated people.") Neither, maybe, is the story of how I found my own way home thanks to the Olympics. But it's true.

Decatur is part of metropolitan Atlanta. When I was growing up there, as I have mentioned, it was kind of like *Leave It to Beaver*, only with lots of black people tucked away in little ghettos with names like Eskimo Heights. Decatur was desegregating, slowly and awkwardly, when I moved away in 1968. My sister left in 1971. After my father died in 1974 and my mother in 1981, my roots attenuated.

But every so often my travels brought me to Atlanta, and I would drive out to Decatur Square, where the old courthouse stands. I would stop to look at the bronze plaque that says ROY A. BLOUNT PLAZA. DEDICATED TO THE MEMORY OF A GREAT BUILDER OF HOMES AND SCHOOLS, AND THE RAPID TRANSIT SYSTEM WHICH LIES UNDER THIS PLAZA.

"You hear more stories around town about your dad," John Randall told me. He is a native Decaturite, and his wife, Linda Harris, is the daughter of my father's late friend Robin Harris. Linda Harris stayed on in Decatur to become marketing director of the Downtown Development Authority. Randall is immediate past president of the Decatur Business Association, which, along with the city government, took the Olympics as an occasion for a seventeen-day festival in the courthouse square. The Irish delegation, which has also been adopted by Decatur, installed a bar, made of green wood, in the old county courtroom. When I was growing up, the whole county was, like my prominently Methodist parents, staunchly dry. The courthouse an Irish pub! Would wonders never cease?

Budweiser, one of the festival's sponsors, sent actors from its commercials out to make appearances. The "I love you, man" guy from the Bud Light ads was, I regret to say, not a hit. He brought a large entourage, reportedly resisted saying "I love you, man" and did not want to be hugged. Can't blame the poor son of a bitch.

But the Burkinabe athletes—the two I met were Franck Zio, a long jumper, and Chantal Ouoba, a triple jumper—were highly popular around town. I got a sense that Franck was, in fact, cutting a certain interracial swath among young Decatur ladies. He had been living in Paris, spoke English and had a good deal of presence. "He could go right to Hollywood," said Linda Harris.

"One of the Burkinabe asked me to marry him," said Melissa Kirby, who worked at the Decatur Recreation Center, headquarters for the Burkinabe delegation. "He made me shake his hand. I may *be* married to him."

I would learn about the Burkinabe for a while, and then I would learn about Daddy. "You hear about little kindnesses," Randall told me. "Little nudges of the levers of power, things that people like your dad and Linda's did for all sorts of people, black and white, that nobody knew anything about at the time. It makes you feel like you can't do enough."

Yes, well, of course Daddy was the second-best person in the household at making you feel like that. But maybe there were nudges I didn't appreciate.

No little nudges in the Bonogo dance troupe's repertoire. They presented, to quote from the program, "screams of rejoicings" and "grace, strength, finesse and virility showcased through the charming contest between young men and women as they challenge each other by way of dance."

In 1985 Gary Gunderson, a Decatur resident who works for the Carter Center in Atlanta, returned from a visit to Burkina Faso and talked, in the Atlanta media, about how public-spiritedness and family values had prevailed among the Burkinabe in the face of drastic drought, disease and poverty. Mike Mears, then mayor of Decatur, got the notion that my hometown and Burkina Faso should get together.

Not so incongruous, so far. "Much of what I am, for better or worse," Mears, a white Southerner, told me, "comes from what people from Africa brought over." And the student body of Decatur High School—all white when I went there in the fifties—is now 63 percent African American.

Certainly Decatur is more prosperous than Burkina Faso, but it faces analogous challenges. Elizabeth Wilson, an African American, is the current mayor of Decatur. I got the impression from her that she and my father communicated well. On her visit to Burkina Faso in 1985, she said in a speech to some Burkinabe, "What strikes me here is the unity of families, and so many people who could make other choices but choose to stay here because they're going to make things better. I wish I could bottle that spirit up and take it home."

Just before Mears got his notion, there had been a Burkinabe living sixty miles from Decatur. "It helps," says Gunderson, "that the first Burkinabe to come into this relationship was smarter than all of the Americans put together." Mouhoussine Nacro was a visiting biochemist at the University of Georgia in Athens. He was looking for ways to produce energy from the bacteria in a soil sample he had brought from home—it resembled red dirt like north Georgia's, only drier, lighter and less stable because his country lacks north Georgia's moisture.

The summer heat in Georgia, the Burkinabe said, was about like that at home, but they had a little trouble adjusting to the humidity. They also found certain contemporary Atlanta-area customs strange. The extensiveness of body piercing, for instance. Nose and ears, okay, they said. But navels? "The very first Saturday I spent in Athens," said Nacro, who had become the Burkinabe ambassador to Canada but was ensconced in Decatur for the Olympics, "I walked onto the campus to go to the lab, and on my way I noticed that most of the people were wearing red-and-black shirts. The closer I got to the lab, the more I thought, People in this country very much like red-and-black shirts. I went to the lab and worked, and when I opened the door to leave, the campus was full of people in red and black! What's happening? I thought. I didn't feel exactly threatened, but on Monday I asked, 'Was this something traditional, a tribal thing?'

" 'No,' I was told, 'it was a game'! A home game of Georgia football!" Nacro became a Bulldogs fan. In 1984 he returned to Burkina Faso; the next year another Georgia professor, a close friend, contacted him on behalf of the Burkinabe-fan Decaturites.

With Nacro clearing the way, a delegation from Decatur traveled to

Burkina Faso and established a sister-city relationship with Boussé, a town whose population is roughly equivalent to Decatur's 17,300.

"Thanks to money and assistance from Decatur," says Nacro, "Boussé was able to build a tower, drill a well and have tap water for the first time." Before, they had only surface water, which they might have to walk four miles to get to and which was often infested with microscopic guinea worms that grew—talk about a curse—within people's bodies until they burst out horribly through the skin. "Now people can get water in the center of the village, and it is clean water," Nacro said. "There are clinics, so that people can have doctors and nurses. There is a new school building."

And thanks to Burkina Faso there were, as Linda Harris put it, "fertility dances—and no doubt about it, either: those movements—on *Decatur Square!*"

Maybe that wouldn't seem remarkable on your town's square. But if you'd grown up in Decatur! The official language of Burkina Faso is French. Decatur has a cop now who speaks French. I saw him doing it—interpreting back and forth between his fellow officers and Ouoba, the triple jumper. When I was growing up in Decatur, I'm not sure we had cops who spoke English. I studied French under Miss McGeachy at Decatur High School, but I haven't kept it up. Emily Hanna-Vergara, a historian of African art and the president of Decatur's sister-city committee, translated as I spoke with the dance troupe's director, Jean Ouedraogo, and with Lamber Ouedraogo (no relation), vice-president of Boussé's sister-city program.

Jean was wearing a shirt hung with horsehair tufts and goat-horn danglers. "A shirt worn by priests," he explained through Emily. "Priests that outsiders typically call sorcerers. The priest acts as a liaison between the world of the living and the invisible world of ancestors and spirits."

It occurred to me to suggest that he and I and several of the dancers step over to the Roy A. Blount Plaza plaque.

Emily translated the inscription for the Burkinabe.

"My father would be honored," I said, "that you are here." In fact, if you had told me before the Olympics that there would be an African seduction dance on my father's plaza, I might have said he would be turning over in his grave. But he was a genial man, even I know that. And maybe people in the grave like to turn over.

The two Burkinabe gave me looks that communicated well. "They are very touched," Emily said. "They say that for them, your dad has not gone, he is here with us speaking your name to them. When they dance again, the first dance will be in honor of your dad."

It would be appropriate in this situation, Jean told me, to make an offering to my father of a chicken or some beer.

"Unless he's changed his habits in the Hereafter," I told John Randall later, "I think he'd appreciate the chicken more."

"Should it be a live chicken?" Randall asked. That opened up all sorts of theological and practical questions that hadn't occurred to me when the Burkinabe were telling me my father was there, with us, speaking my name, at his plaque. Because I was crying, then.

When the Burkinabe danced again it was Burkina Faso Night on the square. Susan came in from Houston. She ran into a couple of friends from high school. Surrounded by heartily sweaty dancers and drummers in the band shell on the square, Mayor Wilson called me up to say a word. I looked around and realized that while I was off escaping the strictures of Decatur, Decatur had become the kind of place I wish I lived in. Academic types, post-hippies with babies, black folks and white folks mingling. Someone in the *Journal-Constitution*, I'm told, described Decatur as "a cross between Mayberry and Berkeley."

"This is exactly the kind of thing I like," I said. I felt . . . integrated. "Please don't spoil it by expecting me to dance."

But what I was thinking was, I loved you, man.

CHAPTER 25 / The Family Curse

The more sentimental a man is, the less is he helpful, the more loath is he to cancel the cause of his emotion. —MAX BEERBOHM

Couldn't you just kill 'em sometimes?" my mother used to say to her women friends about children. And to us, "I'll skin you alive." "I'll beat you to within an inch of your life." "I'll snatch a knot in you."

Always tongue-in-cheek. Figures of speech. But behind them lurked the family curse:

A wife and mother, whose husband is devoted and whose children are turning out, by most standards, well, is so unhappy that not only won't she admit that her loved ones love her, she also leaves her children with matricidal guilt.

"You'll probably write about me someday," my mother told me when we were arguing about something. Well, I'll tell you what we were arguing about. It had transpired that it was the policy of Agnes Scott College to have no Jewish professors. This was back in 1968. I wrote a sort of matter-of-course editorial in the *Atlanta Journal* criticizing that policy. "The Atlanta area's educational institutions would never be respectable as long as they clung to such parochialism" sort of thing. To my astonishment my mother jumped all over me about it. I don't even know how she knew I wrote the editorial. Maybe somebody called up the *Journal* and found out, and called my father and his feelings got hurt, and it was my mother's role to magnify those feelings and pass them on to me. I guess she saw it as a matter of my being snotty about her community's hard-earned values. She and my father were great supporters of Agnes Scott, she said, and it wasn't a matter of prejudice, my father was friends with the owner of Rich's department store in Atlanta and several other fine local Jewish men, and why couldn't Agnes Scott have all Christian professors, Brandeis had all Jewish ones. "You are starting to write things that sound *snide*," she said.

I guess I should have realized that she was afraid I was getting so far off her wavelength that she'd never be able to get through to me. In fact, that was happening. But I flashed back—grown man that I was—on all those times when I was a kid and she said, "Don't you talk back to me." "Don't you use that snippy tone to me."

And I said, "I *want* to sound snide." That really set her off.

"What have you ever done for anybody?" she demanded. I couldn't come up with anything offhand. She gave me a withering look. "You'll probably write about me someday," she said, "and you don't know anything about me."

I guess there should have ensued a long heart-to-heart that would make a great scene in this book, but at that moment I didn't feel like I wanted to know anything more about her. I don't think I ever asked her about her childhood. She was too likely to come out with her single reminiscence of her stepmother: "Used to beat me till the blood ran." Come out with it in a voice that sounded not at all maternal, but frighteningly childish and full of implication: the implication, for instance, that I, Mr. Social Conscience, ought to feel responsible for *that*, if anything.

She would volunteer an old family story from time to time. Her aunt Annie, before dying, unmarried, of yellow fever around the turn of the century, published poems in the local paper and wrote a novel, *Bound by Honor's Chains*. She didn't know anything about getting a book published, so she wangled an invitation to a ball at Governor Vardaman's mansion, thinking that someone there would have connections, and sure enough she met a lady from New York who took her manuscript back with her and got it published, all right, but under her, the New York lady's, name—*she* wasn't bound by honor's chains.

Aunt Annie was left with a false address for the lady and a beaded evening gown and big plume she never had any occasion to wear again. The family's maid, Kate (you didn't have to have much money to have a maid back then in Mississippi), eyed the gown in the closet for years, and when her husband, Jack, died, she borrowed it for the funeral.

Three days later she turned up still wearing the gown and still carrying the plume. She said, "I was the hatred of all the women, and the dee-light of all the men."

My mother would tell us how good it was to come home from school and have a snack of cold corn bread broken up into buttermilk, and she confessed in a mischievous tone to having fed liniment to a black playmate to see what would happen, and once after I moved to New York and got curious about the fact that the sole classic movie I was ever exposed to, growing up, was *The Birth of a Nation*, which my grammar-school class was taken to see a special showing of at the Fox Theatre in Atlanta back in the early fifties, she wrote me this reminiscence, from the early twenties, after she went to live with her aunt Pearl and uncle Archie:

Roy you asked about your trip to see *Birth of a Nation*. At that time the race issue was practically nonexistent so far as we knew in our area. It was not sponsored by any one group and you-all were carried to see it from a historical standpoint only. The Ku Klux Klan was nearly dead at that time—rarely heard from. Your father and I saw it, and I remember it being a magnificent movie and we did not at that time consider it as racial. I've now forgotten the details of the movie, but the scene at the end about shipping the Negroes back to Africa was not shown, I'm sure. Even when I was a small child the Klan had lost the respect of most decent-thinking people. I remember once when Uncle Archie was chairman of the board of stewards at old Phoenix Park Methodist Church, now nonexistent, the Klan came to visit our little church in robes. We were raising money to build Main Street Methodist Church. They came to show approval of the building and to make a contribution. One of the ushers came and whispered to Uncle Archie. He went to the door and asked them not to enter unless they unmasked. They said several of their members were active in our church and this was a goodwill gesture. He didn't let them come in—and they didn't leave the contribution, which was sorely needed. Auntie Pearl didn't sleep all night for fear they would come in the night and tar and feather Uncle Archie. Also, everyone in church spent the rest of the service looking around to see who wasn't there, and debating about whether the absent ones were members of the Klan. This is my only brush or memory of much mention of the Klan. I thought little of it then, but I look back now and think how much courage it took for that small, rather mild little man to stand there and turn them back.

Archie was a railroad bridge tender. Pearl was the daughter of a railroad worker. Archie enjoyed her column in the railroad's house organ so much, he paid a call on her. They never had any children of their own. After he died of a heart attack on the job, Aunt Pearl tried to keep her thumb on my mother, tried to keep her from marrying my father, but in that she was unsuccessful, because they gave up on having a wedding and slipped off for a quick, small ceremony. Aunt Pearl did manage to become an invalid and move in with the newlyweds.

My poor mother, orphaned, abused, saddled with a mean aunt, denied any anesthetic when she had her tonsils out ("I held a silver basin to spit the blood in"), deprived of an eye, afflicted with arthritis. Couldn't afford higher education, didn't get to wear her wedding dress, kept an immaculate house and cooked three hot meals a day for thirty-some-odd years (which alone is enough to drive anybody crazy)—and then her son, for whom she did all she could, puts her on the defensive about one of the greatest films of all time and a fine Christian college!

But that doesn't add up to a family curse. There had to be something more ferocious gnawing at her, making her not only resentful of her children but sometimes venomous toward us. Surely the roughest figure in Louise's rough childhood was the stepmother who beat her and abandoned her to relatives whom she overheard saying that they didn't want her.

So I figured what I would do, specifically, to lift the family curse was go spit on my mother's stepmother's grave. First I had to find it.

I traveled from Scoby, Mississippi, to Ola and Little Rock, Arkansas, and back to Jackson, Mississippi, by way of Monticello, Mississippi, tracking my mother's background.

My great-grandfather George Henry Floyd was born in 1839 in Vermont, came to Mississippi to work on the railroad. In 1860 he was living in a boardinghouse with twelve other railroad bridge builders from Norway, New York, Canada, Ireland, Ohio, Wisconsin, New Hampshire and Georgia. Must have been interesting when war broke out. George Henry had a brother who fought (according to my mother) for the Yankees, but George stayed in Mississippi with the rebels. (Maybe he was already courting Eliza A. Lawson, whom he married after the war and whose widowed mother had ten slaves.)

In 1869 George Henry, employed as a wagon maker, was taxed forty cents for his dog. Apparently he didn't own anything else. By 1891 he was a farmer who owned one cow assessed at $15, one horse at $25, three mules at $180, two carriages at $35, one piano at $25, one watch at $15, for a total worth of $270. He's never listed as owning a home. Sharecropping, maybe. George Henry Floyd Jr., my grandfather, was born in 1887. He got a traveling job on the railroad—he was a brakeman, like Jimmie

Rodgers, the father of country music, though given the poignantly (to us) imperfect pitch of my mother and me, I doubt he could sing. In 1911 in Yell County, Arkansas (where Mattie Ross, the heroine of *True Grit*, is from), he married Ida Prichard, daughter of a railroad tie maker. In 1913 they had a daughter, Pearl, and in 1914 they had my mother, Mattye Louise. In 1915 Ida died. Of what, I couldn't determine. But I did find records of her successor. In 1917, according to an index of Mississippi marriages kept in Arkansas, George married Nellie Burk. But that must be wrong, because in the 1920 Mississippi census his wife was identified as Lettie.

Susan has most of the old family photographs. We found one on which someone—presumably Lettie—has written, "Dad, two old cronies, Nellie and me." If you hold that photograph up to the light, you can see a faint inscription, "Lettie," on the older girl—and from later pictures you can see that this clearly was Lettie—and "Nellie" on the younger.

Was Nellie a witness of the marriage and her name wound up in the index as that of the bride? At any rate, Lettie is clearly the notorious stepmother. In 1918, when George and Lettie had been married for only five and a half months, Pearl—not the mean Aunt Pearl my mother would wind up with, but the only sibling she would ever have—died of peritonitis.

Little Louise was not yet four. She kept wandering around looking for her sister (so she confided once to Ennis, never to Susan or me), because no one told her what had happened. And in 1922, when she was not quite eight, her father died.

I found the notice of his death in Monticello's daily paper, the *Lawrence County Press*, which was full of patent medicine ads: "Mineralized Water Routs Chicken Lice," "Women Need Swamp Root," "Mother! Move Child's Bowels with California Fig Syrup," and "You Can't Trust Calomel At All. The next dose of calomel you take may salivate you. It may shock your liver or start bone necrosis. It is mercury, quicksilver. It crashes into sour bile like dynamite, cramping and sickening you. If you feel bilious, headachy, constipated and all knocked out, just go to your druggist and get a bottle of Dodson's Liver Tone."

Right next to a huge ad for Tanlac ("promotes energetic action of all the bowel muscles and glands and enables the food to pass through the digestive canal in the normal time") was the daily Sunday school lesson, entitled "The Downfall of Israel." On another page was an installment of *Ramsey Mulholland*, by Booth Tarkington, and an anecdote picked up from the *Philadelphia Ledger*:

LESSER EVIL, AS IT WERE

Darky's Excellent Reason for Pre-
Ferring to Take His Chances
With the Bear

A New York man tells of an exciting bear hunt in Mississippi. The bear
was surrounded in a small cane thicket. The dogs could not get him
out, and the gentleman who was at the head of the hunting party
called to one of the darkies:

"Gus, go in there and get that bear out."

Gus hesitated for a moment and then plunged into the cane. A
few moments later the negro, the bear and the dogs were rolling on
the ground outside. After the hunt was over the man from the north
said to the darky:

"Gus, weren't you afraid to go into that thicket with the bear?"

"Colonel," said Gus, "it was jest dis way: I neber had met that
b'ar, but I was pussunally acquainted with the old boss, so I jest
nachurally took dat b'ar."

My grandfather's death was announced simply as follows:

"The many friends of Mrs. Floyd and Mrs. C. B. Walker deeply sympathize with them in the loss by death of George Floyd, son and brother
respectively, which sad event occurred in Jackson yesterday."

That struck me as odd, because the other obituaries ran on along
these lines:

"**Death of Mrs. May Carlisle Noland.** The Death Angel entered the
home of Mr. E. C. Nolan in this place last Saturday p.m., just as the evening shades began to gather, and took from it the wife of his bosom. She
had been lying in a stupor the last week, constantly attended by him and
other family members . . ." and on and on and on.

At the state capitol in Jackson I applied for a copy of his death certificate. It came in the mail.

Under "HUSBAND OF OR WIFE OF," the certifying physician, Dr.
W. E. Clark, had written "D.K.," for "Don't Know." Aha! Abandoned by
mean Lettie! His final residence was given as "Hospital—Charleston, Mississippi." That was near Scoby, in Yalobusha County, where he and his parents and siblings are buried.

Mumu always said he died with the alcoholic d.t.'s, so I figured he must have been hospitalized for that. But the newspaper had said he died in Jackson, over a hundred miles away. So did the death certificate—Hinds County, Jackson, address, "State Insane Hospital."

Well, the d.t.'s, I guess. Paternal grandparents met working in one loony bin, maternal grandfather died in another. That must have been the institution Eudora Welty mentioned in a *Paris Review* interview, talking about the time Henry Miller came to visit her.

"He was so dull," she said. "He never looked at anything. I guess he was bored by being in Mississippi. That day they were going to move the hospital for the insane down on North State Street . . . to a bigger place. The patients were helping move themselves. I thought that that would be a funny sight for Mr. Miller, especially since the superintendent was named Love. Superintendent Love, moving the insane hospital patients from Jackson to across the river. It meant absolutely nothing to him. . . . It's not every day there's something like that in Jackson to offer anyone. These poor old crazy people carrying their own beds out, and putting them in a truck and driving away. . . . I thought it was a gift that I could offer as a hostess."

Dr. Clark had attended my grandfather for three weeks at the state insane hospital. The CAUSE OF DEATH, the certificate stated, "was as follows: General Paralysis Insane."

CONTRIBUTORY cause was "Syphilis."

Ah.

You know, you can be funny about dying, you can be funny about the d.t.'s, but it's kind of hard to squeeze much humor out of syphilis. Let's see, self-loathing, syph-loathing. . . .

> *Here's to all my critics,*
> *You rotten syphilitics. . . .*
>
> *I said to her, "If, Phyllis,*
> *You're sure you have syphilis,*
> *Then we're in a heck of a mess."*
>
> *Oh grampaw couldn't keep it in his pants,*
> *The startup of my family romance.*
> *Things just do not come about by chance.*
> *Grampaw couldn't keep it in his pants.*

The family curse was just a disease? Something a traveling railroad man picked up from a prostitute? Or maybe, I'd prefer to think, from a wild girl like the one Barbara Hershey played in *Boxcar Bertha*. At any rate, from fucking. What they call the act of love.

Papa boo-boo bye-bye.

And you can bet people back then, even more universally than people now, saw that disease as God's vengeance on abominable sin. No wonder my mother saw lipstick on my collar as playing with dynamite. Or did she ever know what killed her father? Even if she didn't, she probably saw him rant and rave. I think of the times when Susan and I would be babbling rowdily and she would jokingly call us "blithering idiots" or "raving lunatics." "You're talking like a man up a tree." "Have you taken leave of your senses?" "Have you gone stark, raving mad?" And the biblical expression she often cited with a certain relish: "There will be weeping and wailing and gnashing of teeth."

"This is the craziest family!"

Syphilis, even in those days before antibiotics, didn't necessarily advance to the point of dementia and death, but the eminent child psychologist Bruno Bettelheim's father died of it in 1926, four years after my grandfather, and Bettelheim later said the final stage was "horrible to see."

The elder Bettelheim had been diagnosed as syphilitic nineteen years before. "This projected him and my mother," Bettelheim wrote late in life, "into a state of deep anxiety which was not lost on my sister and me. . . . From this moment on the life of my parents was a nightmare for them which they kept hidden from everybody, even their parents and siblings."

As a child Bruno didn't know the cause of the pall over his household—he was afraid he had caused it. He was marked for life, by depression and sexual conflicts.

The father of Dora, Freud's most famous hysteric, had syphilis. "A *strikingly high* percentage of the patients whom I have treated . . . ," Freud wrote, "come of fathers who have suffered from . . . general paralysis. . . . Syphilis in the male parent is a very relevant factor in the aetiology of the neuropathic constitution of children."

Around the time my grandfather died, in fact, many medical authorities believed that a father's syphilis, even if the mother was not infected, could become hereditary—could even skip a generation. Just about anything might be blamed on syphilitic parents. The French physician Leon Daudet wrote that "the vast majority of neurasthenics, melancholics, misanthropists . . . and, in a word, misfits, are . . . a product of that terrible miniature destroyer which is also called the pale spirochete."

During the 1920s more than 9,000 Americans died of syphilis, and 60,000 babies a year were born with it. My mother was not, but did she suspect—or did her relatives suspect—that she might have been? "You get treated like lepers," says a man whose father was an unwitting participant in the U.S. government's Tuskegee Study of Untreated Syphilis in the Negro Male. "People think it's the scourge of the earth to have it in your family."

Given the time it takes syphilis to progress to the stage of insanity, her father would have been well beyond the infectious stage when he married either of his wives, and his first wife may have died without knowing the disease was in him, but then, when the tertiary symptoms came upon him . . .

"Many were so light and giddy that they could not stand," wrote a physician. "Some run mad, and not only their hands and feet but their whole bodies trembling." Maybe that's when the stepmother became wicked. Maybe she screamed at her husband that *he* had made *her* life a double-jointed hell. Maybe she took her abhorrence out on her stepchild.

It may even be that my mother's memory projected the ravings of her loving father onto the convenient figure of the stepmother.

I never found Lettie's grave. Maybe it's over in Arkansas somewhere, where she came from. Somewhere along the line I lost interest in spitting on it, anyway. Spitting on a grave is not the kind of thing people get any real satisfaction out of, I'm afraid, in my book.

What I did find, going through my mother's old photograph album with Susan, was a picture of me on a horse on a farm in Mississippi in the summer of 1948. "I remember that," I said. "We visited Daddy's uncle Josh's farm, and ate great huge country meals at a big table, and I rode that horse into town and back by myself, it knew the way. Daddy wanted me to see what farm life was like. In 1948 . . . Mumu would have been pregnant with you then, and before long she would find out about her eye."

"No," Susan said, "this is Mumu's family. It was her uncle Will's farm."

"Oh. Well, I'll be. I wonder why I've always thought—"

"Uncle Will is the one Lettie married after Mumu's daddy died."

"She did?" She did. According to census records, she was his third wife. She must have raised Uncle Will's third, fourth and fifth children, by his late second wife, whose name was Edna, according to one census, or Edner, according to another. Uncle Will lived to be ninety. There's another picture in the album, of a sour-looking woman with big buck teeth, on which my mother wrote "Aunt Lettie." I stayed at her house! Nobody was mean to me there. Aunt Lettie must have cooked those wonderful country meals.

Whoever heard of a wicked aunt? Surely nobody told me that this was the woman who abused my mother. Maybe my mother had mellowed toward her by then. In the Monticello town library I read an unpublished history of Lawrence County, which includes this testimony about "slavery time" by a man named Jim Robertson: "Dey wasn't mean to us, 'n' dey never 'lowed nobody to whip us but dem, 'n' yuh know de ole missus couldn't whip hard, so dey wuz boun' to a' been good to us."

But no, "beat me till the blood ran" flashed out again after that trip to the farm. Susan heard it. Maybe that kind of memory isn't one that you can incorporate into your behavior and stay sane, so you go visiting folks as if it didn't happen. Can it possibly be that my father took my mother to see Lettie so she could shake that demon? If so, it didn't work. "You've got to put that behind you," Susan heard him tell her once, when she was going on about her childhood.

All we know is that Lettie sent little Louise away to her paternal grandmother, Big Mama, in Monticello, who was kind but a widow in her seventies and may have felt imposed upon by this extra child. Who carried a stigma? Who moved on to other relatives, at any rate, finally mean Aunt Pearl.

None of them are alive to answer questions, but in New York I happened to meet a woman from Monticello. She called her mother, who remembered when Louise came to live there after her father died. "Very pretty, with dark hair and eyes, and dressed in purple and black—she was so fascinating the other girls would follow her everywhere, even to the bathroom."

They jiggled the door maybe, and a little voice came out, "There's someone in here."

And whatever she was thinking in there in her purple and black, I'll bet it wasn't "I'm the dee-light of all the men."

Poor little girl. I'm trying to imagine how she felt, but I'm not trying as hard as I ought to, because I don't know that I could stand it. Maybe all the stuff she laid on Susan and me as kids went toward insulating us against ever feeling that bad. Or maybe she *wanted us to know*, so we would never do that to a child. A couple of years ago we were all in Austin, Texas, for Susan's stepdaughter, Audrey's, wedding to her longtime boyfriend, Wendell. By "we all" I mean Susan, and Audrey's father, Gerald, and his first and third wives, Donna and Pat, and Audrey's brother, Stuart, and his wife, Leigh, and Audrey's half-brother, Edward, and Ennis and my son-in-law, David, and my grandson Jesse (his brother Noah was present fetally), and Kirven and his girlfriend, Carrie, and Ellen, and Ellen's daughter by her second marriage, Myra, and Roland and Lois, and Gerald's and my old mutual friends Vereen and Jane Bell, and Ennis and Audrey's mutual friend Debbie, and Debbie's parents even, and Joan was going to come but she got sick. It's amazing, really, there we all were just moiling and thrashing amongst ourselves in all our divorce-riddled extensiveness, and getting along and having fun. At Ennis's wedding in the Berkshires, just about all those people, plus Joan, and David's parents and sister of course, and the Swans, were all out on the floor together *dancing*. Dancing *sweatily*. Kiss my ass if my broken-home daughter, Ennis, and broken-home niece, Audrey, don't have the gift of getting people together.

And in Austin the day after Audrey's wedding, little old Jesse Roy, who was somewhere between one and two then, suddenly said, "Where is Boppoo?" Which is what he calls Kirven. He loves Boppoo, who flings him around a lot.

"Remember?" Ennis said. "Boppoo told you good-bye. He had to go back to where he lives."

Jesse's face contorted with grief. I'm not exaggerating. There he was surrounded by two loving parents and two of his four loving grandparents (if I'd had *one* grandparent who took any real interest in me I'd be sitting on the Supreme Court right now), and he was genuinely stricken—if you saw a photograph of him at the moment you'd have thought he'd just been suddenly orphaned.

We assured him that he would see Boppoo again in his lifetime, and he got over it. But that's how sharply little children feel things. Can you imagine losing your mother, for good, when you're Jesse's age, and your only sibling, for good, when you're not yet four, and your father when you're not yet eight, and wicked stepmother aside, you're in the middle of a bleak part of Mississippi in 1922?

The terrible thing, though, is that we would not have been having such a good time if Mumu had been there in any other form than spirit. We'd all have been bothering about her, as she kept saying, in various tones of voice—light, barbed, tragic, combinations of all three—"Don't you all bother about me."

H. P. Lovecraft, whose morbidly eldritch story about a nameless infectious menace, "The Color from Outer Space," struck me forcefully in adolescence, was the son of a traveling salesman who began to evince syphilitic dementia when Lovecraft was two. The father died in an insane asylum when the boy was seven. The boy grew up to be an etiolated, sexless recluse whose life work was tales—"The Myth of Chthulhu," "The Rats in the Walls"—of creeping, unspeakable horrors.

And my mother grew up to describe herself to her children as "a freak of nature." And I have grown up to be a jack of various trades but primarily a fool by profession.

What is the connection? What is, after all—after all this—the connection?

Let me answer that question with a question. Why have I found myself, in this book, twice getting a glow on about my father and yet I can't quite seem to join forces with my mother even against a wicked stepmother?

One reason, I believe, is that once we were established in separate metropolitan areas I could have whacked my father on the back, done good work in my field, asked his advice from time to time on matters in his field, avoided adding to his worries (which is to say, avoided getting my mother on his back—I remember him saying to me, in a beat-up, pleading kind of way, "You just don't know how vitally interested she is in you") and asked him to go fishing with me once, and his heart would have overflowed. Whereas I would have had to pump twelve hours a day to keep my mother's heart less than a quart low.

Men and women don't even have the same working notion of what the word *heart* means. Among men heart connotes staunchness, tough vitality in the face of resistance—"With a heart for any foe." A fighter on the ropes who keeps battling back, keeps refusing to get in touch with his feelings, keeps putting effect before affect, is said to have heart, because this is the male idea of generosity; whereas a man who claims to be giving something away is disbelieved: "You're all heart." Among women heart is associated with going all weak in the knees—"Be still, my heart." It is quite a trick for any two hearts that *regard themselves* as that different to be one.

And I swear to God my mother had a heart like some drinkers have a hollow leg. Trying to tell my mother you loved her was like trying to tell Michael Jordan you could take him one-on-one.

Another reason is that as a boy, when I heard my parents arguing, I instinctively sided with my mother, and now I believe that although men may be clods, to rail at them about it as frighteningly and unanswerably as my mother did is a form of abuse.

Here's another reason. Remember that vital ingredient of humor, self-loathing? Sefflo may be how a humorist—perverse breed, and I have known them all, from Fran Lebowitz to Jerry Clower—works up a head of self-esteem. My father is the framework I need to get around in. My mother is the magma inside.

To loathe framework is just superficial. To loathe magma is to get *down*. Which is why, ever since I was a young *Sports Illustrated* reporter and that swimmer, Brian Job, told me, "I hated my mom," I have been working toward making the following simple statement, myself—

"You children go run, skip and play," my mother would say. "I better go run fix supper." It seemed so cozy. And supper itself, her cooking, was lovesome. But there was a catch in there, a catch about the playing, a catch about the supper fixing.

"Y'all are going to grow up and forget about me. Yes, you will. You will too," she would say, and how were we going to argue with that statement, as blatantly self-refuting as it was? How can you demand that your children prove a negative, set in the future? If she was truly looking for people to be sweet to her, her approach was so ("to put it mildly," says Susan) *counterproductive*.

How can you expect your children to respond positively to abject pitiability? This confounds every law of human nature. Surely a woman is bound to know better than that. A woman doesn't respond positively to pitiability in men. Handicapped, objectively pitiable people don't expect people to respond to pitiability. Certainly you can't expect the person you're complaining *about* to be sympathetic.

"You don't love me! You don't appreciate me!" That's an *accusation*. A woman would *take* it as one, if it were directed at her—she wouldn't take it seriously, because her assumption would be that women are always so much more loving than men and men are always appreciated so much more than women that it's an accusation not worth considering, but she would take it as an accusation. She'd get defensive. *I* got defensive. And if you got angry at my mother, that, to her, was hatred.

Maybe I'm all wet. Maybe I should draw back, repress my natural response and take "You don't love me! You don't appreciate me!" as an *appeal*—and respond to it with, what? Some kind of *inflected boiler-plate*. Is that what women want? Platitudes with feeling? Genuinely inspirational-sounding greeting-card verse? That goes against my instincts. Which are to follow language as deep as it will go, as long as I can keep up with it. And which I learned at my mother's knee.

Excuse me. I got carried away. I was saying I have been working toward making the following simple statement:

I hated my mom.

There. Now. Whew. You have to be able to *say* that, don't you? You ought to be able to say it when you're a kid, and she knows you don't mean it, and you get over it. She certainly seemed to hate me sometimes. I know she didn't.

Here's the way the story I wrote about Brian Job, the swimmer, whose mother drove him to excellence, ended:

> "I mean, I know I don't hate my mom," Brian says. "She's a smart woman, she's taught us a lot of things that have been valuable. . . . When I got a little older I'd start thinking, 'What would I do if I were a parent?' and I realized it must be hard. But if I had to do it all over again. . . . And as to whether I'll want my children to swim, I don't know. I don't think so."
>
> On the other hand, let it be noted that in the Jobs' scrapbook . . . there is a recent newspaper clipping in which Brian is quoted as say-ing, "The whole race went just like I planned it. About halfway through I said to myself, 'Hey, you feel good, you feel good.' And I did."

I feel that way sometimes when I'm writing. Not at the moment; at the moment I feel like a damn dog (maybe *that's* why our dogs often looked so hangdog, they were walking around thinking, Well, I love these people, of course I love them, they're my people, but sometimes . . .), but a man's got to do what he's got to do. What I got to do—and, hey, to be fair, what I *get* to do—is live up to the strange grip (secret grip, even) on language that I obtained at my mother's knee.

In life, I felt that way for a while in Mill River, Massachusetts, in the seventies.

CHAPTER 26 / When I Was Happy, I Thought

What is it men in women do require?
The lineaments of gratified desire.
What is it women in men do require?
The lineaments of gratified desire.

—WILLIAM BLAKE

In 1989, when my sweet second wife, Joan, and I were going through a divorce, a concerned female friend handed me a new book by George V. Higgins, the author of *The Friends of Eddie Coyle* and other estimable underworld novels. This book was nonfiction—reminiscences involving baseball. Higgins is a Bostonian and a Red Sox fan. "You'd better look at this," my friend said anxiously, showing me the following passage, which had to do with the third game of the 1975 World Series, which the Sox lost 6–5:

That game was one of the toughest I have ever watched. For one thing, the press office had seated me next to Roy Blount, Jr. I do not know quite how to characterize Blount's occupation. The usual sobriquet is "humorist," but it's too tame for him; he's more of a cynic gone antic, with occasional intervals of utter battiness, and it's very difficult to devote full attention to anything else while sitting next to him. He introduced his lovely companion as the reigning Possum Queen of Georgia, airily declaring that as one of the contest judges, he had been instrumental in her selection. He confided that she had assisted him in choosing the most beautiful possum among the animals shown at the second part of the pageant. He did not seem to be troubled by the inference that his vote might have been impaired by lust—indeed, he specified that lust had been his sole motive. He went on to describe in detail the superiority of the Georgia Possum Pageant to all other beauty competitions. He grounded this opinion in the candor of its rules, which openly admit that the judges intend to eat at least one of the two winners. Blount's voice has solid timbre, and it carries well. He does not like to hurtle to the end of things, especially when he finds himself surrounded by an appreciative audience. The fact that he knows at most three or four of his perhaps fifty or sixty listeners hinders him not at all; indeed, it seems to impel him to shift from narrative to aria, his almost caloric Southern accent coagulating like a big warm muddy river choked with catfish in the sun, eddying and swirling, seeming never to progress but always and inexorably moving on. It must have taken him close to the end of the regulation nine innings to complete his monologue.

When I had read the above passage, I said to my friend, "I'm not all *that* ethnic, am I? Molassic even when manic? I remember it as a night when I wished George had told more underworld stories. Anyway, the possum show was in *Alabama*, and—"

"But what if Joan sees it?"

"Well, I can see she might not care for it much, but I didn't write it."

"But she could *use* it."

"I don't see how."

"You running around with this . . . lust bunny."

"Oh. Well, firstly, we're not going to have that kind of divorce. Secondly, in 1975 we weren't married. When I'm married, I'm married. I have enough trouble giving one woman as much undivided attention as she expects and presumably warrants. How anybody manages to two-time, I don't know. And thirdly—"

"Yes, but you were *living together*. And you're at the World Series with that—"

"Thirdly, that was Joan."

To be sure, the portrait doesn't do her justice. She wasn't Miss Georgia Possum, she was Miss Possum International. We were at this possum show together—I was covering it for *Sports Illustrated*—and the local girl who was to be the Possum Queen had discovered boys and didn't show up, so the organizers asked Joan to be Miss Possum—*International* because she is not from down there in Alabama, or Georgia either, she is from Cambridge, Massachusetts. Her mother was *mayor* of Cambridge. Joan may have struck Higgins as merely lovely, but she wrote some great first-person stories for *Sports Illustrated* herself, about playing the organ in big-league parks, swimming with a Polar Bear club, and delving into the whole phenomenon or construct of throwing like a girl. She started a local theater when we were together, and now she writes plays that are produced all over the country.

In point of fact, it struck me as kind of nice that although we had known each for more than a year and were living together and were well on our way to getting married and staying together for ten years and remaining friends after that, evidently we acted around each other in such a way as to cause Higgins to assume that I had just dragged her up out of the darkest Bible Belt—as who wouldn't who could—in a fit of animal heat.

Personally, I don't think Higgins did justice to all of my personality's nuances either. But then, I wasn't quite myself at the time. I was happy.

The mid-to-late seventies were the only time in my life when I even *thought* I had everything together. I'd fallen in love with Joan, and we had gotten a house in the country where I could have joint custody of Ennis and Kirven. They lived with us half the time and their mother half the time, back and forth every other week or every other half-week, various schedules. How strange their two-household childhood was for them I leave to their memoirs, but we kept adjusting to suit each of them individually as best we could, and at least they were relieved, perhaps, of the burden of growing up expecting life *not* to be strange.

When Ellen wanted to travel, we kept the kids, and when we wanted to, she kept them. My first marriage in its last several years had been like an albatross nestled (no, trapped and thrashing) in the heart. "Better to marry than to burn," said that disastrously seminal asshole the apostle Paul. He never mentioned that you can marry *and* burn. But Ellen—thank God, in retrospect—was anything but the clinging type. The albatross had been purged belatedly but about as cleanly as could be. The offspring were troupers. Once Ellen and I were apart, and grateful to each other for being apart, we attained, at the point where we still overlapped, something much like—yes—mutuality.

Blessedly unemotional as that mutuality was, it was not easy, I realize now (belatedly), for a young wife to live with.

But I had become what I'd always wanted to be—self-employed. I'd had a book published and a couple of pieces in *The New Yorker* and was still on good enough terms with *Sports Illustrated* that they were sending me not only to possum shows but to the 1975 World Series. Which was a corker, you may recall.

My first date with Joan, by the way, was to see *Young Frankenstein*. In that movie the song "Ah, Sweet Mystery of Life," which Nelson Eddy and Jeanette MacDonald sang so feelingly on my parents' first date, crops up, in a carnal, low-comic context. Cool.

So what the hell happened?

One day when I was managing, if I may say so, somehow or another to keep a roof over all of our heads by dint of a thousand-dollar-a-month *Esquire* sports column and a contract to write a book about country music (which evolved eventually into *Crackers*) and various other bits of catch-as-catch-can freelancing, I was in the room where I worked, and my wife and my children were home, and I came out of the room to show Joan this bit of verse I had written:

> *My only employee*
> *Is me, old Roy,*
> *And also my only employer.*
> *I don't have a lawyer.*
> *My livelihood rests on one column*
> *And research into a volume*
> *On music—though nary*
> *A tune can I carry.*
> *But I'm blessed with my life*
> *In my house with my wife*
> *And my girl and my boy*
> *   —signed, Roy.*

She didn't seem to care for it much. I see now that it was self-centered. True, she from time to time would tie knots in my pants and fill the legs with whatever that caustic substance is that women use for the purpose, and when I slid my legs into them in the morning (my offense being that I had left them on the floor overnight) she would laugh as I hopped around in agony, but at one time or another they've all done that, all the women I've loved; I shrug it off. Or rather, I get so mad at them sometimes that you'd *think* they had done something that awful.

Or no, they get that mad at me, and I start arguing with them. . . .

I don't mean to suggest for one moment that women are all alike. In fact, when you try to do what you thought you weren't doing with the last one, that doesn't seem to be the thing you should do with this one.

You know one thing that's wrong with me as a husband? I can't get over feeling that a certain anecdote from Hodding Carter's 1950 book *Southern Legacy* is sexist.

A male pedestrian dashes across the street just as the light is turning yellow, and a woman comes along just behind him and tries to do the same thing. A policeman bent on enforcing the town's jaywalking ordinance blows his whistle and tells her to get back.

The woman complains:

> "Look at that man ahead of me," she raged.
> "You let him go across without stopping him. But you whistle and yell at me and embarrass me to death—"
> The policeman might have argued the point. Instead, he grinned admiringly and drawled:
> "Shucks, lady, I don't care if that ugly old man wants to get his head knocked off, but I can't let a pretty young lady like you get hurt." The pretty young lady smiled the smile of properly regarded Southern womanhood and said no more. As she crossed the street under the double protection of a red signal and admiring Southern manhood, the policeman winked. "Best way is to perk 'em up," he observed.

That anecdote is set in Jackson, Mississippi, where my maternal grandfather died, insane. And I be John Brown, as my father used to say, if the first and most formative woman in my life, my mother, or the second one, my first wife, was that readily perkable.

I respect that. Don't I? Shouldn't I? I don't know. I'm fifty-five years old, and I have known a *bunch* of women, and I am not *stupid*, and I don't know.

Maybe my mother *could* have been perked. Maybe it was all Daddy's fault. Maybe there is some kind of secret code that Daddy was supposed to take me aside and clue me in on. Maybe his daddy didn't clue him in, because . . . maybe it was all my grandmother's fault.

Mama Blount, we called her. Rawboned, six feet tall, thin upper lip, deaf and a puddle of frets and whines.

"Poor soul, Mama wasn't *much* fun when she was young," my mother would say, when her mother-in-law was visiting and she had to entertain her. Or she "wasn't the *best* of company when she could see and hear." Once I wrote down some dialogue that was actually spoken by my mother (M), my grandmother (GM), and my aunt Betty (B). My grandmother had been staying with Aunt Betty and Uncle Charles (Charles is my father's brother). My mother felt Aunt Betty had gotten a little *too* religious, she was trying herself. It was time for my grandmother to shift over to our house. Anna Livia (not her real name) was one of my mother's church friends, very sweet, who I later found out had a bad diet-pill Jones:

M (*loudly*): Anna Livia has invited us to lunch Thursday, Mama.
GM (*vaguely*): Did . . . ? Well . . . that's nice.
M (*loudly and too brightly*): We'll go frolicking.
GM: Well . . . If you'd *rather* go Friday.
EVERYBODY IN THE ROOM BUT GM AND ME: Friday? Friday?
M: Would *you* rather go Friday, Mama?
GM: No, I just thought . . .
ME: I think she thought—
EVERYBODY IN THE ROOM BUT ME AND GM: Oh, "frolicking."
M: No, Mama, I said we'll go *frolicking*.
GM: Oh. Frolicking. Well, I need some of that.
B: Well, Mama, if I'd known you wanted to *frolick.* . . .

It's not easy, dealing with other people's blood kin. Joan is my children's stepmother. The antithesis of my mother's wicked one. My sister is a (now single) stepmother, and I remember her telling me the night before my wedding to Joan, "Being a stepmother is *hard.*" I got angry, I wouldn't hear it, I said, "*Everything* is hard." I should have heard it. If anybody in the world doesn't seem to need perking up, it's Joan, but the plays she writes tend to involve women finding ways to perk themselves up.

I wasn't sweet enough. When I realized that the family situation I was so pleased with didn't make Joan happy, an abyss opened up.

I felt like Olivia de Havilland in *The Snake Pit*: When will I be real?

I can't make an *effort* to be sweet.
Maybe I'll learn to yet.

Here's another thing wrong with me as a mate. It's kind of chilling, but I'm going to tell it on myself anyway.

It's late one autumn Monday night in 1979. The children are at their mother's house. My column for *Inside Sports* is overdue. (I don't know that there has ever been a moment in my adult life when some deadline wasn't nagging at me.) I'm wandering around in our house in Mill River, switching on the Monday Night Football game for a while, staring at my typewriter for a while, trying to write one more time about the Super Bowl.

These days the Super Bowl is not a factor in my life, but in the seventies, I covered it nearly every year. I had sneaked down onto the sidelines and celebrated victory with my friends the Steelers—taking a little run and butting Mean Joe Greene right in the numbers. I had crouched in the end zone with the halftime show, I had hustled around the Superdome in New Orleans with a ticket scalper, I had drunk sangria and danced the bump with the Steelers' defensive line and their wives, and, back when I was single, I had in collaboration with the (now late), great Pete Axthelm of *Newsweek* bought out the stock of a flower girl (who wore a chenille bedspread, flip-flops and nothing else) and roamed the French Quarter streets on Super Bowl eve, the three of us dispensing free jonquils and blowing kazoos.

One more time, into the breach. I was thinking about how Warren Bankston of the Oakland Raiders had, during the week before the 1977 Super Bowl, tried to explain to me how the Raiders were going to foil Minnesota's efforts to block their field goals.

He had drawn a little circle with two dots in the middle of it.

"This is my body," he explained, "standing over my feet."

Ever since then, I had been trying to firm up my own self-concept by drawing little pictures. This is my mind, standing off to one side of my mouth. This is my soul, standing in need of something. This is my mission, standing under my misunderstanding.

Pete Gent, author and former Cowboy wide receiver, in a visionary mood had told me once, "I always wanted to win the Super Bowl so I could take it and hold it and see what lies beyond it. I think it may be the sun."

In Mill River, a long stretch of rain was just ending. A full moon had emerged. Joan wanted me to take a walk and admire the moon. I said no, I had to work. I switched on the TV again. There, on the BarcaLounger, was my body, sitting level with my feet. An ugly piece of furniture. I inherited it. My father died in it. I looked out the window. I sprang up, ran to my typewriter and wrote:

"On this Monday night, the purpose of the Super Bowl dawns on me. It is to make us unfulfilled by pro football. There are things, the Super Bowl hints, even harder to cover than this. I cry out, spring up, break away from the TV game as it is entering sudden death, and sprint out to walk foot-foot-foot with my wife in the drying, clearing night under the orbic moon. There are two dots in the middle of it."

Here's the bad part. I wrote those words, but I didn't do what they said. I developed them into a column. Stayed inside and cranked out and polished my column.

What lies beyond the sun and the moon for me is the language. You've heard of "a love affair with the language"? The expression, itself, is cheap, anybody can pick it up. And call it up on behalf of the next schmuck who comes through town to promote his book on the romance of etymology. A real love affair with the language is dirty, Lord knows, but it's *expensive*. You think a *person* you're involved with body and soul (insofar as you are up to it) demands a lot of attention? You just let the language get its hooks into you.

Warren Bankston, the aforementioned Raider, wrote a poem once about sticking your head in there, sucking it up, sweating blood, reaching back for whatever it takes to win. The opening stanza:

> *When all the rhetoric is over and done,*
> *And it's time to face your opponent,*
> *You've got to face up to the challenge*
> *And say to yourself, "I want it."*

The challenge of rhetoric—rhetoric with no ulterior motive, if that is not a contradiction—is what I want.

Where the tip of the tongue meets the back of the mind, I am forever turning over language. I am also forever talking to loved ones, in the same place. If I speak to them from the heart, aloud, it will come out wrong, they'll take it wrong, it won't be what I meant exactly—you know what I mean?—and it will rankle in their bosoms. Ten years later, whatever loved one I said it to will say, as my mother did to Susan once, "You told me the only reason Daddy took me on business trips was so I could wash his socks."

What?

Even at that tongue-mind nexus I can't bring myself to say obvious, hackneyed things with words like *love* and *appreciate* in them. Except every now and then when nobody is listening I blurt out, loudly and almost Tourettically, *"I love you, Porgy!"* Why Porgy, I don't know, except that it's a musico-literary allusion, and I guess there is a kind of switcheroo element in his being black and male, and he was crippled, and so in various ways was my mother.

My being an unattached grandfather is my own damn fault, which is to say my mother's: If your own mother would never believe that you loved her, what is to be believed?

Here are lyrics I wrote for the Julie Kavner character to sing in Nora Ephron's movie *This Is My Life*:

I Don't Believe in Love

> *From* Can-Can *to* La Traviata,
> *In song it's assumed that you gotta*
> *Give romance priority.*
>   *(Here my voice*
>   *Should go misty-moist . . .)*
> *Hey I'm singing, right? Will we*
> *Hear that same old jive from me?*
>
> *No, no,*
> *Romeo,*
> *Truthfully, I don't think so.*
> *I don't believe in love.*
> *Yoo-hoo,*
> *Juliet,*
> *You and he are both all wet.*
> *I don't believe in love.*

Hey, all the best and mazel tov,
But I don't believe in lov.

Oh sure, between mother and daughter.
And also I think that you oughter
Love thy neighbor if thou can.
  (And of course
    A girl loves a horse.)
But love twixt a sane woman and,
Like, an unrelated man?

Har, har,
Lochinvar.
You and I ain't going far.
I don't believe in love.
Well, jeez,
Heloise,
Dote on Ab'lard all you please—
I don't believe in love.
Marla to Donald, push to shove,
But I'm not drawn to love.

Oh sure, when he's wooing you, then you
Are dancing with fairies and elves.
But the least little change in the venue—
You both turn into yourselves.

A cheapskate, in love, is a spender.
A slugabed's up with the dawn.
What is love but two gods on a bender
Which ends, and where have they gone?

So, no,
Romeo,
Truthfully I don't think so.
I don't believe in love.
Yoo-hoo,
Juliet,
You and he are both all wet,
I don't believe in love.

In the end, of course, since *This Is My Life* is a comedy, that character does find someone. My lyrics didn't quite work; they were never set to music.

The other evening, with an estimable woman whom it has been my privilege to be seeing sporadically (she lives out of town, and travels a lot), I took in an Australian movie called *Love Escapade*, something like that. *Love* something. It was all right, sort of fanciful. A couple of days later, I found the ticket stub in my pocket. It has the name of the theater on it, and the day and the time of the showing, and the ticket price, $8.50, and this:

Love

One

Adult

All right, already!

CHAPTER 27 / **I'm Not Here Right Now**

That it will never come again
Is what makes life so sweet.
Believing what we don't believe
Does not exhilarate.

—EMILY DICKINSON

If there is any question of my lying in state—not that there would be—I'd like to do it *before* I die. See who would file by.

"What you doing there?"

"Lying in state."

"Oh. How's it going?"

"Kind of slow right now."

"That's a nice coffin. What'd it cost you?"

"I'm just renting it. I'm not dead."

"No, I didn't think you were."

I'm afraid it would be too much like the Christmas trade show in Raleigh, North Carolina, some years ago. I was sitting in a booth next to a poster with my picture on it and a stack of whatever book I had out then, with a big sign over my head that said AUTHOR HERE TODAY. Next to me was a booth where someone was selling little people—snowmen, Santas—made out of pinecones. They were moving a lot faster than my book.

A nice-looking woman came by and stopped. She looked at me, she looked at the poster, she looked at the books, she looked at the sign and she looked at me again.

"I married Eddie Goodloe," she said.

Well! Eddie lived down the street from us in Decatur in the fifties. He and I would go down to the creek and shoot crawfish with these blowguns and darts we made out of various materials. Then, one year in high school, when our yearbooks were just out and we were all passing them around to friends who'd write little inscriptions in them—"May the road always rise

261

to meet your feet" sort of thing—according to custom, Eddie wrote in mine, "Keep it in your pants."

In ink, you know—there it is, for life, in your yearbook, and my mother saw it. I had to come up with a tortuously innocuous interpretation. "We used to shoot crawfish, down at the creek? And . . . one time I lost my pocketknife. . . ." She gave me a grave look. I wasn't the little boy who used to call her Sugar anymore.

So I sold Eddie Goodloe's wife a book and wrote in it, "To Eddie. Keep it in your pants. What goes around comes around."

Forget lying in state. How would I like to die? The best way to go would be along these lines (I quote from the *New York Daily News* of April 6, 1996):

"As the audience gasped in horror, a singer fell ten feet from a ladder to the stage of the Metropolitan Opera House last night after apparently suffering a fatal heart attack.

"The singer, tenor Richard Vesalle, 63, had just sung 'You can only live so long.' "

It certainly beats "being found dead on his kitchen table, wearing fishnet stockings and with a plastic bag tied over his head and half an orange in his mouth after a failed attempt at ecstatic autoeroticism," as *The New Republic* described the demise of a British member of Parliament in 1995.

This might be a good time to mention that if by chance I am found in the street with a flyer for Madame Satan's Palace of Pain clutched in my hand, it will be only because I was too nice to reject it—someone was handing them out and I always feel, hey, those guys have to make a living.* And I didn't want to litter the street, so I was looking around for a trash basket when the safe fell on my head.

People have come up with humorous terms for death. The great

*When you're an author, people always ask you what you're "working on next." Sometimes I don't mind. For instance, a woman who was bounteous and attractive all over asked me that question, and when I told her I was contemplating a book called "New Tricks," she suggested that I tie her up sometime. She liked the idea for herself. Just a matter of finding a bed with the right knobs. On reflection, I couldn't think of anything I wanted to do with her that I didn't like doing more with her having the full use of her limbs; all the same, a part of me responded to the idea. But then I neglected to send her a Valentine, and she didn't want any more to do with me. Story of my life. Sins of omission.

proto-R&B musician Louis Jordan spoke of "coppin' that eternal nod." But can you die *on* humorous terms? Cop an eternal twinkle?

Flann O'Brien breathed his last on April Fool's Day ("an irony that would not displease him," as a critic has rather presumptuously asserted), but probably not on purpose. Comedy is not that easy.

The actor Bill Bixby died in 1993, of prostate cancer after a great deal of suffering, but a year or so before, as he was about to be anesthetized for exploratory surgery, he *pretended* to expire. When he opened one eye and grinned at the doctors, they were highly annoyed. *They're* the ones who are supposed to do the joking, after the patient is unconscious—the patient is supposed to be the straight man.

But that could hardly have been their *stated* objection to Bixby's levity. "Now," they must have grumbled, "when you *do* die, no one will believe you."

At my funeral I would like for there to be some really trashy special effects:

- When someone makes a complimentary remark ("Well, the old boy was sweet to dogs, anyway"), we hear from the coffin a recording of my voice saying, "Can I get an a-men?"
- Right in the middle of the service somebody sees the faces of Princess Di and Elvis, intertwined, in the grain of my coffin: "Praise Jesus! It's *them!*"
- You know the vision at the end of Flannery O'Connor's story "Revelation"? ". . . a vast horde of souls were rumbling toward heaven. There were whole companies of white-trash, clean for the first time in their lives, and bands of black niggers in white robes, and battalions of freaks and lunatics shouting and clapping and leaping like frogs." (A scene which, incidentally, I suspect was inspired by the end of the "Zippety-Doo-Dah" number in *Song of the South*.) I want that scene *staged*.

I would like for all my friends to gather, however far they have had to travel. I would like for Garrison Keillor to imagine for me a Lake Wobegon burial, Pastor Inkvist presiding. Then—Bill Murray can follow *anybody* at a funeral. I saw him follow Ziggy once. We attended the observances for Louis Goldman, a movie-set still photographer who had escaped from a concentration camp. Louis's old friend Ziggy got up and told the story of how he and Louis had seen a chance to escape, and first Ziggy's father and then Louis had made it over the wall and eventually gotten out of Germany, but Ziggy had been caught right after giving Louis a liberating boost. Then years later Ziggy and Louis had been reunited in America.

And I thought, How in the name of God is my man going to follow *that*? Murray got up, strode to the front of the room and said, "That's not how I heard the story."

Then he proceeded to tell it as the deceased had told it to him—Louis had stopped every now and then at the most suspenseful moments to say mildly, "But you don't want to hear any more of that," before letting himself be urged to go on—and somehow, thus framed, the story was hilarious and yet ethno-historically sensitive and moving. In closing, Murray recalled a time when Louis's daughter visited the set of our movie, *Larger Than Life,* and how, when Louis saw her face, his eyes lit up.

At my funeral I want people to cry their eyes out, *and* I want those eyes lit up.

At the party afterward, I want the food to be good, and I want everybody to take turns reading my entire published works aloud until everybody thinks *they* are going to die.

But I know in my soul, what is going to happen is just whatever will happen. *Happen.* There's an interesting word I never really noticed before. A lot like *hoppin'*. I see by the dictionary it has the same root as *happy*. Imagine that.

When my father died, sentiments were loosed. My mother said, "He was the only man I ever loved," and I said, "He was the only man I ever loved too," and we hugged each other, and I told her, "All those obituaries, those tributes to him, they're tributes to you too," and it was a good moment. When she died, furies were loosed. Her survivors got drunk, something we'd never done in her house before, and Susan and I had angry arguments with our spouses that presaged the ends of our marriages.

In other words, we got on with our lives.

It wasn't Mother's fault, and it won't be mine. I have had so many sweet moments, which in my obliquity or perversity I haven't acknowledged—maybe when I die sweetness will be loosed. If so, it won't be to my credit. Y'all go run, skip and play and forgive me.

CHAPTER 28 / Sweet Bye and Bye

Assessment of what makes something funny depends on an
awareness of two conflicting contexts: an expected, "appropriate" context, and a logically possible but very odd one.

—TERRENCE W. DEACON, *THE SYMBOLIC SPECIES*

"It's just so odd to think that people are walking around in
Heaven and Hell."

"Yes, but it's odd to find ourselves walking around here,
too, isn't it?"   —CHARLES PORTIS, *THE DOG OF THE SOUTH*

I think the reason people where I come from drink so hard, when they
do—drink so hard they get to *sweating*—is they believe in heaven.
That's the reason they abstain so hard, too, when they do. They believe
there is a better land somewhere. They believe in getting *beyond* this
sphere, here, where not only does everybody not understand everything,
nobody understands a single goddamned thing. They believe there is a
sphere—the sphere we stand under, now—where everybody understands.
Why else is there the whole notion of understanding?

"Everything human is pathetic," wrote Mark Twain. "The secret
source of Humor itself is not joy but sorrow. There is no humor in
heaven."

Of course Mark Twain soured in his old age, whereas P. G. Wodehouse,
who remained funny up into his nineties, offered this observation in his
essay "Some Thoughts on Humorists":

And if any young writer with a gift for being funny has got the
idea that there is something undignified and anti-social about making people laugh, let him read this from the *Talmud*:

265

. . . And Elijah said to the Berokah, "These two will also share in the world to come." Berokah then asked them, "What is your occupation?" They replied, "We are merrymakers. When we see a person who is downhearted we cheer him up."

These two were among the very select few who would inherit the kingdom of Heaven.

But then, Wodehouse *would* say that.

In the Sunday school of my adolescence, when we might so much more usefully have been discussing how to make responsible and considerate love, we discussed, instead, whether you had to be a Christian, not to mention a good one, and most precisely a Methodist one, in order to get into heaven.

For all I know, contemporary Methodist adolescents where I come from are examining both sex and heaven in the same light; the girls are deconstructing the expression "Saint Peter" from a feminist perspective and the boys are coming up with droll but nonobjectifying double entendres about the Pearly Gates. But in those days we would get hung up on the question of how God could in all good conscience justify denying eternal salvation to everyone but us.

It didn't seem fair. Pets were an issue—we were encouraged to cling, on no scriptural authority so far as I know, to the *possibility* of a separate dog and cat heaven. Less pressing—since we didn't know any—was the question of devout believers in other religions. One teacher laid on us the revelation that Jews didn't *believe* in heaven.

I don't know how that squares with Wodehouse's reading of the Talmud, but at any rate, our teacher didn't hold disbelief of heaven against Judaism (we made field trips to Jewish and Catholic services to broaden our perspective), just thought it odd. Without heaven, where was self-denial getting you?

Well, he wouldn't have put it in such bottom-line terms. He would have said something more like what a character named Melba says, during a religious discussion, in *The Dog of the South*: "It's amazing what people will do. Look at the ancient Egyptians. They were the smartest people the world has ever known—we still don't know all their secrets—and yet they worshiped a tumblebug." That was the teacher whose advice with regard to social drinking was to go ahead and attend cocktail parties, when necessary, but to hold an empty glass. One member of our class—not me, I have never been at my best on Sunday mornings—suggested it would be a more forthright testimony to hold the glass upside down.

But if Jack Benny couldn't get in, and didn't even want to. . . . Later, when I learned that Jews didn't believe in Jrs., either, I thought: good thinking on that account, probably on the other too. Still later—if heaven was like the country club my parents joined after my father's position in greater Atlanta started requiring them to get more ritzy, then the hell with it. We had always been *against* ritziness, in our family. Against exclusiveness. And yet . . .

Dramatic irony entails exclusion. The speaker knows something that the audience doesn't. You know what has just occurred to me? Ironists hone their irony with the pain of having been excluded themselves. Irony is a way of reaching out beyond the excluders to an audience of the excluded.

My mother was excluded.

My friend James Hamilton, the photographer, has spoken of forming a support group called CHIPS—Children of Ironic Parents. I can see that, but I wouldn't qualify. My father wasn't ironic at all; my mother was quasi-ironic, in a raw, vulnerable way. It has been pointed out to me that one of my drawbacks as a significant other is that I hate to exchange an outright knowing look—certainly in the company of any third party, but even with any third party conceivably in mind. Not a lot of exclusionary eye contact. Not a lot of eye contact, period, maybe. I don't like it when anybody present is the third person.

Ennis was saying to me the other day that she hates it when people go along talking about somebody when they know that another person in the group doesn't know who that person is. I hate even this kind of mock-third-person reference: when somebody refers to someone present as "this one." You know what I mean? "This one here never notices what anybody is wearing." What is that, "this one?" Is that supposed to be *fond*, or something? Well, it isn't. Can't we face up to *he* and *she* and *you*? Not that it's easy.

My mother was an orphan, bounced from family to family. I don't want anybody to be cut out of a joke. I want everybody to get it—even, or especially, if it's *on* them. If I tell a joke about Rush Limbaugh, I want him to know about it—I want it to *gall* the narrow-minded son of a bitch, but I don't want it to be over his head. If I tell a joke *to* anybody I *like*—even partly like—I don't want that to be over his or her head either. (And yet I don't want to exclude any levels of allusion.) I do of course sometimes tell jokes behind the back of someone who I am glad is not there because I'm violating a bit of humor trust between me and that person—or that category of people—but it's always a guilty pleasure.

"The most insidious part of sexual abuse," writes Michael Ryan in his autobiography *A Secret Life*, "is in the creation of desire in the molested child, the way it forms a shape for desire that can never again be fulfilled, only compulsively substituted for and repeated."

In that sense my mother conceivably desired exclusion. Exclusion infused with a heavy moral-erotic charge. And she passed that desire on to me, and I have twisted it as best I can.

The most awful thing about my mother was her peculiar kind of wistful freak-of-nature, or-shall-I-go-fuck-myself crestfallen non-laugh—a way of excluding everyone by insisting upon her own exclusion. Or her abject appeal: "I've lost you, Bucky, and I don't know what to do about it," she would say to me, not *to* me but *at* me, or so *intensely* to me as in effect to be at me.

A humorist believes, in some twisted but heartfelt way, that irony should be available to everybody.

If there is a heaven, it probably has a V.I.P. area. Otherwise millions of souls would be elbowing each other to get close enough to watch Fats Waller and Mozart jam.

At one point I tried to write this book fictionally, in the form of a father writing a letter to his children from heaven:

> I never saw the point of reincarnation. If I consisted of my body and my awareness, and reincarnation meant coming back in another body without being aware of it—what's the point? (If there were reincarnation, though, I wanted to be reborn as a dog free to roam on a small college campus.) And I was right, about that. What I wasn't prepared for was this. Heaven. You suffer from postmortem depression for a little while, but then . . . Eternity! You can get used to anything, I guess.
>
> I can't describe it to you, and even if I could, I wouldn't, because it would be a form of abuse. It would be like describing sex to a six-

year-old. Let's just say that the harps and clouds and long white robes are the equivalent of the stork. And when I say sex, I don't mean just romance, either, or just getting hot or just doing it, even; I mean the whole shebang, the ups and downs.

It's a little bit like prison, in that you're not supposed to ask people how they got here. Also, you don't think about who might be getting here next—you're liable to start wishing your friends would die.

It's not like reverting to childlike innocence—why the heck would it be, when you think about it. It's like being an advanced adult. Something that's even harder to figure out how to do right. Great, just what I need, after life. But I'm just griping. What it is, is on to the next level, and if I were to make you apprehensive about it, I'd be like the kids who've gone on to high school who try to scare grade-school kids by telling them, "Everything has to be in ink! You can't erase!"

You should see some people trying to be cool when they walk through the Pearly Gates—acting like a rookie in the end zone, as if you've been here before.

Ghosts, by the way, are dead people who won't grow up, like the kids who used to come back and hang around high school after graduation. I won't be haunting you. The whole point is to unhaunt you.

I remember walking down the street after finally accepting that your mother and I had to break up, and it suddenly hit me: "I don't have to be married!" What a relief. I just had to figure out a way to stay family with you, and we managed it, didn't we?

Well, now I don't even have to make money. Or shave. I just have to figure out a way to stay in touch with you. You won't receive this letter, as such, but some of it may filter through. The main thing I wish I could tell you is that anything you may be feeling bad about, which happened or didn't happen between you and me, it wasn't your fault. From "up" here ("Uptown," we call it), everything looks pretty much no-fault.

They say only about 35,000 souls, throughout history, have actually been condemned—and yes, Hitler's was one of them. I was talking to Jesus the other day, and I said, "I understand there's one theory that Hitler was just the product of a dysfunctional family—his father beat him."

"How can you criticize somebody for beating Hitler?" Jesus said.

His understanding has limits, as on the cross.

But that's just gossip.

Getting down to cases with God doesn't exactly clear everything up. He says that on earth I was actually depressed, and wouldn't face up to it. *He* was depressed for one day, after finishing the creation—which is why Sunday afternoon is so gloomy; he hopes every week that worship services all over the world will cheer him up, but they don't.

Turns out he's a Methodist God. I had trouble accepting that. He said, "So do I." Then I realized: everybody has the supreme being he or she deserves. Mine is Methodist/agnostic. Male. Other guys, who stayed married longer, get female ones, which I realize now would be a lot more interesting. Oh well, He it is.

In life I always hated hearing people say things like "Dessert was sheer bliss," or "Three weeks in Provence. Ah, heaven!" or "You look divine."

Perhaps accordingly, my heaven borders on anhedonia. (Woody Allen's term for what he suffered from. Humorist syndrome.) I still don't feel that anybody's heart is ready to be lifted unless it's down where it ought to be.

Here's something I've been thinking about. Nobody in our whole complicated extended family was a downright asshole. We were all strange in one way or another, most of us could be hurtful, but . . . Of course they say if you're playing poker and you can't figure out who at the table is the sucker, it's you. Maybe the asshole was me.

God is not all that helpful on that question. "You were a flibbeti-gibbet," he told me. "And you know it too, don't you?"

Flibbetigibbet? I've got plenty of time to figure it out.

"I kind of thought you were going to be the one," God said, "to write the book."

That's as far as I got, with writing this book that way. I couldn't keep my disbelief suspended any longer. And I didn't know how to deal with what the narrator and his parents would say to each other up there. Would we finally be on an equal footing? All dead, we could talk things through? I could easily imagine Louise saying to Jesus, "No, no, don't mind me, you run along and enjoy yourself." Would she still slip up occasionally, even in heaven, and say, "You children ruin everything we try to do"? Or, "See,

Smarty, I tried to tell you. You just don't realize how hard I prayed, and how worried I was, night after night after your father died, and who knew where *you* were, you wouldn't call me just to ease my mind. . . ." Or would we fall into each other's arms and there would be weeping and wailing but no gnashing of teeth? The prospect is too raw, like Barry Fitzgerald's reunion scene with his old mother in *Going My Way*.

Susan and I were talking about Mumu the other day on the phone, reminiscing about her last days, when the cancer had altered her mind.

She lay on the fold-out couch in the den of the condo just outside Decatur that she'd moved into after my father died. She was worried that things weren't right, somehow, that she wasn't doing right.

"All of a sudden," Susan remembered, "she said, 'Well! You might as well go marching up and down the street with a sign saying, "We Have No Supper Tonight." ' "

Perhaps so she could bear the notion of not cooking supper for us, she started talking as if we were in someone else's house. "I was cleaning out her medicine cabinet, getting rid of old stuff," Susan remembered, "and she said, 'Do you think those people will mind us taking all that away? The people whose house this is. How did you get those people to let us stay in their house?'

"And then it was as if she were actually willing, for the first time, ever, to accept that I was someone who was being nice to her, trying to help her," Susan said. As if she had let go of her bad childhood, finally, and was having a new one. All of a sudden a big smile lit up her face. "I know," she said. "You have a puppy in the attic."

Susan said, "Puppy, Mom? No, I don't believe there's a puppy anywhere around."

She kept smiling, like we were planning a surprise for her. "I know you have a puppy in the attic. I can hear it." She didn't even have an attic, there in the condo. She looked puzzled, but she was smiling.

"I *like* dogs," she said. "Why don't you bring the puppy down?"

Remembering all this on the phone, my sister laughed a pleased, puzzled laugh, a laugh that reminds me of my mother's, only less conflicted. When Louise laughed she would look down and shake her head, as if embarrassed to feel that she deserved to laugh.

Imagining that puppy, though, she smiled unashamedly. As if she were what she always was in a way but never felt right about being. A little girl.

My mother.

Ennis at six (after experiencing a bit of culture clash while staying with her grandmother): "Now I never say 'fart' in front of
anybody until I've heard them say it first."

Kirven at four (told to pick up his clothes): "It's my life!"

There's a dwarf who plays at the Hollywood Y. He's not bad, he can keep
the ball away from people. I blocked his shot. I don't let anybody
inside," says Blount.

Not Corie Blount, who plays for the Lakers, nor Elvis Blount, who used
to play for Martin Luther King High School in Manhattan, but Kirven
Blount, the 6'4½" center of the Nukes in the Walt Disney Intramural League.
The Blount whose hoops credits include a shoving-and-yelling match with
Denzel Washington. It was that Blount who looked back after the Nukes'
solid 60–45 victory over Disney Channel the other night and said . . .

Forget it. Hey, I'm an old sportswriter, I could turn any athlete—well,
any athlete but Harmon Killebrew—into good copy. For Kirven Blount, I
will do this much, because, after all, I am a father: every young man would
like to see his name in a box score, so here it is (admittedly incomplete):

Nukes 60, Disney Channel 45

Nukes	m	fg	ft	reb	a	pf	pts
Mike	32	7–?	0–0	?	?	?	14
Miguel	32	3–?	4–?	?	?	4	10
Blount	32	3–?	5–6	10	6	1	11
Jim	32	2–?	3–?	?	?	?	7
Artie	32	7–?	2–?	?	?	?	18
Totals	160	22–?	14–?	?	?	?	60

Three-point goals: 2–4, .500 (Artie 2–3, Blount 0–1). Steals: Several (Blount 2). Turnovers: Not all that many.

Disney Ch	m	fg	ft	reb	a	pf	pts
Big guy	32	?–?	?–?	?	?	?	?
Guy	?	?–?	?–?	?	?	?	?
Big guy	32	?–?	?–?	?	?	?	?
Good shot	32	?–?	?–?	?	?	?	?
Small guy	?	?–?	?–?	?	?	?	?
Reserve	?	?–?	?–?	?	?	?	?
Reserve	?	?–?	?–?	?	?	?	?
Reserve	?	?–?	?–?	?	?	?	?
Totals	160	?–?	?–?	?	?	?	45

Three-point goals: Good shot: quite a few. Blocked shot: One of the big guys: at least one.

The reason it's incomplete is that I was worried, during the game. You can't help it, as a father. Over the course of Kirven Blount's career I had watched him play every damn sport imaginable (including hockey—jeez, being a hockey father gets cold), except basketball, so I thought: I'll fly out to L.A., watch the kid play, write him up, make him feel like a real player.

And I have done the box score. Incomplete, yes. Because I was worried. And also because, during the warm-ups, the Nukes were one man short and it looked like I might have to play.

Basketball is not my forte. I know it's trite, but I can't jump. If there is any less saltatorial race than the white one, then that is the one I must belong to. At eleven, I couldn't jump. At fifty-five, I'm proud I can still stand up straight. Still, I considered playing. Then the fifth Nuke showed up. But all through the game I kept thinking, What if Kirven's teammates were not Artie, Mike, Jim and Miguel but me, and my father, and his father, and his? And we're playing against the seven dwarves. . . .

So, I didn't get every little stat down. Still, there's the box score, a father's gift to his son. But I'm not going to break my neck to write a full-blown professional-quality profile of Kirven Blount, 6′4½″ center of the Nukes, and here's why.

I fly out there, I see the Nukes play, I worry, I fly back to New York, I'm tired, but I'm a pro—I call Blount up and put it to him, "Okay, the dwarf quote is good for color, especially because we can tie it into the Disney angle, and the Denzel story is good for name recognition, but neither of those things is pertinent to the Nukes' victory. What we need is a good postgame quote. Anything you want to say, as if it's right after the game. Doesn't have to be off the top of your head, take your time and call me back."

I'm letting him in on the process, see? Because he wants to be a writer. In fact, when I met his fellow Nukes there in the Hoover High auditorium in Glendale, where the Disney league games are played, his fellow Nukes said to me, "You're a writer too?"

Okay, so, he wants to be a writer—so much that, in fact, he is quitting his perfectly good job, with health insurance, in the Disney Studios creative department to move to Austin, Texas, to write a novel. Did I quit my job when I was twenty-five and just take off to an interesting city to be a writer? No, because I had a family. But that's okay. We'll work together on this story.

"Okay," he says. Okay.

Then two minutes later he calls me back and says, "I don't think I will. Make up a quote like that."

"Why not?"

"It wouldn't be fair."

It wouldn't be fair! To whom? Hakeem Olajuwon? "Don't you want to say anything about how your father painstakingly put up a backboard for you and taught you how to shoot—well, encouraged you to fling the ball up there—when you were a little kid, so that now, every time you soar through the air and by golly, *whoomp*, dunk one, though of course you didn't actually manage to dunk one in the game I flew three thousand miles to attend, but you did hit that reverse layup, so, okay, every time you soar through the air and by golly hit a reverse layup, you remember back to when . . . ?"

"No."

Hey. If a guy won't meet me halfway (Harmon Killebrew, for instance—a private person), then I'm going to write what's really interesting. I'm going to write what a father feels.

The father flies back from L.A., calls up his son, his son won't give him a quote, okay, the father is on West Coast time anyway so he stays up till five in the morning trying to finish some other work he has to do, he goes to bed tired but thinking cozily to himself, Hey, my children who won't give me a quote have lives of their own, I can sleep till noonnnn . . .

And right in the middle of a dream about trying to catch a child who is stepping out into traffic—the phone rings.

Wumf? Ungh? It's 8:15. Just let the answering machine deal with it. Won't even listen to the . . .

"Dad, if you're worried, I'm fine; got to go out and w——."

That's all.

Go out and wAVE FROM THE TOP OF A PRECIPICE? Go out and wALK A TIGHTROPE? Go out and wAKE UP THE NEIGHBORHOOD, WHICH IS SLIDING DOWN THE SIDE OF THE HILL?

For it is my son Kirven, who not only won't take the opportunity to give his father a quote but who also, when an opportunity to break every bone in his body arises, does not know the meaning of Maybe this isn't such a good idea. Who, for instance, climbs up the outside of buildings.

He used to do it at the University of North Carolina. Entered his dorm room that way, by climbing up the brick wall to the window. Perhaps because (I read somewhere) Lawrence Taylor used to do the same thing. I don't know. I don't want to talk about it. I don't want to encourage him. Last New Year's Eve he climbed, by way of fire escapes and balconies and ledges, all the way to the top of the Hollywood Tower, a tall apartment building. Why? I don't know. I never climbed the outside of buildings.

He lives in the Hollywood Hills. When it's 8:15 in New York, it's 5:15 there. Why is he up, even? I used to have to threaten him with eviction to get him up at 12:15.

I leap to my feet and punch the Play button . . .

". . . I'm fine; got to go out and watch." Oh. Watch what?

. . . dial his number . . .

Ring . . . ring . . . ring. He is, of course, out watching something, and his machine is not picking up. Power out? Nuclear strike?

. . . then turn on CNN:

". . . our bureau in Los Angeles, where just over forty minutes ago a major earthquake . . ."

If an earthquake occurs anywhere, one of my children is likely to be fairly close to the epicenter. My daughter, Ennis, was in the big San Francisco quake. I was talking with her on the phone a couple of days later, providing a steadying post-quake influence, when she said, "On TV they showed a home video somebody was making when it hit and THINGS ARE MOVING AROUND ON THE TOP OF THE REFRIGERATOR, OHH WAW!" An aftershock had hit while we were talking. I almost felt it through the phone. Get back into this house right this minute! was what I wanted to say, but she was three thousand miles away.

A daughter, though, you can talk to, you can tell her the ground will stop lurching eventually, and she will appreciate it. A son—a son, if he should become Chief Justice of the Supreme Court, you are still afraid that he is going to step out into traffic. With good reason. I don't mean that he will step out into traffic with good reason—though that is how it will seem to him—I mean, you are afraid with good reason that he will.

Because he did once, in Pittsfield, Massachusetts, when he was little. I let go of his hand for one instant and the next thing I know I'm snatching him—and of course he will probably hold it against me, for the rest of his life, that I got him out of the way of a speeding minivan just in time.

I could tell you stories. Once in high school he borrowed my car to drive to New Jersey to a schoolmate's house, with other schoolmates, for the weekend. Okay. So Sunday night, he calls from school. Could he have a ride home?

Well, I thought he had my car. I mean, he left with my car.

Yes, yes, he did have my car, but he doesn't right now.

Well, okay, uh, why?

"Because I don't have the keys."

Well . . . when he left he had the keys. What . . . became of them?

"Well, I gave them to a girl to hold."

Yesss, and . . .

"And she forgot she had them, and she left to go back to school before I did, and . . ."

So, of course, my car is still in New Jersey. But, uh, why did he give the keys to a girl to hold?

"Because I didn't have any pockets in my pants."

Finally, I lost my fatherly calm: *"What kind of pants don't have any pockets in them?"*

"Some pants you don't know about."

A youth loves to play all kinds of sports, but he's little in high school. His father goes to watch him play football, and the youth is hurling himself into people of literally twice his weight. The youth is game, the youth is crazy, is what he is, the youth, in fact, hits huge people low and stops them, but every football season, the youth breaks some small bone. And in baseball he is stylish but small. And basketball, forget about it.

And the father thinks, If we had waited a year before we put him into first grade . . .

Furthermore, to compensate for his father's rushing him into first grade when his birthday is in December, the youth does things like bounce himself off a trampoline in such a way as to create on his forehead a gash which is literally in the shape of his first initial, J (he was going by his first name, John, then, instead of his middle one, Kirven), with the little horizontal mark on top even. The scar is there to this day, the scar which stands for Jesuswhatkindoffather . . .

And the youth graduates, and begins to grow. Two inches in three weeks. At least nine and a half inches after high school. The youth doesn't even get gawky, he just becomes a force on the softball diamond and on the court, because he is picking up basketball on his own, playing in Worcester, Massachusetts, and San Francisco, and Sun Valley, and Austin, and Lee, Massachusetts, and in an inner-city gym in Chapel Hill, North Carolina, where a family race-relations milestone is achieved:

Blount is playing with black youths, and he goes up and takes a rebound away from one of them, who turns to a friend and says—by way of describing my son, *my* son who must, sometimes, instinctively know the way to an old Southern liberal father's heart:

"That nigger is *tall*."

Still, a father worries. I'm standing at courtside at the Nukes versus Disney Channel game, and Blount misses two or three layups—he's getting rebounds and assists, and all, but he hasn't dunked (I have, in fact, seen him dunk in warm-ups, and he says he has done it in games off a pass, and let me tell you, he is the first person, by a margin of a good eleven inches, in his family line to dunk). Disney Channel has a couple of big guys too, so he is not dominating, not scoring thirty-four points the way he did in a game a while back, and he misses a three-pointer, and I'm thinking: I've put too much pressure on him by showing up here to write a column, he's going to be so pissed at himself for missing shots—ooh, another one—and it's my fault probably, but . . .

But he comes over and slaps hands with me and he's smiling, his team is winning, they really are working well together. Mike, the forward, is not only good but also has the techniques of somebody who was big enough in high school to have received coaching, unlike my son, whose father rushed him into the first grade . . . and Artie can hit from outside . . .

Actually Blount did have an on-the-spot postgame quote: "I attracted a lot of attention under the basket and I kicked the ball outside. A Sha- quille move."

But, I mean, that's so positive. He likes himself as an athlete.

My son does.

I never really did. I was always conflicted as an athlete, anxious—with flashes of brilliance, sure, but always preoccupied . . .

Blount organized the Nukes himself (though what inspired the team's name is not clear), and, hey, it's not a big deal, but they move the ball around. . . . You'll notice Blount had six assists. "I've become a pretty pass-able passer," he says.

It's almost as if Blount is a grown man, a centered center, who enjoys the game. He's kidding with the refs about missing his layups. One of the opposing big guys blocks one of Blount's shots and says, "Don't bring that shit around here anymore," and the next time they're down the court Blount says to him, "Did you actually say, 'Don't bring that shit around here anymore'?" And they both chuckle.

Maybe I've been thrown all out of whack by writing stories about pro-fessional athletes, which is to say cutthroat athletes—many of the greatest and most quotable of whom had absent fathers or no fathers at all, they had to somehow create themselves with no models. . . . Maybe Harmon Killebrew had a wonderful father, that's why he didn't like me.

The reason Blount had a shoving match with Denzel Washington, in a pickup game at the Hollywood Y, is that Denzel Washington "acted like he thought he was a star." On the court. Blount says L.A. pickup basketball generally is awful because guys are always acting out, arguing on and on about fouls, they're trying to signify something that has nothing to do with the game. L.A. basketball is "poserish," he says. I think I mentioned that he's leaving his secure job in L.A. in a building supported on the out-side by enormous stone representations of the seven dwarves, to freelance in Austin, Texas.* Hey, I like Austin, myself. I didn't take off and start free-lancing till I was thirty-four.

---

*Since I wrote that sentence, he has spent time in Austin and moved on to New York, where he is bartending and pursuing his muse, and we do stuff together.

A father is all set to write about realizing he has the son he always wanted to have (I mean, we do agree on things, we both love dogs and George Jones and despise Rush Limbaugh), but what hits him, instead, is that maybe a father has the son he wants to be.

It's not fair.

In the summer of 1970, when Ennis was about the age that her elder son, Jesse, is now, I dispatched this to the *Atlanta Journal*:

> Being in an airplane with two children under four and a meal is like being in an elevator with two horses and an armload of pies, but with one child barely under four on her way back home after a visit to her grandparents, it is possible even to conduct an interview.

THE JOURNAL: Why do you like just the yellows of your hard-boiled
   egg?
LITTLE GIRL: I just don't like the yellow part.
T.J.: No, you do like the yellows, you don't like the whites.
L.G.: I know.
T.J.: How do you like flying?
L.G.: Not too well.
T.J.: Why?
L.G.: Because I hate flying!
T.J.: What's wrong with it?
L.G.: We're up and we ought to be down!
T.J.: Don't you like anything about it?
L.G.: The pilot gives us food. And jelly and beddy.
T.J.: Beddy?
L.G.: Betty.
T.J.: What's that?
L.G.: Betty and beddy and baddy.
T.J.: Well, you mean the stewardess gives us food.
L.G.: *Nooo.* She's Betty.
T.J.: What did you do in Georgia?
L.G.: Heard a record, *Peter and the Wolf.*
T.J.: What was it about?

L.G.: About Peter and the wolf ate the duck.

T.J.: Then what?

L.G.: And they took the wolf to the zoo and cut him open and get out the duck.

T.J.: And was the duck all right then?

L.G.: No.

T.J.: What did you do then?

L.G.: Nothing. I just cried.

T.J.: Then you stopped crying.

L.G.: No. *Are we rolling on the buildings? Are we in the river? Where are we, for goodness' sake?*

T.J.: About to land.

L.G.: *If we're down we should be down. If we're up we should be up. We're supposed to be down but we're up.*

T.J.: Now we're down.

L.G.: I know.

A year and a half before my mother died, she and Ennis and Kirven and Joan and I and Susan and her husband, Gerald, and their kids, Audrey and Stuart, had Christmas in Gambier, Ohio, where Gerald was teaching English at Kenyon College. Ennis was twelve. The night before Christmas, Ennis and I were walking through the snow. Mumu and my kids were enormously fond of each other. She had taken them to Disney World twice. Whenever they arrived to visit her in Georgia, they would rush to the bedrooms they always stayed in and Mumu would have covered their beds with presents. Christmas morning had always been the high point of my mother's year. Seeing the children's "eyes light up"—Susan's and mine, when we were kids, then Ennis's and Kirven's when they came along—when we first saw what Santa had brought was my mother's greatest earthly reward. Imagine, then, how scary it was the Christmas morning somewhere in the mists of my childhood when, for some reason, I hate to think what, she stayed in bed.

This Christmas Mumu had been making us all feel that we were making her miserable, while insisting that we not give her another moment's thought. Ennis was distressed.

"You have to understand . . . ," I said to her as we crunched across the campus snow.

"I'M TIRED OF UNDERSTANDING," Ennis shouted.

A healthy reaction. But understanding has become her vocation. She majored in psychology—what Mumu always said she wished she could have studied—at Stanford. For a while she taught variously blighted children at a school in a San Francisco neighborhood that was so rough Domino's refused to deliver pizza there, and now in North Carolina she is not only a crackerjack mother (at least I can say I helped raise someone to be a better parent than I am) of two crackerjack boys, she's a social worker whose speciality has been early intervention—helping hapless welfare mothers understand how to care for their children before it's too late. My daughter. One of her clients, a mother who couldn't tell time or count money, wrote her this letter:

> Hello Ennis How things with you fine I Hope Well the same Old
> thing with me Ennis I call that Lady Back from over there by Dr
> Winegar Office But She Was'nt in Because she Act like don't Want
> to help Me Ennis Because I need some help what I want would She
> Come to my House and work with Me Cause Just Give Me One day of
> her time Cause the other day Charles bring some Math Home and
> Ennis I Could'nt help him cause I did'nt No How I did'nt Ennis
>
> For me going Back to school Ennis to Be Honesty with you that's
> Out the Question I don't want to Be in embrass to them
>
> Ennis I guess you tired of hearing my Promblem But Ennis Right
> Now You and Only One I can turn to Ennis Please bear with me
> Ennis And understand Me So Please Ennis understand Me Cause
> when I talk to you Ennis I get So Upleaf Please take care Ennis
> Love

CHAPTER 30 / **What the Author Has to Tell Us**

One is one, two is two,
Never love a woman like she say she love you.

—"KANSAS CITY BLUES"

What do you want from me, closure? I know how you feel. I can't go to sleep at night, myself, until I hear someone say "closure" on TV. But a family curse is not lifted in a generation.

It's absorbed gradually. Like a stain that seeps down from layer to layer. You can realize how interestingly the stain sets off the presumption of stainlessness around it. You can discover the face of Jesus or Elvis or somebody in it. You can convert unconditional self-loathing to steam or charity or humor. You can't push the stain back up into your parents' layer.

Just don't be a flimsy tissue, don't let it all pass on down to the next generation. Absorb as much of it as you can.

My mother would look at a sweet little child and say, in a tone of voice that still makes me shudder in recollection: "How could anybody ever hurt one?"

Come on, Mom. It's hard not to.

"Your job is to be my sunshine," Mother told Susan when she was a girl. She also said doctors had advised her to abort Susan because pregnancy would make the tumor in her eye worse.

"I had an epiphany one day walking down the street," Susan says. "I realized that children love their parents not because of what the parents do for them but because of how they make them feel about themselves. I don't think Mother understood that at all."

You can't demand gratitude. Neediness and generosity—selflessness with its hand out—doesn't add up. Susan went into math and business. Looking, we might say, for a clear-cut bottom line.

282

"She was mean and hateful and drove us all away," Susan blurted out once a couple of years ago after we had watched a video of *The Heiress*, in which Ralph Richardson withholds affection from Olivia de Havilland. For a moment, I thought the family curse might have been lifted by the sheer rational audacity of that declaration.

But Susan's choice of words was in part ironic homage. "Mean and hateful" was one of Louise's expressions.* She did genuinely hate meanness and hatefulness. (I saw somebody wearing a T-shirt the other day that said, "Fuck Hate.") And Susan is the one who will say, when lots of us in the family are having fun together, "Mumu would have loved to be here for this."

She's a sweet girl, my sister.

She tries to think how things might have been different between Mumu and us:

"Imagine if instead of 'You'll just grow up and forget about me,' she had said, 'I hope we can still be close after you're grown and have your own home and family,'" Susan says. "Or better yet, just assumed we would because we liked each other.

"What could we have said in response to 'You'll grow up and forget about me'?

"'Mother, why do you fear that? What precedent is there in our family for that? Your words sting because they imply coldheartedness and ingratitude on my part, which doesn't reflect well on my character. Do you think I'm that kind of person? Do you realize your statement hurts my feelings and pushes me away?'

"Ha—what a fantasy."

Anyway, who would want to read—let alone write—a book in which people talked like that?

There was one occasion when I thought we might actually have a curse-lifting while our parents were alive.

It was 1970. Susan had been out of school for a year, doing computer work at Decatur Federal. I was still married to Ellen, living in New York, working for *Sports Illustrated*. One night I got a phone call from— Susan? Daddy? I don't remember. At any rate, Susan had announced to our parents that she was going to Germany for the summer with a young man she wasn't planning to marry.

---

*"Ashley is so mean and hateful!" says Scarlett in *Gone With the Wind*. Later, when both Scarlett and Melanie are talking him into something, he says, "I can't fight you both." My mother was both Scarlett and Melanie. Maybe every woman is.

Family shame! First Roy Jr. gets an F in conduct, and now this! Double-jointed hell had broken loose. Louise had swallowed a bottle of aspirins.

When I heard that, my conscience, or at least my mind, cleared somewhat. If she would try to kill herself over something so silly, how culpable was my nearly killing her at birth?

Then she had thrown up the aspirins.

We have strong stomachs in our family. I have thrown up once since 1969; my children never hurl. We can stomach a lot. I am friends with several people who are widely regarded as difficult. Not compared to my mother.

But we will swallow only so much. Once we decide we are fed up, watch out. Our stomachs don't have a death wish.

I was fed up. I took the red-eye to Atlanta and waded into the fray. I told my parents they were being ridiculous.

"Men don't want a girl who has been around the track too often," my mother insisted.

"Where did you get *that* expression?" I asked her. Whom I had tried to shield from the word *pee*.

As for Daddy, at one point while we were arguing, he was sitting on a kitchen chair with his *back* to me. "Look at your body language!" I said. (Thinking to myself, I never thought you'd use *that* expression.)

"I can talk to all kinds of people," he said, shifting just slightly around toward me.

"That doesn't mean you can talk to your son!" I cried.

I felt that I was standing at Armageddon, clearing the air.

Ha.

Susan went to Germany. But our relationship with our parents remained pretty much the same.

Susan and I got closer, though.

The other night, Susan and I were discussing that confrontation.

"I remember us all arguing there in the kitchen," Susan said. The room where my mother so suffered and shone. "I'll never forget one thing Mother said:

" 'You have ripped out my heart and jumped up and down on it on the kitchen floor.' "

Ooo.

Let's have that one more time.

"You have ripped out my heart. And jumped up and down on it. On the kitchen floor."

Wasn't funny at the moment, but . . .

What *else* could a boy turn out to be but a humorist, whose mother could come up with such a *cri de coeur*? With a straight face! For me the only career paths commensurate with my mother's extremity were saintliness—becoming a sort of Bubba Teresa, washing the sores of syphilitic railwaymen, for which I lack the character— or folly. If my father had been the nebbish or cipher that most male humorists' fathers have been, I might have become a *great* fool. But then I might have been denied some of the gratifications of fatherhood. Robert Benchley missed both of his sons' college graduations and one son's *wedding*. I can't imagine that.

If Mother had carried that expostulation one phrase farther—"and jumped up and down on it on the kitchen floor *with your muddy shoes on*," say—it would have been too much. We would have had to laugh *then*. Louise would have been the humorist.

Have I mentioned all the expressions she had that substituted for "I'll be damned"?

"Glory-osky." "Golly Ike." "Well, bless Pete." I'll probably remember another one tomorrow. For "goddamn" my father said "dag-nab" or "dad-gum" or "dad-blast it."

Do I miss my parents? A day seldom goes by, I would say. . . .

The preceding sentence is shaping up as a fusion of my mother's emotional syntax ("A day never goes by that I don't think of you children, and it ties me up in knots") and my father's judiciousness. Sometimes when I am writing I feel like my mother bustling about amongst savory kitchen smells and agonizing over whether the meal would turn out right or anybody would *get* it: "I spent all day cooking this mess," she might say when it was on the table, "the least you can do is eat it." (I have reformulated that notion into the Latin motto on my stationery: *Si legetis, scribam*. If you'll read it, I'll write it.)

And sometimes I feel like my father down in the basement poking through a pile of hardware odds and ends, whistling to himself.

Generally, I feel both ways at once.

You could think of "upleaf" as turning the page. I've turned a million of them, thanks in great part to my mother, but don't expect me to turn over a new leaf.

"Have you learned anything from writing this book?" my daughter, the psychology major, asked me last night. If anybody else asked me that I would jump down his or her throat, but since it was Ennis I laughed sardonically and then we laughed sweetly together.

Maybe the daughter of Sophocles asked him the same question when he was getting down to the short strokes of *Oedipus Rex*.

The other day I leafed through a book about male depression (*I Don't Want to Talk About It* is the title). I was struck by the author's assertion that "a healthy parent, barring some true catastrophe, does not bid for his child's pity."

Well, bless Pete, I thought to myself.

I miss my parents, in the sense that a day seldom goes by, probably, when I don't feel a pang about not having gotten to know them better. Maybe writing this book has helped me feel less sorry for them, finally. I wouldn't call that unconditional love, but at least it will help me deal with the probability that they would have hated a great deal of what I have written.

If a parent *does* bid for a child's pity, according to *I Don't Want to Talk About It*, he or she "injects into another the disowned aspects of his [or her] own personality." Causing the child to internalize shame, disempoweringly. The parent "also models, through example, a shameless way of being in the world." For instance, if your father beats you, he makes you ashamed about being who you are, but not about doing to others what he did to you. There are various ways, however, of being shameless in the world. One is to write a memoir. Tracing your shame, publicly, all the way back to when you were a little bare baby—farther back, in fact, to when you were a twinkle in your father's eye as he looked at your mother.

You should have heard me screaming at my computer just now. It *froze* on me, I had to reboot, and some of what I had written was lost. "I am going to finish this *goddamned* book," I told the computer (I have been around professional athletes too much, maybe), *"if I have to shove it up your ass."*

This book has by no means redeemed my character entirely, then. But I have to say that exposing the mystery of my life has rendered the mystery sweeter to me.

So you, the reader who has made it all possible, deserve some dessert. A quick story:

The other night I was talking to my friend Jan Yusk on the phone. She's a pediatric dermatologist down in Louisville. I was telling her that I was thinking of calling this book *There Are No Free Lullabies*, or maybe *Lullabies Don't Grow on Trees*. My theory being that my mother's harsh childhood left her with no sense of give and take. She thought she could make her children's childhoods be the antithesis of hers. Give us everything, ask nothing in return. Except that we be sweet. She had an idealized idea of love, which therefore corrupted. There was never one moment when I realized that my mother's love was bad for me; because where would I be without it? But I would have been a better person if I had realized long ago that there's no such thing as an unmixed blessing or a free lullaby.

That did not sit well with Jan. I didn't mean to be cynical, I assured her. By way of analogy I cited something I'd learned from another friend— Caroline Seay, a biochemist who does research into DNA down in North Carolina. A bit of "lore among scientists," as Caroline had put it. (Lore is better than data if you ask me—it doesn't pretend to be unconditional.)

The lore, Caroline had told me, is that *pure* DNA doesn't work well in experiments: "There are two ways you can prepare a DNA sample. You can do an ultraclean prep, distill it down to its absolute, just pure DNA, or you can do a quick and dirty prep. The quick and dirty prep seems to work better. Whatever the impurities may be—traces of salt or tissue or plasma or serum—I don't know how they help the reaction go right, but they do."

"The analogy," I told Jan Yusk, "is that love doesn't work when people expect it to be pure. It's a personal transaction. It's—"

"Let me tell you a story," Jan said. "There was a little baby—I swear to God his name was Adam, do not laugh. No, no, it wasn't Adam, it was— don't use his name. The point is, he had a skin condition called transient bullous dermolysis—breaking apart of the skin. His skin literally sheared off in your hands. You changed his diaper and you wound up with his hide to discard along with the used diaper.

"In terror, the nurses kept him in an incubator. They called me and said, 'We can't *stand* the way he cries whenever we touch him.' I said not only do we have to clean him so he won't get infected, we have to touch him and love him and hold him while we feed him. Or he's going to die. He won't see any reason to live.

"They said, 'Nobody will be able to stand it.' I said, 'I don't care whether we can stand it or not, we have to do it.' So I'm holding that baby while they're taking his dressing off to bathe him, and he's shrieking—even though we were giving him medicine to help him with the hurt, it wasn't enough medicine to help that kind of hurt.

"The nurses are undressing him, I'm holding him. We're wearing gloves, gowns, all he can see is our eyes. He must have thought he'd landed among Martians and they peel your skin off. Who would want to stay?

"I'm trying to bear that anguish. Literally bear it, I've got him in my hands.

"For one split second, I wanted to throw that little dude against the wall.

"I'm thinking, Oh, God, and tears are flowing out of my eyes. But I knew it was a *transient* condition.

"I started singing Brahms's 'Lullaby.' And holding that baby with my eyes. And his eyes are gorgeous, huge.

"He stopped crying. Just stared, transfixed.

"From then on the nurses would rock him and they would sing that lullaby, or they'd play a little tape recorder—he learned to love classical music, but his favorite was Brahms's 'Lullaby'—and he got out of there, grew skin that adhered. Now he's two or three and comes into my office. . . . He doesn't have any scars. He does have the oldest, wisest eyes—you talk about eyes that know how to hold irony.

"And he exults in himself. Runs around the office nekkid like he and I both think he's the cutest human being that ever hit the planet.

"And we do."

I don't. I *would* say this, of course, and maybe they will curse me for it someday, but I have a right to brag—I think the cutest are Jesse and Noah. Ennis and David's little boys. Mumu's—Mother's, Louise's, Sugar's—great-grandchildren. (If only they would *do what I tell them* . . .)

I wish Sugar could see them.

She absorbed the most.

Acknowledgments

Thanks to my agent, Esther Newberg, and my editor, Peter Gethers. May this book reflect as well upon them as do their cats.

Apologies to those friends of mine who are mentioned insufficiently or not at all in this book. (Consider this: Henry Adams didn't mention his estimable wife in *The Education of Henry Adams*, and that is why we remember her today.)

To Slick Lawson, Hal Crowther and Vereen Bell: Do you realize that when we were off in the middle of the Okefenokee Swamp for three days together, the fact that *all four of us* are juniors never even came up?

To Lee Smith: In Mill River once you said, as I recall, "Be sweet, and do whatever you want to." (Uncle John Hulley noted the similarity to Saint Augustine's "Love God, and do what you will.") You would like Esther's and Peter's cats.

To the Jayneses: Thanks for the use of the dog.

A NOTE ABOUT THE AUTHOR

If there is one thing that Roy Blount Jr. prides himself on, his modesty aside, it is this: that he has done more different things *than any other humorist-novelist-journalist-dramatist-lyricist-lecturer-reviewer-performer-versifier-cruciverbalist-sportswriter-screenwriter-anthologist-columnist-philologist of sorts he can think of. A single grandfather, he hails from Georgia and lives in Manhattan and western Massachusetts. Right after finishing this book, he turned fifty-six. His preference would have been to turn fifty-four, at most, but you can't go back except in a memoir.*

A NOTE ON THE TYPE

*The text of this book was set in a face called Clearface,
designed by Morris Fuller Benton in 1907. Benton has been
credited with being the most prolific type designer in
American history. In addition to designing original
typefaces, he expanded existing type into families,
including eighteen variations on Century, a face that was
designed by his father, Linn Boyd Benton, and
Theodore L. DeVinne.*

Composed by Creative Graphics, Allentown, Pennsylvania

*Printed and bound by The Haddon Craftsmen,
Scranton, Pennsylvania*

Designed by Iris Weinstein